Election Administration in the United States

This book tells the story of how the way we conduct elections has changed after the Florida recount litigation of 2000. Some of the nation's leading experts look at various aspects of election administration, including issues of ballot format, changes in registration procedures, the growth in the availability of absentee ballot rules and other forms of "convenience voting," and changes in the technology used to record our votes. They also look at how the *Bush v. Gore* decision has been used by courts that monitor the election process and at the consequences of changes in practice for levels of invalid ballots, magnitude of racial disparities in voting, voter turnout, and access to the ballot by those living outside the United States. The editors, in their introduction, also consider the normative question of exactly what we want a voting system to do. An epilogue by two leading election law specialists looks at how election administration and election contest issues played out in the 2012 presidential election.

R. Michael Alvarez is professor of political science at the California Institute of Technology. He earned his BA from Carleton College and his PhD from Duke University. He is the author of numerous books, including *Evaluating Elections: A Handbook of Methods and Standards* (Cambridge, 2012).

Bernard Grofman is Peltason Chair in democracy studies and professor of political science at the University of California, Irvine, and the immediate past director of the university's Center for the Study of Democracy. He is the author or coauthor of five books and the editor or coeditor of twenty books. He has written more than 200 research articles and research notes. He is a member of the American Academy of Arts and Sciences and the recipient of an honorary doctorate from the University of Copenhagen.

Election Administration in the United States

The State of Reform after Bush v. Gore

Edited by

R. MICHAEL ALVAREZ
California Institute of Technology

BERNARD GROFMAN
University of California, Irvine

CAMBRIDGE
UNIVERSITY PRESS

CAMBRIDGE
UNIVERSITY PRESS

32 Avenue of the Americas, New York, NY 10013-2473, USA

Cambridge University Press is part of the University of Cambridge.

It furthers the University's mission by disseminating knowledge in the pursuit of education, learning, and research at the highest international levels of excellence.

www.cambridge.org
Information on this title: www.cambridge.org/9781107625952

© Cambridge University Press 2014

First published 2014

Printed in the United States of America

A catalog record for this publication is available from the British Library.

Library of Congress Cataloging in Publication data
Election administration in the United States : the state of reform after Bush v. Gore / edited by R. Michael Alvarez, Bernard M. Grofman.
    pages cm
Includes bibliographical references and index.
ISBN 978-1-107-04863-8 (hardback) – ISBN 978-1-107-62595-2 (paperback)
1. Elections – United States – Management.   2. Election law – United States.
3. Bush, George W. (George Walker), 1946 – Trials, litigation, etc.   4. Gore, Albert, 1948 – Trials, litigation, etc.   I. Alvarez, R. Michael, 1964–, author, editor of compilation.   II. Grofman, Bernard, editor of compilation.
JK1976.E437   2014
324.6'30973–dc3   2014009740

ISBN 978-1-107-04863-8 Hardback
ISBN 978-1-107-62595-2 Paperback

Contents

Contributors

R. Michael Alvarez, California Institute of Technology

Stephen Ansolabehere, Harvard University

Lonna Rae Atkeson, University of New Mexico

Danny Boggs, U.S. Court of Appeals, Sixth Circuit

Mark Braden, Baker/Hostetler

Khalilah L. Brown-Dean, Quinnipiac University

Bernard Grofman, University of California, Irvine

Paul Gronke, Reed College

Thad E. Hall, University of Utah

Samuel Issacharoff, New York University School of Law

Martha Kropf, University of North Carolina, Charlotte

Jan E. Leighley, American University

Kathleen Moore, University of Washington

Jonathan Nagler, New York University

Charles Anthony Smith, University of California, Irvine,Richard Pildes, New York University School of Law

Nathaniel Persily, Stanford Law School

Amy Semet, Columbia University

Charles Stewart III, Massachusetts Institute of Technology

Robert Tucker, Baker/Hostetler

Foreword

Judge Danny Boggs, U.S. Court of Appeals, Sixth Circuit

Professors R. Michael Alvarez and Bernard Grofman and the authors of the individual chapters in this book have given a finely detailed study of many of the crucial aspects of election vote casting, administration, counting, and litigation. In particular, they have developed the granularity of the stories of individual American elections that lead to discussions over these issues. That is, each close or mismanaged election is like Tolstoy's statement: every unhappy family is unhappy in its own way. The broad issues only come to life in individual disputed races and practices. Each contested election, or controverted election practice, depends mightily on the individual circumstances and the positions of the contesting parties. If you win on a machine count, you disparage hand counts; if you are behind, you want hand counts.

A second key point is that these issues are endemic to elections, but rise to the surface only in very close elections. In assessing Florida 2000, it needs to be noted that Florida was unique in being the closest state presidential result (in percentage terms) in American history, rivaled only by Henry Clay's four-vote margin in Maryland in 1832, out of 38,000 votes cast. Florida was equivalent to counting 10,000 votes and having the count come out 5,001 to 5,000 – 500+ consecutive times! By contrast, the somewhat controverted result in Ohio in 2004 was exceeded in closeness hundreds of times in past state presidential elections – eleven times in 1960 alone.

A message that should be taken from this solid academic work, and taken to heart by all political participants and administrators, is that forethought on issues of ballot design, election administration, and voter education can be just as crucial as other campaign elements and ballot design deserves the same degree of forethought at a time when action can be taken in the interests of all voters and of the candidates and participants themselves.

Ballot design can be especially crucial, as the very interesting discussion of the Florida Thirteenth Congressional District race in 2006 sets out. Much less known is the fact that it is almost certainly the case that far more votes were lost to Gore by means of the "caterpillar ballot" in Duval County, Florida, than could possibly have been affected by the much more publicized butterfly ballot in Palm Beach County. Duval County attempted to solve the problem of the large number of candidates by placing the candidates on two facing pages. However, this design apparently resulted in tens of thousands of over-votes in Duval County, many perhaps by voters who had been advised to "vote every page," and thus voted for one of the candidates on the first page and another candidate on the facing page. Regression analysis indicates that it was extremely likely that this ballot design cost Gore thousands of votes.

Both legislators and voters, as well as voting administrators, would do well to examine this volume carefully with an eye to understanding and fixing, or at least avoiding, the many potential traps that can arise in a process that involves fallible humans undertaking hundreds of millions of individual choices and physical actions, and yet whose smallest mistakes can, on rare occasions, affect the course of history.

Acknowledgments

With one exception (an author whose schedule did not permit her to attend), earlier versions of the essays collected in this volume were given at a conference on "*Bush v. Gore* Ten Years Later: Election Administration in the U.S." held at the Hotel Laguna in Laguna Beach, California, April 16–17, 2011, co-organized by R. Michael Alvarez and Bernard Grofman, and held under the auspices of the University of California, Irvine, Center for the Study of Democracy. Funding for the conference came from the Jack W. Peltason Chair at UCI, with supplemental funding from the UCI Center for the Study of Democracy (CSD). The conference reflects a combination of the interests of the Caltech/MIT Voting Technology Project and those of the Center for the Study of Democracy in electoral reform issues in the United States and worldwide.

The conference was long in the making. A decade ago Grofman and Henry Brady had planned a volume dealing directly with the panoply of issues in the 2000 *Bush v. Gore* recount controversy. But the proliferation of articles and books on that topic soon made it clear that yet another book on that topic was not really needed. Instead they decided that it made sense to wait until the dust had cleared and scholars could investigate how *Bush v. Gore*, the case and the controversy, had affected election administration in the United States in the longer term. Because of the press of other commitments, after his election as president of the American Political Science Association, Brady had to drop out of the project and was replaced by another leading expert on election administration issues, Mike Alvarez. We are deeply indebted to Shani Brasier, staff administrator of the Center for the Study of Democracy, for her remarkable organizational skills in putting the conference together, and to Ines Levin, currently an Assistant Professor at the University of Georgia, for her invaluable help in manuscript preparation. Alvarez wishes to thank his colleagues on the Caltech/MIT Voting Technology Project and Gloria Bain and Barbara Estrada for their support and assistance with this project.

Editors' Introduction

R. Michael Alvarez and Bernard Grofman

"*Bush v. Gore*" means different things to different people. To some it is a 2000 presidential contest during which the winner received fewer voters than the loser and during which the election outcome was not "decided" until more than a month after the election. Some at the time (and some today) saw the election as "stolen."[1] To others it is a still highly controversial Supreme Court case, *Bush v. Gore*, 531 U.S. 98 (2000) that stopped an ongoing recount in Florida on the grounds that the different standards(or lack thereof) for ascertaining voter intent in different parts of the state violated the equal protection clause of the Fourteenth Amendment, and that a statewide recount could not be conducted fast enough to offer Florida the ability to take advantage of a federal "safe harbor" deadline for disputed presidential outcomes. And many see "*Bush v. Gore*" as a poster child for problematic U.S. election administration practices, including partisan and localized control of the voting process, inexperienced election officials and polling place workers; and an absence of validated information of who was eligible to vote, uniform ballot formats, uniform technology for recording the vote, and uniform standards for recount practices. In Mark Braden's apt phrasing, the Florida litigation revealed the "soft underbelly of American elections" and cast doubt on their legitimacy.[2]

The chapters in this book come neither to bury *Bush v. Gore* (the case), nor to praise it; rather they seek to trace the consequences of "*Bush v. Gore*" (and *Bush v. Gore*) for election law and election administration in the United States during the past decade. As the various chapters in this book demonstrate, in addition to sparking major changes in election practices in Florida, disputes about voting and vote counting in the 2000 election have served as a catalyst for a wide range of election reforms throughout the country that have been very similar to what happened in Florida.[3] While the change is at a local level, it has been triggered by one of the most significant federal election reform efforts in recent decades, the Help America Vote Act (HAVA), passed in 2002, which mandated major changes in the election process and provided a carrot of substantial federal funds to motivate state compliance.

HAVA came about almost entirely because the deep flaws in how elections are conducted and in how votes are tallied that the 2000 election revealed provided a brief window of opportunity for electoral administration reform to be squarely on the national legislative agenda.

Moreover, while reforms like voting by mail are not directly linked to *Bush v. Gore*, issues related to absentee ballots, both those internal to the state and from overseas, arose in counting ballots in Florida in 2000, resulting in litigation in state or federal courts during the Florida recount controversy,[4] and the election controversies in Florida stimulated the search for alternative voting technologies (see Stewart, Chapter 4, this volume, and Gronke, Chapter 6, this volume). In particular, we have seen the greatly increased use of DRE (computer-based modes of recording ballot information/images such as touch screens) and the replacement of punch card machines.

However, while great progress has been made on some fronts (e.g., in choosing technologies for recording votes that reduce voter errors leading to invalid ballots), there are still many areas (like ballot design) where little has changed; these topics are discussed in contributions to this volume by Charles Stewart III and Martha Kropf. Moreover, the virtual elimination of punch card machines and their replacement by computerized voting technology or optical scanning devices has not been without its problems, and the rise in absentee voting by mail has created problems of its own (see Alvarez and Hall, 2008). Furthermore, despite improvements in election processes, both preelection and postelection disputes have risen – in part, perhaps, because the revealed flaws in past election processes make challenging procedures in advance look like just being sensible while making election outcome challenges look less like merely being a sore loser.

STRUCTURE OF THIS VOLUME

The first section of this volume, placing *Bush v. Gore* in historical context, consists of three chapters. The first chapter, by Mark Braden and Robert Tucker, looks at how recount disputes have (or have not) changed after 2000. The second chapter, by Charles Anthony Smith, looks more broadly at the long-run legal impact of *Bush v. Gore* on election law, and potentially on other legal issues as well. The third chapter in this section, by Amy Semet, Nathaniel Persily, and Stephen Ansolabehere, traces the impact of *Bush v. Gore* on public opinion about the Supreme Court.

The next section has four chapters. The first of these, by Charles Stewart III, offers a broad overview of election administration reforms over the past decade. The second, by Lonna Rae Atkeson, examines the determinants of voter confidence, focusing attention especially on how the political and legal context shapes confidence. The third chapter in this section, by Paul Gronke, considers the extent to which the 2000 election controversy in Florida can be linked to the greatly increased proportion of voters who now cast their votes early (e.g., via ballots that are sent by mail). The last chapter in this section, by Jan E. Leighley and Jonathan Nagler, traces the changes in registration laws and in voter turnout since 2000 and compares the amount of change to what was observed in earlier time periods.

The final section of this book looks at a number of issues that remain highly troubling and, as discussed in the last two chapters, much more controversial. The first chapter, by Martha Kropf, looks at the potential for improvement of ballot format to minimize voter confusion and make it more likely that voters will complete a full ballot. The next chapter, by Thad E. Hall and Kathleen Moore, looks at the front line of election administration, poll workers, and at how what happens at the polls affects voter confidence in the election process. The chapter by R. Michael Alvarez and Thad E. Hall argues for improved voter registration procedures that allow some degree of "transferability" with change in residence and that shift the burden from the voter to the government to assure that voters who wish to vote can easily do so. The concluding chapter, by Khalilah L. Brown-Dean, identifies mechanisms to foster ex-felon re-enfranchisement and shows how ex-felon disenfranchisement has had especially pernicious consequences for minority communities.

We now turn to a more detailed discussion of the arguments and findings of each of the chapters.

CHAPTER-BY-CHAPTER OVERVIEW

We are very pleased to include in our volume a foreword by Judge Danny Boggs and an epilogue by Samuel Issacharoff and Richard H. Pildes. Judge Boggs is a longtime member of the U.S. Court of Appeals, Sixth Circuit, who is highly knowledgeable about constitutional law and about elections worldwide. Issacharoff and Pildes are two of the country's leading election law specialists, and each played central roles in the preelection and election day litigation efforts of the Obama campaign in 2012, in areas such as voter lists, voter identification, and other issues of ballot access. Both are at New York University Law School (Bonnie and Richard Reiss Professor of Constitutional Law and Sudler Family Professor of Constitutional Law, respectively).

Judge Boggs's foreword emphasizes the importance of election administration for democratic decision making. We agree fully with Judge Boggs that "issues of ballot design, election administration, and voter education can be just as crucial as other campaign elements and ballot design deserves the same degree of forethought at a time when action can be taken in the interests of all voters and of the candidates and participants themselves." A central point made in the Issacharoff and Pildes postscript, which brings the U.S. election administration story though the 2012 elections and considers how close or potentially close elections raise legal issues, is about the legacy of *Bush v. Gore* vis-à-vis the spotlight it cast on "pervasive and structural dysfunctionalities of the American electoral system." In their view, these include a winner-take-all electoral college system that created the cliff effect necessary for Florida 2000, the "control of federal elections left in the hands of the states and, ultimately, in those of local county administrators," election day staff who are volunteers, "generally with inadequate training," and "partisan control of the machinery of elections."

In the opening chapter of this volume, Mark Braden and Robert Tucker look in detail at three of the most publicly visible recount disputes since *Bush v. Gore*: one gubernatorial (Washington, 2004), one for the U.S. Senate (Minnesota, 2008), and one for the U.S. House (Florida 13, 2006) and at one local-level recount dispute (a county-level juvenile court judge in Ohio) that would normally fly well below the radar were it not for the fact that, unlike these other cases, the trial court explicitly drew on the equal protection argument in *Bush v. Gore* to frame its ruling and that the Supreme Court may hear the case again after district court proceedings are completed. In their chapter, Braden and Tucker offer a template for classifying election law issues and alert us to the wide variety of election law controversies. They remind us that *Bush v. Gore* was only one of a number of presidential-election-related lawsuits in Florida, that Florida was only one of several states where presidential recount controversies were taking place (e.g., it is often forgotten that in New Mexico the presidential race in 2000 was even closer than in Florida), and that there were in 2000 (as there are today) many election challenges affecting all levels of public office and that these will primarily be litigated and decided on state law grounds, not in federal courts.

In addition to issues about who is eligible to run for office and procedures for getting candidates listed on the ballot (e.g., signature requirements), or about campaign funding legalities, or about election fraud in the narrow sense (e.g., ballot stuffing), among the many litigated election issues are polling place closing times; alleged discriminatory effects in purging the electoral rolls of dead and moved voters; voters turned away at the polls because of registration lists that wrongly omitted their names, or because of failure to present proper identification, or because of eligibility issues linked to supposed felony convictions or lack of citizenship – the flip side of which is voters wrongly allowed to vote; the handling of overseas military ballots and of other mail-in votes; issues of voter intimidation; ballot design problems (think of the "butterfly ballot" in Palm Beach), and so forth. In none of the three major recounts Braden and Tucker look at did the deciding court rely on *Bush v. Gore*. Braden and Tucker suggest that, even without the explicit disclaimer about the case's precedential value in the *per curiam* opinion, because *Bush v. Gore* was primarily about standards for a statewide recount based on equal protection, it will simply not be relevant to most election law disputes, even recounts, although it might apply to other domains where statewide equal protection issues might arise, such as those involving differential standards and practices for offering/validating provisional ballots.

Charles Anthony Smith looks at the precedential value of the *Bush v. Gore* opinion and tracks the degree to which courts, both federal and state, have subsequently cited the case. He identifies three different strands of the Supreme Court's views of the Florida recount. Some justices emphasized equal protection (with two believing that there should be statewide recounts held under uniform standards). Three justices asserted that the Florida Supreme Court had made "new law" when it ordered the recount and thus subverted the authority of the state legislature. But even more generally, as other commentators on the case have emphasized, there was also apparently great concern on the part of a number of justices that any further delay would obviate the state's "safe harbor" deadline and force a purely partisan political resolution of the dispute that would keep the dispute alive for even longer and cast doubts on the bona fides of the next president. Smith notes that only the first strand has struck a responsive chord with later courts. Despite the claim in the *per curiam* opinion about the decision only being applicable to the specific case facts at issue, substantial numbers of courts at all levels are citing *Bush v. Gore* in cases where equal protection issues can be said to apply. However, while Smith finds more than 100 federal cases in which *Bush v. Gore* has been cited, only a handful of these cases have actually treated the case as a relevant precedential authority. Moreover, with one key exception, a case still pending, the cases where judges made the greatest use of *Bush v. Gore* as precedent have been reversed on appeal. As Braden indicated in his comments at the conference, litigators of election law disputes continue to attempt to link some of their arguments to *Bush v. Gore* even though in almost all instances this proves unconvincing to the court before which they are arguing. Smith argues, however, that the claim that *Bush v. Gore* is without teeth is premature in that the idea of disparate impact as an equal protection violation (without a necessary showing of discriminatory intent) remains resonant with many attorneys, and may eventually gain more traction with judges, even in areas that are far removed from election law.

Amy Semet, Nathaniel Persily, and Stephen Ansolabehere look at public opinion regarding the *Bush v. Gore* decision, both in the immediate aftermath of the decision and more recently. While examining 2000 NAES data, their contribution also focuses extensively on recent survey data that they collected in 2010 on opinions about the fairness of this seminal decision by the Supreme Court. What is quite interesting and important about their contribution is that they find that among those survey respondents who have an opinion about the decision, the same factors – race, partisanship, political ideology, and Bush approval – that ten years ago polarized opinions about the decision continue to divide Americans about *Bush v. Gore*. They also find that *Bush v. Gore* has lingering effects on Americans' views about the Court. These findings, of course, open the door to many other questions that Semet and her coauthors pose; in particular, whether *Bush v. Gore* is unique in its effects on American public opinion or whether these attitudes about the case arise from more general opinions about the Court.

In the opening chapter in the next section of this volume, on the voting process, Charles Stewart III provides a synthetic overview of changes in election procedures over the past decade. Changes he discusses include access to ballots by the disabled, changes in ballot technology, and use of provisional ballots. Stewart views HAVA as the direct result of the Florida election controversy because, without that controversy and the deep flaws in election processes it revealed, there would never have been the pressure to do something about election technology that tended to frustrate voter intent. But Stewart, in the process of tracing the links between the 2002 passage of HAVA and the 2000 presidential election controversy, shows how *Bush v. Gore* served as an icebreaker (our word, not his), which once having opened the way to putting reform of election administration on the congressional agenda, allowed issues that were not of great moment in Florida to be key elements of the new legislation. While some parts of HAVA were directly responsive to problems that came up in Florida (e.g., funding for new election machines to replace punch cards, requirements to guarantee that voters not found on electoral rolls would have the opportunity to cast a provisional ballot that would be sequestered until a postelection-day determination of the voter's eligibility could be reached), what went into HAVA was affected by the agendas of various interest groups (e.g., lobbying for special ballot access provisions for the disabled) and by the particular agenda of key political actors (e.g., raising concerns about fraud at the polls by voters who were not legally entitled to vote – leading to language in HAVA about voter identification requirements).

It is commonly asserted that citizens and voters must have confidence in the outcome of an election so that the government taking power after the election has legitimacy. The Court in *Bush v. Gore* noted this, faulting Florida's contest provision by saying it was "not well calculated to sustain *the confidence that all citizens must have in the outcome of elections*" (emphasis added). However, while such normative concerns have often been stated about elections, prior to *Bush v. Gore* little attention was paid to the question of how confident voters and citizens were with the outcomes of elections, or with the process that produced those outcomes. Discussions about whether voters were confident in the American electoral process continued during the debates about HAVA, and that was about the time that scholars began to devise means to study voter confidence.[5] Hasen (2005) used what little survey data existed on voter confidence, and Alvarez, Hall, and Llewellyn (2008a) developed innovative survey questions to measure voter confidence in the 2004 presidential election.

More recently, a healthy and vibrant literature has arisen about voter confidence, as Lonna Rae Atkeson summarizes in her contribution to this volume. Instead of looking primarily at demographic divisions in voter confidence and at whether balloting technologies are associated with differing levels of confidence (as has been the primary focus of the literature on voter confidence), Atkeson uses voter confidence to study opinions about photo identification and fraud, as well as the changing context of elections. Her study is built on innovative surveys conducted in New Mexico, part of a longer-term project evaluating election administration reform in that state. Atkeson's study shows how sophisticated the state of research has become in the short period of time since *Bush v. Gore* and also provides important substantive results that will factor into current debates about voter confidence, photo identification, and fraud. One of the most interesting of these findings is that many voters who claim to be familiar with election fraud are using the term *fraud* in a very broad way to include virtually any form of elite activity that is seen as violating the spirit of free and open elections. And the fraud they are referencing is not something they have experienced firsthand.

Next, Paul Gronke tackles another important issue that has arisen since *Bush v. Gore*: early voting. Prior to the 2000 presidential election, few states allowed for widespread in-person early voting or voting by mail; the few academic studies that existed in the literature at the time looked mainly at how such procedures affected turnout and the composition of the electorate.[6] But, as Gronke notes, while the *Bush v. Gore* decision did not really bear on the question about where Americans would cast their ballots, whether in person on election day, in person before the election, or by mail, the 2000 election seems to stand as a watershed in the deployment of "convenience" voting innovations (defined loosely as efforts to make voting easier beyond election day voting). In Gronke's argument, *Bush v. Gore* is a catalytic event in the recent history of election administration; after the decision and the public attention this election generated about flaws in election administration, election administrators were much more willing to turn to new ideas like early voting. And there has been a slow but, in the longer run, dramatic increase in the proportion of the electorate voting elsewhere than in a polling station on election day, although clear regional differences appear in the likelihood that early voting provisions will be adopted.

In close elections, the side that is more efficacious in getting its voters to the polls will be advantaged. Even in elections that, on election day, are not so close, turnout issues might well affect election outcomes, which is why parties (and candidates) are so concerned about mobilizing the vote. But we also need to understand how election procedures themselves may affect turnout. In their chapter, Jan Leighley and Jonathan Nagler look at how absentee voting procedures, in particular the exact procedures associated with getting a ballot prior to an election, affect voter participation. The logic of their chapter is straightforward; they argue that absentee voting reforms should work like other reforms that lower the cost of voting (like election day voter registration). While they show that allowing easy absentee voting does increase participation, they do not find evidence in their analysis that permanent absentee voter registration procedures increase participation above and beyond the allowance of absentee voting, per se. However, they note that the data they use may lack the statistical power to distinguish an additional effect of making absentee voting status permanent.

In the last four chapters of this volume, authors discuss unresolved issues and proposals for reform. In her contribution, Martha Kropf discusses problems of ballot design. Oddly enough, despite the evidence of significant ballot design problems in the 2000 presidential election in Florida (for example, the Palm Beach "butterfly ballot"), questions about ballot design were not a factor in *Bush v. Gore*, nor were they much of a focus of HAVA. Instead, issues of ballot design have been left to states and counties, and, as Kropf discusses, this is an issue where very little progress has been made. It is the case that scholars like Kropf and her colleagues have studied ballot design issues, and that entities like the U.S. Election Assistance Commission have issued guidance to election officials about ballot design. But in her chapter Kropf notes that despite this attention, the empirical evidence she presents shows little sign that ballot design has improved dramatically. This stands as an area in need of more research and policy-making attention.

Thad E. Hall and Kathleen Moore look in detail at another largely overlooked topic, the human side of election administration, where the rubber meets the road, namely poll workers. Earlier research by Hall has noted that poll workers are "street-level bureaucrats," and in that capacity, they have been delegated substantial authority over the local conduct of elections (Alvarez and Hall, 2006; Hall, Monson, and Patterson, 2009). For example, research has shown that poll workers apply this discretion with regards to the application of voter identification procedures (Atkeson et al., 2010a). Here, Hall and Moore show that voter experience at the polls has a direct impact on voter confidence in the electoral process, identifying demographic characteristics of voters and specific aspects of the voting experience that affect confidence in election procedures. Hall and Moore conclude with suggestions for improving the training and performance of poll workers. This is but one important example of how better election administration could substantially improve a voter's experience at the polls (see also Gerken, 2009).

Another relatively unresolved issue at the state and local levels concerns voter registration. Like with ballot design, the *Bush v. Gore* decision was silent about voter registration issues. But as many of the studies and reports published in the aftermath of the 2000 presidential election note, a variety of voter registration problems cropped up in 2000, and by some estimates problems with voter registration might have accounted for more lost votes than bad ballots or faulty voting machines in that election.[7] These concerns led to many proposals for reform, and HAVA mandated two significant voter registration reforms: states were required to allow some form of provisional or "fail-safe" voting for those individuals who were not on the rolls, and states were also required to develop statewide, computerized voter registration databases.

R. Michael Alvarez and Thad E. Hall discuss these reforms in their contribution and argue that much work still needs to be done. In particular, they contend that states should consider modernization of their voter registration systems, to move those systems away from the current standard where voters need to be proactive to get on the voter rolls and for their information to stay current; rather, Alvarez and Hall argue that states should adopt more automatic and portable procedures so that eligible citizens who move to or within the state, who turn eighteen years of age, or who otherwise become eligible to vote are automatically added to the voter rolls in a way that makes them potentially eligible to vote in future elections. They argue that such reforms could minimize errors in voter registries that prevent people from participating or that lead them to have to cast provisional ballots; these reforms might also lead to higher levels of voter participation if implemented well. In their view, the primary effort for registering to vote should be moved from the voter to the government.

Khalilah Brown-Dean looks at one of the consequences of the initial decision by the framers to leave suffrage issues in the hands of the states, namely the tremendous variation in suffrage eligibility across the different states linked to state provisions for felon (and even more important, ex-felon) disenfranchisement/re-enfranchisement and reviews the unsuccessful legal challenges to felon disenfranchisement practices. Brown-Dean points out how both felon and ex-felon disenfranchisement affect African Americans to a much greater degree than they do non-Hispanic whites. The rules in place in many states are tantamount to a barrier, in that those who served time as a felon face a daunting task of returning to eligibility. She also looks at how felon disenfranchisement affects those of Spanish heritage and considers how various states have changed their laws affecting ex-felon voting. She argues that: "The automatic restoration of civil rights for eligible current and former felons, particularly where application for restoration is intended to be mostly perfunctory, should be sought as a crucial advancement over existing laws."

The focus of the chapters in this volume is either descriptive (e.g., identifying changes in election law over the past decade) or explanatory (e.g., using process tracing to look at the impact of the 2000 election controversy on subsequent changes in election administration, attempting via multivariate regression to assess the impact of particular election law changes on voter turnout), but it is impossible to write about elections without at least touching on central normative issues in democratic theory. In the remainder of this introduction we draw on the discussion at the 2011 conference that led to this volume to consider some of the more normative aspects of election administration.

A number of conference participants highlighted three of the frequently identified goals for an election:

1) An election must provide a winner (or winners).
2) The winner (or winners) should be known in a timely fashion and with finality.
3) An election contest should produce an outcome that is seen as legitimate both by the voters and by the losing candidate(s).

The first two of these seem relatively straightforward, and some variant of them is found in virtually everything written about election administration. For example, the 2001 Report of the Collins Center on the 2000 election in Florida commissioned by Governor Jeb Bush asserted that "Elections must achieve two competing goals: certainty (making every vote count accurately) and finality (ending elections so that governing can begin)."[8]

The third might seem equally straightforward and noncontroversial. Similarly as with the first two criteria, concern for the perceived public legitimacy of outcomes is found widely in the literature on election administration. For example, the 2001 Report of the Collins Center on the 2000 election in Florida asserted that "procedures for counting and challenging votes should be open, transparent, and easily documented to ensure public confidence in the results."[9] Related, the Report argued that "Voting methods … should meet uniform statewide and national standards for fairness, reliability and equal protection of voting opportunity."

But while these assertions seem completely unobjectionable, in determining what constitutes a legitimate outcome, we must recognize that legitimacy (a) involves a multiplicity of factors; (b) is in part based on perceptions about fairness (and the competence of election officials), which are subject to manipulation by elites; (c) may generate issues of trade-offs between legitimacy and the timely and unambiguous resolution of outcomes; and (d) is not synonymous with having an outcome that is identical to the preferences of the voters in the jurisdiction, or even an outcome that corresponds to the preferences of the voters who were actually at the polls if there are "legitimate" reasons why some preferences were not registered or had to be disregarded.[10] In particular, despite the many facts that problematize the 2000 election result, recognizing that there are virtues to finality, and having a greater degree of trust in the U.S. Supreme Court as the appropriate agency to resolve the conflict than they had in any other state or federal entity, after *Bush v. Gore*, most voters found it reasonable to accept the declared winner of the 2000 contest in Florida as our forty-first president, although partisan affiliations were strongly linked to how Americans evaluated the merits of the Supreme Court's decision.[11]

Five additional and more specific criteria for judging election administration were also discussed at the conference:

4) Choose election procedures that minimize the number of invalid ballots.
5) Use methods that maximize the likelihood that voter intent will be reflected in the tally of votes cast.
6) Choose election procedures that will enhance the likelihood of full citizen participation.
7) Implement procedures that make voting easy and convenient.
8) Make citizens' experience with elections one that reinforces confidence in the system and ensures that the process has a high degree of integrity.

The fourth criterion raised issues that were central to the Florida recounts because a number of votes were invalidated either because of over-vote (i.e., voting for more candidates than were eligible to be elected) or because a vote was not recorded for reasons such as incompletely cleared punch card chads. The criterion of minimizing invalid ballots has been widely used to compare different election technologies and to argue for the superiority of one over another. It has most often been operationalized in terms of what is called the "residual vote," that is, the difference between the number of voters who went to the polls on election day and the actual number of valid votes for a particular office, usually the highest office on the ballot, such as the presidency (see Stewart, Chapter 4, this volume).[12]

The fifth criterion is another one that became prominent in the Florida presidential contest in 2000. In the Collins Center 2001 Report on Florida elections, one normative goal asserted is that "Voting systems should be designed to determine voter intent, to the extent that is humanly possible."[13] Florida showed the potential difficulties in reading voter intent (the numerous varieties of hanging chad) and the mess that can be caused by confusing ballot formats such as the infamous "butterfly ballot" in Palm Beach that led to at least 3,000 ballots being recorded in ways that did not match the intent of the voter (Wand et al., 2001).

The sixth criterion, full citizen participation, is a staple of civic discourse and is used as a component of cross-national measures of a country's degree of democratization (e.g., Vanhanen, 2004). Because the United States has very low turnout compared to most other established democracies (Franklin, 2004), it scores somewhat lower than most other established democracies on Vanhanen's measure of functioning democracy. However, in a world where a book entitled *Don't Vote, It Just Encourages the Bastards* (O'Rourke, 2010) can become a best-seller, citizen duty, on the one hand, and concerns about electorates being unrepresentative of the overall population, on the other, run up against voluntaristic notions of political participation. For example, when the Collins Center 2001 Report asserts in seemingly the strongest possible terms: "The goal is perfection: every registered voter should have the opportunity to vote and every vote should count,"[14] the language of full participation and full ballot efficacy is couched in terms of those voters who are already registered, not in terms of eligible voters (much less potentially eligible voters, such as ex-felons).

The seventh criterion, ease of voting, is also widely supported. For example, the Collins Center 2001 Report claimed that "Voting should be a simple, convenient and friendly process that encourages each responsible citizen to express his or her choices."[15] While this goal, too, is admirable, it runs up against two realities: the blanket-sized ballot that characterizes many U.S. elections and the frequency of U.S. elections of diverse types – both features of elections rooted in a republican model of government that requires there be elected officials from a multiplicity of jurisdictions at all levels of government. Taking into account these two features of the United States in conjunction with our low turnout, A Wuffle once quipped about U.S. elections that "Nowhere else in the world do so few vote so often for so many" (personal communication, April 1, 1984).

Finally, one cannot have a discussion about elections and election administration without mention of voter confidence and the integrity of elections (or the inverse, which is a discussion of election fraud). One of the chapters in this volume, by Lonna Rae Atkeson, focuses attention on voter confidence and the integrity of elections, and there has been some discussion in the research literature about voter confidence (see Alvarez, Hall, and Llewellyn, 2008a, for more discussion). This connection between concerns about fraud and voter confidence has been made recently in litigation (*Crawford v. Marion County*),[16] and scholars have carried out significant research in recent years – spawned in part by questions arising from the *Bush v. Gore* controversy – about how to conceptualize and measure efforts to illegally manipulate election outcomes (Alvarez, Hall, and Hyde, 2008).

In looking at reforms of the voting process, once we moved beyond ballot technology, the recent public debate has largely been about fraud, for example, on issues such as the potential for computer hacking of electronic forms of ballots and even greater fears about the potential for manipulation of ballot tallies were there to be Internet voting, as well as the debate for the need for voter ID requirements at the polls as a means to combat alleged election fraud. Pursuing these issues is beyond the scope of the present volume because we wanted to focus on what has actually happened in the decade plus since *Bush v. Gore*, thus allowing our chapter authors to be primarily factual rather than speculative.

In particular, the volume editors opted against commissioning a chapter on photo ID (and similar) laws because issues connected to voter ID are very much in a state of flux, both legally and politically. Laws requiring voters to show identification are nothing new, but "they are becoming more numerous and more stringent" (Eversley, 2012). In 2011, for example, eight states (Alabama, Kansas, Mississippi, Rhode Island, South Carolina, Tennessee, Texas, and Wisconsin) either enacted new laws about proof of identification (usually photo ID) needed at the polling station or toughened existing laws (Eversley, 2012). At the time of writing (March 2012), although the new Wisconsin law mandating government-issued photo ID was implemented during the 2012 primary elections, its further use was enjoined by a state court (Smolka, 2012), while in South Carolina a new photo ID law was denied preclearance under Section 5 of the Voting Rights Act – a decision that is being appealed to a federal court. The U.S. Department of Justice is apparently considering preclearance denials for the new voter identification requirements in states such as Texas that fall under Section 5 coverage, with other legal challenges, for example, to the Kansas law requiring voters to provide proof of citizenship, which went into effect January 1, 2013, also likely (Eversley, 2012).

In Kansas, the secretary of state asserted that his office discovered thirty-two noncitizens on its voter rolls, out of 1.7 million registered voters. How many other voters who are not U.S. citizens are illegally registered in Kansas but remain undiscovered remains in dispute, as does the more general question about the magnitude of the illegal voting problem in the nation as a whole for which voter ID is the supposed remedy.[17] Other questions, for example, about the magnitude of the burden on voters in obtaining an appropriate form of identification and remembering to bring it with them to the polls and about appropriate trade-offs between Type I and Type II errors (although provisional ballots are intended to deal with voters who are legally registered but were unable to prove that fact on election day), as well as about the claim that racial and ethnic minorities are discriminatorily burdened by the requirement to have government-issued photo ID, are all in dispute.

While we do not wish to directly address any of these questions about the potential for fraud, what we can say is that we believe that the much greater potential for fraud associated with mail-in ballots as opposed to voting at the polls has gone virtually unaddressed.[18] Also, issues of other types of manipulation, for example, improper purging of eligible voters prior to an election, has not generally been a matter of public discussion, nor have allegations of voter intimidation.[19] Thus, while dramatic progress has been made in some respects, for example, improved ballot recording technology, many issues in election administration remain unresolved ten years after *Bush v. Gore*.

GLOSSARY

For readers who may be new to the area of election administration and reform, in the pages that follow we provide a glossary of terminology.

absentee ballot – see **absentee voting**.

absentee voting – most commonly used as synonymous with any form of voting that does not require the voter to be physically present at a polling station in order to cast a ballot. In some jurisdictions, voters who wish to vote absentee must attest that they will not be physically present in the jurisdiction on the day of election or are incapacitated from coming to the polls. When voters are not required to give specific reasons why they wish to vote absentee this is sometimes referred to as *no-excuse absentee voting* or as *no-fault absentee voting*.

active voter registration system – the compilation of a "permanent" statewide database that places more of the onus on the state to seek out and register new entrants to the state and to adjust registration enrollment when information is provided about relocations within the state of previously registered voters (for a more detailed treatment, see Alvarez and Hall, Chapter 10, this volume). Also see **EDR**.

advance voting – see **early voting**.

ballot – used (rather confusingly) to refer either to the way choices are presented to the voters in a given election (see **ballot format**, **ballot design**), or as synonymous with *vote* (e.g., I cast my ballot for Boss Tweed).

ballot design – the art and science of structuring ballot format so as to minimize voter confusion and to reduce the number of invalid or wrongly entered votes.

ballot format – the way ballot choices are displayed on the ballot, for example, by office, starting from the top of the ticket, with vertical columns indicating candidate names, and instructions for voting at the top of the ballot page. This term is also sometimes used to refer to the medium in which the ballot is presented to the voter, for example, paper, punch card, or electronic screen display, although the term *ballot technology* is more commonly used for this purpose.

ballot stuffing – adding fraudulently filled-in ballots so as to affect the election outcome. (NOTE: Ballot stuffing is but one of a bevy of fraudulent devices, including misreporting of ballot returns, destruction of ballots thought likely to be going to the "wrong" candidate or candidates, and failure to provide ballots to some of those eligible to vote, for example, by selectively removing subsets of the population from the registration lists.)

ballot technology – the medium in which the ballot is presented to the voter, for example, paper, punch card, electronic screen display, sometimes also called *election technology*, though the latter term has a broader connotation.

convenience voting – forms of voting that do not require the voter to go to the polls on one single election day, for example, absentee mail voting, **Internet voting**/absentee Internet voting, **early voting**.

covered jurisdiction – see Section 5.

disenfranchisement (also written as **disfranchisement**) – the removal of the right to vote, most commonly applied to those in prison or those who have been convicted of a felony, but also applied to someone convicted of treason. Re-enfranchisement rules vary widely by state in terms of how easy it is for those convicted of a felony offense who have completed their sentence to regain the right to vote after leaving prison or parole.

DRE – a direct recording electronic device, that is, a computer-based mode of recording ballot information/images, such as via a touch screen.

EAC – the Election Assistance Commission created by **HAVA** (q.v.) to serve as a clearinghouse for election research, but with no rule-making authority. (Under the Obama administration this agency has been impotent because Republicans wish to eliminate it.)

early voting – voting rules that allow a voter to cast a ballot at designated locations at times in advance of a single scheduled election day (often, however, used as synonymous with **convenience voting**, q.v.).

EDR – election day registration, that is, allowing voters to come to the polling place and to register the day of the election rather than having to preregister days or weeks in advance. Also see **active voter registration system**.

election administration – the art and science of conducting elections.

election contest – a challenge to the legality of procedures/outcomes in a given election. The contest phase of an election dispute normally comes after the recount phase and is distinct from it. Typically, a contested election is a formal challenge to the outcome of an election – a charge that the declared winner is, for any number of possible reasons, not the true winner. A *recount* is a retabulation of the vote, simply another count (see Braden and Tucker, Chapter 1, this volume, for further clarification of the legal issues involved).

election fraud – a general term for any deliberately fraudulent attempt to corrupt the outcome or process of an election, with **ballot stuffing** (q.v.) one of the most blatant techniques used. (As noted in the Atkeson chapter in this volume, the public sometimes uses this term in a much more inclusive fashion to include "virtually any form of elite activity that is seen as violating the spirit of free and open elections.")

election law – the body of state and federal law that regulates the conduct of campaigning, campaign finance, election technology, vote counting, recounts, registration procedures, suffrage eligibility, and so forth.

election technology – a general term used variously for the mode in which the ballot is presented to the voter, for example, paper, punch card, electronic screen display; the way ballots are tabulated, for example, by hand, electronically from computer input, electronically after scanning of ballots; and the mechanism(s) for validation of the vote count.

ex-felon disenfranchisement – see **disenfranchisement**.

felon disenfranchisement – see **disenfranchisement**.

HAVA – the Help America Vote Act, passed in 2002. It mandated major changes in election technology so as to minimize the likelihood that votes would not be recorded or would be recorded wrongly, required that procedures be put into place for **provisional ballots** (q.v.), and required the creation of statewide computerized registration data lists. Accompanying the passage of HAVA, Congress provided a substantial carrot of federal funds to motivate state compliance with its provisions.

Internet voting – voting involving ballots that are provided to voters electronically and returned to election officials electronically. (This form of voting may be done in such a fashion so as to eliminate the need for polling stations entirely, by handling the entire election electronically.)

lever machine – a machine, usually a bulky one, where a set of candidate names were visible at the same time on the front of the machine, and voters indicated their vote by moving a lever below (or to the side of) the candidate (s) they chose from an off position to an on position. In many of these machines a single larger lever allowed voters to cast a partisan ballot, returning a vote for all candidates of a given party for all partisan offices, that is, a **straight ticket vote**.

mail ballot – a form of **absentee voting** (q.v.) that involves ballots that are sent to voters and returned to election officials via the U.S. mail. (This form of voting may be done in such a fashion so as to eliminate the need for polling stations entirely, by handling the entire election via the mails.)

minority vote dilution – see **vote dilution**.

no-excuse absentee voting (also known as no **fault absentee voting**) – see **absentee voting**.

NVRA – the National Voter Registration Act, passed by Congress in 1993, sought to ease the registration process for eligible voters by providing incentives for states to adopt **election day registration (EDR)** or to make registration forms available in state agencies.

optical scanning device – a device that scans paper or punch ballots to transfer the information on them to computer readable form.

overseas military ballots – **absentee ballots** (q.v.) cast by military personal who were not resident in the United States on election day.

over-vote – a ballot that records a vote for more candidates than there are seats to be filled. Normally this results in an invalid ballot.

partisan polarization – at the voter level, a pattern in which Republican and Democratic identifiers differ substantially on candidate or ballot proposition choices, or on issue preferences, or on beliefs about ostensibly factual matters.

polarization – see **racial polarization**, **partisan polarization**.

polling place – the location in which voting takes place if voting is done in person (also known as *polling station* or *precinct*). When referring to the tabulation of votes from a given polling station these are often referred to as the *precinct-level results*.

polling station – see **polling place**.

precinct – see **polling place**.

preclearance review – see **Section 5**.

provisional ballot – a ballot given to a voter who is not shown as registered to vote in that polling station but who claims eligibility. Such ballots are segregated from those of voters known to be eligible, allowing time for the eligibility of the voter to be further investigated and, if the voter is found eligible, allowing his or her ballot to be counted.

punch card machine – a machine that records votes by having voters mechanically or physically punch though a paper ballot so as to leave a hole (punch) by the name of the candidate for whom the voter is casting a vote.

purging – the practice of removing from the voting rolls those individuals who are dead or who have not voted in recent elections and thus may have moved from the jurisdiction. This term is also used for the practice of removing from the voting rolls those individuals who are supposedly illegally on the rolls, for example, because they are ex-felons not entitled to vote or because they are noncitizens not entitled to vote.

racial polarization – at the voter level, a pattern in which non-Hispanic white and African American or Hispanic voters differ substantially on candidate or ballot proposition choices, or on issue preferences, or on beliefs about ostensibly factual matters.

Re-enfranchisement – see **disenfranchisement**.

residual vote – the difference between the number of voters who went to the polls on election day and the actual number of valid votes for a particular office, usually the highest office on the ballot. Also see **roll-off, under-vote**.

recount – the legally mandated recount of ballots when the discrepancy between the first place candidate and the runner-up is below some predetermined threshold. A recount is distinct from an election controversy (q.v.).

roll-on – see roll-off.

roll-off – the drop off in the number of votes that are cast for offices below the top of the ticket. (Normally the highest number of votes is recorded for the most important office on the ballot, though there can be exceptions if that office is not highly contested.) Also see **residual vote, under-vote**.

rolls – see **voting rolls**.

Section 2 – this section of the VRA (q.v.) applies to all jurisdictions. Its most important provision sets standards for what constitutes "minority vote dilution" and allows individual plaintiffs in a protected class to challenge in federal courts election law provisions claimed to violate Section 2.

Section 5 – this section of the VRA (q.v.) applies only to jurisdictions found to have a history of practices that had a discriminatory purpose or effect. It had applied to sixteen states in whole or in part. "Covered jurisdictions," that is, jurisdictions that come under Section 5 review by the Voting Rights Section of the Civil Rights Division of the U.S. Department of Justice (DOJ) must submit any changes in election procedures, from changes in legislative district boundaries down to the level of moving the location of a polling station, to the DOJ for what is called *preclearance*. Only if the change is agreed to (i.e., precleared) by the DOJ or by the Federal District Court for the District of Columbia can the jurisdiction implement the change in election practice. A recent Supreme Court decision has placed the preclearance provisions in limbo until Congress creates a new set of requirements for which states will be covered under Section 5 of the Act.

Section 5 preclearance review – see **Section 5**.

signature requirement – the requirement that, for a candidate to appear on a ballot, the candidate must demonstrate a minimum potential level of support, as signaled by the willingness of legal voters in the jurisdiction to sign a nominating petition on the candidate's behalf. (Sometimes signature requirements are also distributional, for example, for statewide office, requiring a certain number of signatures in a certain number of counties.) In those states that allow popular initiatives, signature requirements also commonly apply before voters can place an initiative on the ballot.

straight ticket vote – a vote cast for all and only candidates of a given party.

top of the ticket – the highest office on the ballot. Normally ballots are formatted so that the first office on which voters are asked to cast their vote is the top of the ticket office. By convention, in the United States, federal offices are regarded as more important than state offices, and state offices more important than local offices.

under-vote – a ballot that fails to record a vote for the (or a) top of the ticket office even though it contains votes for offices lower on the ballot. (Sometimes this term is used even more generally to refer to any ballot that does not contain votes for all offices and ballot propositions for which the voter might have voted, but the first definition we give is the preferred one.) Also see **residual vote, roll-off.**

vote dilution – a term of art in election law referring to election practices that operate to minimize or cancel out the voting strength of minority groups designated by Congress as protected by the VRA (or protected directly under the "equal protection" clause of the Fourteenth Amendment).

voter confidence – in the Atkeson chapter (this volume) voter confidence is measured by a series of questions at different levels of government asking "How confident are you that your vote and all the votes at the XXXX level of government were counted as the voter(s) intended?"

voter identification requirement – a requirement that a voter at the polling station provide one of several specified forms of identification before being allowed to vote. States vary widely in their voter ID rules, and in 2012 some of the most stringent of these that had recently been adopted, often involving the requirement that voters present a picture ID from a state authority, were struck down in federal courts or their implementation delayed until voters have been given more time to familiarize themselves with the requirement and to take steps to satisfy it if they do not already possess a valid driver's license or other official state ID.

voting rolls – the list of voters eligible to vote.

VRA – Voting Rights Act of 1965: the most important federal statute dealing with issues of racial and ethnic/linguistic representation. It has been subsequently amended several times and was reauthorized (with further changes) by Congress in 2006, to be in force for the next twenty-five years. Two of the most important provisions of the VRA are Section 5 (q.v.) and Section 2 (q.v.).

Notes

1 As shown in the National Opinion Research Center (partial) recount, http://www. norc.org/projects/ByClient/Tribune+Publishing/, sponsored by a number of leading news organizations (*New York Times, Wall Street Journal, Washington Post, Tribune Publishing, CNN, Associated Press, St. Petersburg Times,* and *Palm Beach Post*), just as, prior to election day, the Florida presidential result was regarded as "too close to call," and the initial tallied results had the candidates only a hair's breadth apart, so, even with time to count some 180,000 ballots that were not registered as valid – an admittedly incomplete sample of all the votes that might have been recounted – a good case can be made that the election remained "too close to call." Had there been a complete statewide hand recount, some ballots that were not previously counted would have been awarded to one candidate or the other. But given the problem of ascertaining the intent of the voter, seemingly minor variations in what standards were used might have determined the winner of the recount. However, regardless of the controversy over how to count problematic ballots, one conclusion about the 2000 Florida presidential contest is clear, namely that a different result would also have been reached had any of the following counterfactuals

been true: (a) if Ralph Nader was not on the ballot in Florida, (b) if the form of the Palm Beach ballot had not frustrated a substantial number of voters from fill-ing out the ballot in a way that reflected their true voting preference, but with the ballots cast not permitting any reliable way of determining which voters may have been confused by the format (Wand et al., 2001), (c) if Florida's rules for ex-felon re-enfranchisement were not among the harshest in the nation (Manza and Uggen, 2004), (d) if key controversies about the handling of absentee ballots in particular counties in the 2000 Florida presidential election – ones that were not at issue in *Bush v. Gore* – had been decided differently in earlier litigation in Florida and fed-eral courts (Gillman, 2001).

2 Comments at the conference on *"Bush v. Gore* Ten Years Later: Election Administration in the U.S." sponsored by the University of California Center for the Study of Democracy and the Jack W. Peltason Chair, in conjunction with the Caltech/MIT Voting Technology Project, Laguna Beach, California, April 16–17, 2011.

3 In the weeks after the 2000 election debacle in Florida, Gov. Jeb Bush asked the Collins Center for Public Policy to oversee a task force assembled to analyze the state's elections system and recommend improvements. In March 2001, the task force produced a report, "Revitalizing Democracy in Florida," with thirty-five rec-ommendations: https://collinscenter.site-ym.com/resource/resmgr/Elections_docs/Revitalizing_Democracy_in_Fl.pdf. Many of these recommendations have since been implemented. According to "A Report on Election Reform in Florida after *Bush v. Gore*," issued in 2010 by the Collins Center for Public Policy, "all counties use optical scan voting machines rather than the hodge-podge of hardware, including the infamous punch-card machines, used in 2000. The optical scan machines leave a paper trail voters and elections officials can review at the polling place if necessary. The state outlawed lever machines, true paper ballots, punch-card voting systems and touch-screen computers that leave no paper trail. All ballots are now tabulated at the precinct. In many counties that used touch-screen technology, the votes were moved from the precinct and downloaded at a central location. A statewide voter registration system helps weed out duplicate voters, which was a problem in 2000." The state also now has "a uniform ballot design" and "a uniform methodology for recounts" https://collinscenter.site-ym.com/page/voting_home. These reforms have had important effects in Florida; for example, Stewart estimated that between 2000 and 2004 the *residual vote rate* (i.e., the difference between the number of voters who went to the polls on election day and the actual number of valid votes for a particular office, usually the highest office on the ballot, such as the presidency; see Stewart, Chapter 4, this volume) in Florida fell from 2.9 percent to 0.4 percent (Stewart, 2006, p. 16).

4 See, e.g., *Jacobs v. Seminole County Canvassing Board* 773 So, 2d 519 (Florida Supreme Court, 2000), *Harris v. Florida Elections Canvassing Commission* 235 F. 3rd 578 (Eleventh Circuit 2000). Indeed, arguably, the decisions in cases dealing with absentee ballots that sought to make every vote count and to avoid disqualify-ing ballots where the intent of the voter could be clearly ascertained (e.g., allowing overseas military ballots to be counted under a very relaxed standard as to post-mark verification, allowing absentee ballots to count whose voter ID information had been added subsequent to their mail in by Republican election officials) had a decisive impact on the presidential election outcome in Florida (see Gillman, 2001,

esp. pp. 52–53, 108–11, 137–40). Also see Imai and King (2004) on whether illegal overseas absentee ballots affected the outcome of the 2000 presidential election in Florida.

5 For example, two of the most significant federal commissions formed to make proposals to reform the American electoral process after 2000 used the term *confidence* prominently in their materials. The Carter-Ford commission titled its 2001 report "To Assure Pride and Confidence in the Electoral Process," while the Carter-Baker commission's report was titled "Building Confidence in U.S. Elections" (see Alvarez, Hall, and Llewellyn, 2008a).

6 For example, see the early papers on these questions by Patterson and Caldeira (1985), Richardson and Neeley (1996), Stein and Garcia-Monet (1997), and Southwell and Burchett (2000).

7 The Caltech/MIT Voting Technology Project estimated that of the 4–6 million votes potentially lost in the 2000 presidential election, 1.5–3 million were lost because of voter registration problems.

8 https://collinscenter.site-ym.com/resource/resmgr/Elections_docs/ Revitalizing_Democracy_in_Fl.pdf, p. 9.

9 Ibid.

10 Also see Atkeson, Chapter 5, this volume.

11 Moreover, partisan differences in legitimacy attribution for elections in Florida (and elsewhere) persist to the present day. For example, survey research on voter confidence has found significant differences along racial and partisan lines (Alvarez, Hall, and Llewellyn, 2008a).

12 The "residual vote" concept has been used in many studies, ranging from Ansolabehere and Stewart (2005) to Alvarez, Beckett, and Stewart (2011).

13 But as the Caltech/MIT Voting Technology Project pointed out at about the same time, "Reducing the number of lost votes is a very important goal, but it is not the only factor in the choice of equipment. Security and misvotes are also important … (as are) auditability, management, and accessibility" (2001a, p. 24).

14 https://collinscenter.site-ym.com/resource/resmgr/Elections_docs/Revitalizing_ Democracy_in_Fl.pdf p. 8.

15 Ibid., p. 9.

16 *Crawford et al. v. Marion County Election Board et al.*, Certiorari to the U.S. Court of Appeals for the Seventh Circuit, No. 07–21, argued January 9, 2008, decided April 28, 2009.

17 We say "supposed remedy" because there appears a clear partisan subtext to the imposition of voter photo ID laws, which are adopted disproportionately in states under Republican control.

18 At the conference on "*Bush v. Gore* Ten Years Later: Election Administration in the U.S." sponsored by the University of California Center for the Study of Democracy and the Jack W. Peltason Chair, in conjunction with the Caltech/MIT Voting Technology Project, Laguna Beach, California, April 16–17, 2011, Charles Stewart III commented that "The next *Bush v. Gore* will be about absentee ballots." Also see the comments about fraud in the Stewart chapter in this volume.

19 The issue of voter purges came up in 2008 and resulted in a federal district court lawsuit, *Common Cause v. Colorado* (Case 1:08-cv-02321). On voter intimidation, and the more general issues associated with studying election fraud or election crimes, see the EAC's 2006 report (Wang and Serevrov, 2007), and the essays in the volume edited by Alvarez, Hall, and Hyde (2008).

PART I

BUSH V. GORE IN PERSPECTIVE

I

Disputed Elections Post *Bush v. Gore*

Mark Braden and Robert Tucker

INTRODUCTION

The two most vital qualities of any voting system are simple to identify: (1) the winner wins – that is, the candidate with the most lawful votes is elected; and (2) the loser and his or her "reasonable" supporters believe they have lost. All other considerations are secondary.

This chapter provides a broad overview of U.S. practices for the resolution of disputed elections and inventories types of election disputes. Then it examines in some detail four election disputes that took place after the *Bush v. Gore* decision. Three of the disputes are studied because they arguably are the most widely followed and extensively contested election results since 2000: Washington gubernatorial (2004), Minnesota Senate (2008), and Florida Thirteenth Congressional District (2006). The final dispute, an Ohio Common Pleas Court Juvenile Judge contest, is examined because, as of early 2011, it was the only significant decision using *Bush v. Gore* as precedential authority in an election contest or recount.

TYPES OF ELECTION DISPUTES AND MODES OF RESOLUTION

The standard American pattern for determining election results, although not universal, is election night tabulation at each individual polling or precinct location followed by a canvassing of ballots and tabulated results at a central location (usually a county board of election) with an official certification of the results. This is followed by a period during which a recount may be conducted and/or a contest filed. In some jurisdictions, the recount and/or contest must be filed prior to certification of the results.

There is no common law basis for either an election recount or a contest, so the rights of candidates or their supporters are principally set forth in state statutes[1] or regulations. The details vary greatly among the states, but they are similar in general framework. The terms *recount* and *contest* often are used interchangeably, but they are more properly understood as two generally distinguishable processes.

Typically, a contested election is a formal challenge to the outcome of an election – a charge that the declared winner is, for any number of possible reasons, not the true winner. A recount is a retabulation of the vote, simply another count. A recount is usually employed when the challenger alleges mistakes/improprieties in the tabulation of the votes. Recounts are most often not a formal part of a judicial contest procedure, but a separate administrative process.

Recounts have a standard specific resolution, namely a new tabulation of votes with a "new" official result. Election contests can have three possible alternative outcomes: (1) the election result and certification are confirmed (the most common); (2) the election certification is changed and the contesting candidate is certified the winner; or (3) the election is voided with no candidate receiving a certification and a new election is required to fill the vacancy.

Although state election statutes generally provide for an administrative recount procedure, judicial involvement is occasionally set forth in statute, and if not set forth in statute is often sought by the party unhappy with the proposed administration. The most prevalent recount system is mandatory or automatic recounts at the expense of the state or local governments if the difference in votes between candidates is less than a certain percentage figure. The alternative model is a recount done at a candidate's request (a number of states have a hybrid model with provisions for both automatic and candidate-requested recounts).

Because most recounts must be conducted prior to the issuance of any certificates of nomination or election, strict statutory timelines govern the initiation of the recount process. In the states where an election official starts the process, the statutes usually require the official to order the recount as soon as it is clear that the race was close enough and no later than the day set aside for the official canvass of the vote. In practice, election officials generally order a recount as soon as they know one is warranted in order to minimize a delay in the official certification of the election. In states where candidates or voters initiate the process, the law spells out deadlines for filing the recount request or petition. The specified period for filing is relatively short, with no state permitting a recount request to be filed beyond ten days from the date of the canvass.

In seeking to make sense of election administration of recounts and contests both before and after the Supreme Court decision in *Bush v. Gore*, there are a baker's dozen of key points to understand.

First, a very tiny percentage of the individuals who count the ballots on election night are professional election officials. Most hold other jobs. Many are retirees or students. They work at a polling place maybe twice a year, from before 6:00 A.M. to often after 9:00 P.M., for modest pay. Even the observers of the tabulation process are usually party or candidates' volunteers, not professionals.

Second, in comparison to other Western democracies, the United States has many more elected officials and ballot issues. In America, counting the ballots on an average election day is a much more difficult and lengthy process because the ballot is longer and more complex. There are simply many more ballot places (items to count). The vast expansion of mail and absentee voting has expanded and will continue to expand the number of the ballots that are the most problematic to count.

Third, while technological advances hold a hope that, in the future, the difficulties of remotely cast ballots and verifying the eligibility of those casting ballots will be significantly eased, at the current time these "tech" fixes are only theoretical and not practicable. Internet ballot casting and verification processes are still future possibilities, not current programs. Also, faxed and phone voice transmittals of ballots are viable alternatives for the casting of a ballot but, at present, not for the casting of a secret ballot.

Fourth, because of the large number of elected offices and ballot measures in the United States, every election year sees a number of recounts, but only a very small *percentage* of election results in the nation are recounted.

Fifth, very few recounts result in reported judicial opinions because most recounts are administrative in nature, very fact driven, with strict statutory time limits.

Sixth, only a small percentage of recounts leads to contested elections. The candidates who are the apparent losers usually are too physically, emotionally, financially, and politically exhausted to pursue a contest. The "political sore loser" label is not easily shed. The contestant always has the burden of proof and the regularity of election results is a strong presumption to overcome, with judges commonly expressing their desire that the voters, not themselves (judges) decide any election. These factors combine to make actual election contest actions rare in comparison to recounts.

Seventh, very few of these recounts (or contests following recounts) receive national attention because most involve only local candidates or ballot issues. During the 2010 election cycle, for example, despite the fact that the 2010 congressional races were among the most widely and seriously contested races in recent American political history, there were fewer than ten House recounts and only a single U.S. Senate recount.[2] Moreover, despite the existence of recounted congressional elections in 2012, no election contest actions were filed in the U.S. House or Senate. There were also no recounts in gubernatorial contests that year.[3] It is important to appreciate that most of what we think we know about recounts comes from a handful of highly publicized high-stakes recounts, and that these cases are highly atypical. This applies especially to *Bush v. Gore*, where both federal and state issues were implicated and courts construed both federal and state statutes.

Eighth, not only are the implications of a case like *Bush v. Gore* limited for future recounts because of the peculiar nature of the context and litigation history in that case (and the Supreme Court's insistence on its uniqueness regarding its potential use as a precedent), but even without these limitations, it would necessarily be limited in its impact because the conditions for recounts to take place are, by and large, set by state or local statute, and contests that are not close enough to trigger a recount according to those statutes (i.e., the vast preponderance of all contests) will remain not close enough to trigger a recount.

Ninth, in 2000, and especially afterward, virtually all the journalistic attention was devoted to *Bush v. Gore*, but that case was but one of many involving the presidential race in Florida, and arguably not even the most important. Although what is remembered from Florida are disputes about counting procedures (how to interpret dangling and other types of chads as signals of voter intent, whether there was any legal remedy for the effects of the voter confusion caused by the so-called butterfly ballot in Palm Beach), other cases litigated during that controversy dealt with issues like the admissibility of some ordinary mail ballots and many military ballots because of problems like the legibility/absence of signatures, and whether there was reliable recorded information about date of receipt or clear postmarks showing when a ballot was sent. Also there was controversy about registration purges that took place prior to the election allegedly disproportionately deleting minorities from registration rolls, and about Florida's rules for (felon and) ex-felon disenfranchisement that operated to reduce the percentage of African Americans and Hispanics in the electorate.

Tenth, although there are an unlimited number of ways for voting and vote tabulations to be miscarriages, they can be placed into three general categories: (1) malfeasance; (2) mistakes/misfeasance; and (3) acts of God.

It is beyond the scope of this chapter to discuss these three categories in detail; however, a brief outline may be useful.

Malfeasance

A. Candidate/Agents	*Tunno v. Veysey*, H. Rep. Wo. 92–626, 92d Cong. (1970)
	Also see: *Moreau v. Tonry*, 433 F. Supp. 620 (E.D. La 1977)
B. Election Officials	*Stevenson v. Thompson*, In re Contest for Governor, 444
	N.E.2d 170 (Ill. 1983)
	Roe v. State of Ala. Evans (11th Cir. 1997)/*Alabama/ Chief Justice*
	Anderson v. United States, 417 U.S. 211 (1974)
C. Third Parties/Voters	*United States v. Franklin*, 181 F.2d 182 (7th Cir. 1951)
	United States v. Girdner, 754 F.2d 877 (10th Cir. 1985)
	United States v. Clapps, 732 F.2d 1148 (3rd Cir. 1984)
	Dornan/ Sanchez, U.S. House (1998)

Misfeasance/Mistakes

A. Mistake Officials

1) Math/counting. *Thorsness v. Daschle*, 285 N.W. 2d 590 (S.D. 1979)
2) Missed or uncounted ballots (absentee/emergency/provisional/regular)
3) Wrong districts – VA Rep., Dist. 14, 1984
4) Ballot printing errors: *Hendon v. N. Carolina St. Bd. of Election*, 710 F.2d 177 (1984); *Kohler v. Tugwell*, 292 F.Supp. 978 (E.D. Lc 1968); Aff'd 393, U.S. 531 (1969). In Re Election Atty. Gen. of Ohio 569 N.E. 2d.447 (Ohio 1991)
5) Machine failure/voting machine setup. *Buonenno v. DiStefano*, 430 A.2d 765 (1981)
6) Absentee ballots *Akizaki v. Fong*, 51 Haw. 354 (1969)
7) Registration errors. In Re General Election – (531 A. 2d. 836 Penn. 1985)
8) Noneligible voters (felons, aliens)

B. Mistake Voter

1) Absentee ballots
2) Identifying marks
3) Illegible/unclear
4) Over-vote

Acts of God

A. Floods
B. Fires
C. Earthquakes

Eleventh, there are two alternative views as to what a contestant must prove to overcome the presumption of valid official election results. Some jurisdictions require the contestant to show that he or she received the most legal votes – the "but for" analysis: I received the most lawful votes cast for the office, but for the intervening misfeasance, malfeasance, act of God, or a combination thereof.[4] The other view requires that the contestant show only that it is impossible to determine which candidate received or would have received the most lawful votes for the office.[5]

Contest actions focus predominantly on two issues: (1) uncounted ballots; (2) illegally cast/counted ballots.

Uncounted ballots can be simply lost or overlooked ballots common to all large elections. The argument of whether these ballots should be counted when found usually revolves around security or chain-of-custody questions. The most often misplaced ballots are absentee ballots, although election day systems using paper ballots (scan or traditional) also lose ballots regularly.

In every election, absentee and provisional ballots are rejected for specific reasons. The validity of absentee ballots depends on a number of legal requirements such as a signature, oath, witness(es), notary, timely arrival, or postmark. With so many steps, voters and election officials can and will make many mistakes. Decisions on absentee and provisional ballots are at the center of many election disputes because uncounted absentee and provisional ballots are usually from specific precincts, and often an unopened ballot can be linked to a specific individual. These ballots can be placed into various categories from which contestants can conclude with varying degrees of certitude their electoral impact if counted.

Twelfth, illegally cast ballots present especially difficult questions in election contests. Of course, the first issue is the identification of the illegal ballots. Principally, these are ballots cast by individuals not eligible to vote in a particular race[6] or a group(s) of ballots defective under state law for a variety of reasons.[7]

Identifying illegal ballots cast is only the initial evidentiary step. The next step is how to determine the impact of the illegal ballots on the election. Most elections have improperly cast ballots, but are they sufficient in number to be material? Is their number sufficient to change the result or bring it into question?

In some jurisdictions, it will be sufficient simply to show that there are more illegal ballots counted than the margin between the candidates for an election to be voided. However, other jurisdictions require some form of evidentiary presentation on how the illegal votes were cast. This can be in the form of direct testimony, which has obvious problems in the context of secret balloting,[8] or alternatives such as proportional reductions.[9]

Finally, no electoral process is sufficiently exact in design or execution to determine outcomes widely held to be legitimate without recount and contest processes. For example, when the ballot is a piece of paper given to a voter to be marked in secret, the voter's intent can be difficult to determine. As anyone experienced with large recounts can attest, the artistic originality or ingenuity of some voters defy reasonable intent analysis. While a number of methods designed to replace paper ballots have advantages in making recounts easier, each has its own problems.

The optical scan system is now the most widely used balloting system in the United States. All optical scan systems have inherent problems[10] because each ballot is still a piece of paper. Each ballot can be folded, bent, mutilated, gotten wet, or lost. Individual optical scan ballots are pieces of paper that are always lost and/or found in recounts. The misplaced/lost/found ballots are then subjected to security issues. Are these ballots properly cast? Have they been or could they have been tampered with? It is difficult to lose large mechanical lever voting machines; even smaller DRE systems generally are not misplaced. Opposition to electronic voting devices is growing, however, due to a perception held by at least some voters and activists that DRE systems are not secure, and historically there has been concern about proofing mechanical lever voting machines against tampering.

We now turn to four recent recounts and subsequent contests that illustrate many of these points.

FOUR RECENT RECOUNTS

The Washington Gubernatorial Race – 2004

The 2004 Washington gubernatorial race followed the standard textbook path for a disputed election: count, machine recount, and hand re-recount – all administrative but with various court disputes before and during each "count" concerning how or what to count. The certification of the election was followed by the filing of an election contest in Washington Superior Court. The 2008 Franken/Coleman Senate dispute also played out in a number of different court proceedings. It was classic recount litigation. The recount was principally a dispute about uncounted absentee ballots, with the candidate that was behind at each stage seeking to have additional ballots counted.

The basic facts of this dispute can be briefly set forth. Initial tabulations of the ballots cast in Washington's general election on November 2, 2004, showed Dino Rossi (R) receiving the most votes for the office of governor. The margin between Dino Rossi and his opponent, Christine Gregoire (D), was merely 261 votes out of more than 2.8 million votes counted – less than one half of one percent of the total number of votes cast for the two candidates. Washington Secretary of State Sam Reed[11] ordered a mandatory machine recount pursuant to Washington statute.[12] After the machine recount, Rossi led Gregoire by only 42 votes statewide. The ballots were then hand counted, resulting in a Gregoire margin of 129 votes. Of course, these basic facts leave out the ten lawsuits and the continuous roller coaster of changing vote totals.

The initial counting process in Washington is much slower than in most states because of the extensive use of mail/absentee ballots. Washington provides that a mail ballot postmarked by election day must be counted. This results in some valid mail ballots arriving at county election offices two weeks after election day. Washington also provides for a more "liberal" provisional voting procedure requiring that provisional ballots cast anywhere in the state by registered voters be counted in statewide races.[13] The combination of these factors resulted in an estimated 850,000 uncounted ballots remaining following election night tabulations. But, even with such a large number of uncounted ballots, it was quickly clear to all observers that the election result would be extremely close and a recount very likely.

By November 17, all county canvassing boards certified their general election returns. Rossi had "won" by 261 votes out of 2.8 million.

Litigation Pre-recount

The first lawsuit was filed in King County Superior Court on November 12, 2004, before the initial canvass was even completed. The Democratic Party brought suit, seeking the names and addresses of those individuals whose provisional ballots were ruled invalid by county election officials. The county's failure to release this information was argued to be a violation of Washington State and federal constitutional equal protection rights and state public disclosure rules. Although it was far from clear that any county in the state had ever released this information, over the objections of the Republicans, the King County Superior Court ordered that the county release the 929 names to the Democratic Party. Democratic Party workers sought to contact those on the list identifiable as Democratic voters, attempting to qualify their ballots before the completion of the canvass. This process produced few, if any, changes in provisional ballot counts.

Recount I – Machine

The mandatory recount began on Saturday, November 20, 2004. The Washington electorate casts most of its votes on optical scan ballots. In theory, the mandatory machine recount consists of simply repeating the election night process of running the ballots through optical scanning machines for tabulation. This first recount, done by machine, followed a pattern familiar to anyone experienced with disputed elections. Ballots that were not counted in the initial count were discovered and simple tabulation errors found.

In Snohomish County, an election worker discovered 224 properly marked but uncounted ballots sitting in a tray in a secured room. The ballots had been prepared for counting, but mistakenly placed in a stack of empty trays. When additional trays were stacked on top, the ballots were buried out of sight. Despite the newly added votes, the county's recount of more than 350,000 ballots resulted in a net change of only one vote. The "lost" ballots in Snohomish County were evenly divided between the candidates.

Cowlitz County reported that ninety-nine fewer ballots were counted in the machine recount than during the original count. Lost ballots? No, a careful review of the tabulation records showed that a stack of absentee ballots was inadvertently counted twice on election night. The county reported twenty-nine fewer votes for Gregoire and forty fewer votes for Rossi, a net gain to Gregoire of eleven votes. Minor changes were recorded in many precincts around the state; however, the recount outside of King County resulted in very little net change.

By the end of the day on November 22, 2004, the machine recount was completed in twenty-four counties. Most of these results favored Rossi, adding some twenty-five votes to his original 261-vote lead. However, King County had yet to report. The significant net change in the election results following the machine recount was largely attributable to changes in the results in King County, the largest and most heavily Democratic county in the state.

According to the initial count in King County, Gregoire received 59 percent of the votes cast for either Gregoire or Rossi. In the machine recount, King County counted an additional 941 votes cast for the two candidates, of which 66.6 percent were for Gregoire. At each count, more King County ballots were counted and Gregoire's percentage of the vote total of the newly discovered King County votes increased.

Federal Court

Within hours of the machine recount beginning on Saturday, November 20, the Republicans had filed for a temporary restraining order in federal court. The Republicans argued that Rossi was being "irreparably harmed by the King County enhancement and duplication process."

Rossi counsel claimed that the counties had different standards for processing ballots initially rejected by the tabulating machines. "Applying counting standards in selected counties different from those in others violates the equal protection and due process protections of the U.S. and Washington constitutions and ultimately will deny Washington voters ... their fundamental right to vote," the lawsuit stated. This was an express attempt to employ and rely on the analysis of *Bush v. Gore*.

In their pleadings, Republican Party lawyers argued that the plaintiffs were being "irreparably harmed by King County's unconstitutional recount procedure." Because original ballots are being enhanced on the basis of a subjective determination of voter "intent," each "enhancement" is final and cannot be reviewed or reexamined. Moreover, such ballots would be difficult, if not impossible, to locate as King County was simply mixing them back into the general ballot pool once the "enhancement" was complete. In other words, once enhanced, an egg cannot be unscrambled; and as each hour passes, more and more eggs are broken.

On election night workers could enhance or duplicate ballots under state law. The enhancement and duplication of ballots allowed for the ballots to then be counted by an optical scan machine. Washington is a voter-intent state. Thus, even if the voter failed to follow instructions by, for example, circling an oval instead of filling it in, which optical scan machines cannot read, if the intent of the voter was clear, the ballot is to be counted. The enhancement and duplication of ballots allowed for the ballots to be machine counted. According to the Republicans, the recount should only include ballots as tallied in the original count, not new enhancements or additional duplicates.

U.S. District Court Judge Marsha Pechman, during a Sunday conference call hearing, denied the Republican Party's request for a temporary restraining order to stop the enhancement process. The judge did not reject the *Bush v. Gore* analysis, but found that there was no irreparable harm because the duplicated ballots were not being destroyed and could be reviewed later, so there was no need to disrupt the state's process.

Recount II – Hand Count

With the posting of the King County totals on November 24, the machine recount was complete and had Rossi ahead by forty-two votes. The Gregoire campaign and its supporters faced a difficult decision – request a selective recount of only certain districts or seek a full statewide hand count. A statewide hand count required the posting of a $730,000 bond for costs and the bond was subject to forfeiture if the result did not change. On December 3, 2004, with a sub-stantial advance from John Kerry's unspent presidential campaign funds, the Democrats sought a statewide hand recount.

Immediately, the parties disputed how the hand recount should be conducted. At this stage, the secretary of state generally agreed with the Republicans, so the Democrats headed back to state court.

The two Washington Supreme Court decisions involve the most common recount issue of whether to expand the number of ballots counted. In par-ticular the dispute was about King County's absentee ballots. The electoral impact of counting additional King County ballots was easily recognized by all because King County is by a large margin the most Democratic area of the state. More ballots counted in King County meant more votes for Gregoire.

Washington State Supreme Court Round I

The Democrats requested a review of all absentee and provisional ballot rejec-tions. In the first case won by Rossi, Gregoire and his supporters argued that in the recount the canvassing boards were to "consider anew all ballots previ-ously left uncounted." They claimed that King County rejected a higher per-centage of absentee ballots for signature mismatches[14] than did other counties. They contended that various counties used disparate tests and procedures to determine whether to count or reject absentee ballots and that this "suggested or implicated equal protection concerns under the privileges and immunities clause of the Washington State Constitution."[15]

The Washington State Supreme Court rejected this argument on a seemingly straightforward Washington statutory analysis.[16] A "ballot" is a physical or electronic record of the choices of an individual voter or the physical document on which the voter's choices are to be recorded.[17] "Recount" means the process of re-tabulating ballots and producing amended election returns.[18] The proce-dure for recounts is set forth in statute,[19] and starts with the county canvassing board opening "the sealed containers containing the ballots to be recounted."[20] Thus, under Washington's statutory scheme, ballots are to be "re-tabulated" only if they have been previously counted or tallied, subject to the provisions of the statutes.[21] Effectively, the Washington State Supreme Court had moved any issues relating to whether additional absentee ballots that had been previously rejected should be counted to a later contest procedure.

Round II

Eight days later, the parties were back before the Washington State Supreme Court on what from a distance would appear to be the same issue, that is, whether to recount additional uncounted King County absentee ballots. At issue were ballots not counted originally and not counted in the first machine recount. The court's second opinion had the exact opposite effect to its first and led to an additional 573 King County absentee ballots being counted in the hand recount.

During the hand recount, the King County Canvassing Board discovered that 573 absentee ballots that had been specifically rejected and therefore were not counted in either the initial count or the machine recount had been mis-coded by county workers as having "no signature on file" when in fact there were signatures on file.[22] The board decided to count or, as the board described it, "recanvass" these ballots. Rossi's counsel sought and received a temporary restraining order from a superior court prohibiting the "recanvassing" by King County, based on the Washington State Supreme Court's decision of the prior week. Rossi argued that this was a matter properly considered in a contest action, not a recount, effectively the same argument made in the first court case only a week before.

The Washington State Supreme Court reversed. According to the court, the decision was based simply on the Washington statutory scheme. The court said that the Washington recount statute does not permit the recanvassing of ballots rejected and not counted, but when a board recanvasses it may correct errors. In prior cases, these errors had been only arithmetic or omission. Valid ballots that were misplaced and found were counted, but ballots specifically rejected for whatever reason were not "recounted" or "recanvassed."

Although it is logically difficult to reconcile this court's action with its prior decision, the court faced an unpalatable course if it were to remain constant. Without counting the 573 King County absentee ballots, Rossi would be cer-tified the winner of the gubernatorial election. Every party to the litigation and every serious observer understood that, based on partisan voting patterns, counting these ballots would result in the certification of Gregoire as governor. King County wrongly rejected these absentee ballots. The Washington State Supreme Court ordered them "recanvassed" so they would be counted in the second recount.

Notably, no reference to *Bush v. Gore* can be found in the briefs of either party or in the court's opinions.

Contest

On January 7, 2005, Rossi filed suit in Chelan County Superior Court, con-testing the election of Christine Gregoire as governor. The suit asked that the court set aside the election and order a new election. The suit alleged that the number of illegal ballots and the number of valid ballots improperly rejected rendered the true result of the election uncertain and likely unknowable. Rossi made no request, however, to block the swearing in of Gregoire as governor. Efforts to block the acceptance of the returns in the legislature failed on party lines and thus, on January 11, 2005, the state legislature confirmed Gregoire's election as governor.

Gregoire filed a series of motions contesting subject matter jurisdiction and venue that were rejected in early February, but Chelan County Superior Court Judge John Bridges did task Rossi's counsel with delivering to the opposing party "a written list of the number of illegal votes and by whom." The court stated that no testimony would be received as to any illegal votes, except as to those specified on the list.

Also, Judge Bridges critically defined the Republicans' ultimate burden of proof. The judge stated, "no election may be set aside on account of illegal votes unless it appears that an amount of illegal votes has been given to the person whose right is being contested, that, if taken from that person, would reduce the number of the person's legal votes below the number of votes given to some other person for the same office, after deducting therefrom the illegal votes that may be shown to have been given to the other person."[23]

Republicans would have to show that Rossi received more valid votes for the office of governor than Gregoire.

After extensive discovery and a two-week trial, the Washington State Superior Court concluded that at least 1,678 illegal votes were cast in the 2004 general election. This included ballots cast by felons[24] established by Rossi (754), felons established by Gregoire (647), deceased voters (19), double voters (6), illegal provisional ballots in King County (96), illegal provisional ballots in Pierce County (79), and additional votes in Pierce County for which a registered voter could not be found (77).

The trial also confirmed, as was evident by this time to everyone in Washington State, that King County's election processes were seriously flawed. King County could not identify how many ballots were mailed to eligible voters, how many voted ballots were returned, or how many absentee ballots were received and not counted because they were deemed improper. Although many felons were permitted to vote and more than 1,000 votes were cast by persons whom King County had failed to ensure were qualified and registered voters, and whose identities could not now be determined, Rossi proved no intentional fraud in regard to any King County election official.

Judge Bridges concluded "that no matter the number of illegal votes, whether they total 1,678, as determined by this Court, or 2,820, as argued by petitioners in their closing, this election may not be set aside merely because the number of illegal or invalid votes exceed the margin of victory, because the election contest statute requires the contestant to show that the illegal votes or misconduct changed the election's result."

For every illegal vote alleged by Rossi, the court required credible evidence to prove that these illegal voters actually cast a vote for governor and for which candidate. Not surprisingly, Rossi's lawyers concluded that attempting to compel hundreds of felons to admit they had committed another crime (voting), and also who they cast their secret ballot for, was an impossible task to undertake through standard depositions or direct testimony.

In an effort to bridge the gap between simple identification of categories of illegal voters, and actual proof that specific voters cast ballots for Governor Gregoire in the 2004 election, Rossi introduced the testimony of two political science professors[25] who argued that statistical analysis should be used to show that Rossi received a majority of the lawful votes.[26] Gregoire presented conflicting expert testimony. Even the expert witness Gregoire employed admitted, however, that it was impossible to know whether Gregoire actually got the most legal votes.[27]

The court was unwilling to credit any form of evidence other than direct voter testimony on how any individual cast a ballot.

Rossi did not appeal to the Washington State Supreme Court. Neither the attorneys for Rossi nor the attorneys for Gregoire cited *Bush v. Gore* in any of the pleading or argument in the superior court contest action. Not surprisingly, the court did not find any need to reference the case in its opinion.

Minnesota Senate – 2008

The November 4, 2008, Minnesota general election pitted Norm Coleman against Al Franken as the principal candidates for U.S. Senate. On November 18, the statewide canvassing report showed that Coleman received 1,211,565 votes and Franken 1,211,359 votes for the Senate. The margin separating the two candidates was 206 votes, far less than one half of one percent, triggering under Minnesota law an automatic hand recount of the ballots.

Recount
The Minnesota State Canvassing Board[28] directed the secretary of state to oversee the manual recount.[29] The secretary drafted proposed administrative recount procedures and provided them to both campaigns for their review. The board approved the administrative recount procedures as proposed with neither candidate objecting initially to the terms.

The mandatory recount began November 19, 2008, with nearly 3 million ballots to review and hand count. Although a lengthy process, the actual hand count of the individual optical scan ballots was not especially contentious. The ballots were hand counted in each county. The candidates' observer representatives could object or challenge the counting of any ballot that would effectively defer the decision on how to count the ballot to the state canvassing board. The state board members laboriously reviewed the individual challenged ballots. The originality of some voters at times stumped the panel, but the board was usually unanimous when determining the intent or lack thereof on the challenged ballots. The single locus and the total transparency of the process rendered any equal protection or fundamental fairness argument moot in regard to challenged ballots.

Shortly after the recount began, however, it became clear that county election officials had improperly rejected a significant number of absentee ballots during the original count. This became the principal focus of the election dispute.[30] Franken's campaign asked for these ballots to be counted by each county and added to the recounted results. Coleman's campaign argued that the canvassing board did not have the authority to deal with rejected absentee ballots in a recount. Some counties began sorting rejected absentee ballots to find out how many were incorrectly rejected, while other counties believed they lacked the authority to review in any manner prior rejected ballots during a recount. The board voted to recommend that the counties sort through their rejected absentee ballots, setting aside those they concluded were incorrectly rejected, and to resubmit their vote totals with the incorrectly rejected ballots counted. The Coleman campaign petitioned the Minnesota Supreme Court to halt such counting as inappropriate until an election contest or alternatively until "a standard procedure" could be determined for the process.

Supreme Court I
The Minnesota Supreme Court did conclude that county canvassing boards lack statutory authority to review improperly rejected absentee ballots.[31] However, the court ordered the candidates, the secretary of state, and all county auditors and the canvassing board to establish a process as expeditiously as practicable for the purpose of identifying all absentee ballot envelopes that the local election officials and the candidates agreed were rejected in error. The court also ordered local election officials to identify for the candidates' review those previously rejected absentee ballot envelopes that were not rejected on any of the four specific reasons found in Minnesota law.[32] Any absentee ballot envelopes that the local election officials and the two candidates agreed were rejected in error were to be opened and the ballots counted. This statewide "standard procedure" was at least in part a response to *Bush v. Gore* equal protection concerns that Coleman expressed to the court.

During the process, county officials had identified more than 1,300 apparently wrongly rejected absentee ballots. The Franken campaign wanted to count all of those ballots, while the Coleman campaign agreed to a subset, but also wanted to reconsider more than 700 other absentee ballots that they argued were of the type accepted in some counties but not in other counties.

Supreme Court II
After the secretary of state rejected Coleman's request to review these additional absentee ballots, Coleman filed for an emergency order with the Minnesota Supreme Court, seeking an order requiring that local election officials convey all absentee ballots identified by any party as wrongfully rejected to the secretary of state's office for a uniform review by the parties. The Minnesota Supreme Court denied this motion, ruling this issue could be addressed in an election contest.[33]

On December 30 and 31, representatives of both campaigns met with county officials sorting through uncounted absentee ballots. After each campaign rejected some ballots, 953 ballots were sent to the secretary of state. The parties agreed these "wrongly" rejected absentee ballots should be opened and counted. On January 3, 2009, 933 previously uncounted absentee ballots were counted with 481 votes for Franken and 305 for Coleman, effectively changing the prior result.

The board's final report compiled from the hand recount showed that Franken received 1,212,431 votes and Coleman received 1,212,206 votes. On January 5, 2009, the board certified the results of the election, declaring that Franken received 225 more votes than Coleman.

Contest

On January 6, 2009, Coleman filed a Notice of Contest[34] in Ramsey County District Court contesting the certificate of election results issued by the board and seeking an order declaring that Coleman was entitled to the certificate of election as U.S. senator. This action stayed the issuing of a Minnesota certificate of election to Franken. It was clear by this time that the U.S. Senate would not be able to seat any candidate unless they had a Minnesota certification of election in hand to present to the Senate.

The contest was held pursuant to Minnesota law[35] before a special three-judge district court panel. The trial commenced on January 26, 2009, and ended on April 13 with the dismissal of Coleman's contest and a ruling that Franken had won the election by 312 votes.

With the change in vote total between the initial canvass and the recount, the candidates' position on whether additional absentee ballots should be counted changed. In the election contest, Franken argued to exclude any additional absentee ballots, and for the strictest interpretation of the Minnesota absentee balloting law. Coleman's position essentially was the mirrored image. By election day, approximately 300,000 Minnesotans had voted by absentee ballot. Under Minnesota law[36] as in all states, certain requirements must be met before an absentee ballot can be counted. During the initial count more than 12,000 absentee ballots were rejected. Coleman identified 4,797 of these rejected absentee ballots, which he argued should now be opened and counted by the trial court.

Coleman believed he could present evidence that showed local election officials did not uniformly apply the Minnesota absentee balloting laws and that there was no consistency among the counties and municipalities in how ballots were rejected and how ballots were accepted. Coleman's argument was that the constitutional guarantees of equal protection and due process require the uniform application of the statutory standard to all absentee ballots. Equal protection and due process mandate that similarly situated voters be treated the same: whether a ballot is accepted cannot be determined by where the voter lives.

Coleman argued that local county officials applied Minnesota statutory requirements differently and inconsistently in ways that went beyond isolated, "garden variety" errors to be expected in every election – different counties and municipalities made their own decisions on the meaning of the statute and, as a result, reviewed similar absentee ballots differently, accepting ballots that were not in strict compliance with the statute but had sufficient indicia of trustworthiness. As a result, some ballots were counted in some counties while other, identical ballots were not counted in other counties.

From Coleman's perspective, the trial court exacerbated the disparity. Coleman attempted to show that most counties accepted absentee ballots under a substantial compliance standard. He argued that those who had their ballots rejected in jurisdictions applying a more exacting standard and then not enfranchised by the trial court using its strict compliance standard were treated unfairly – two classes of similarly situated voters with different acceptance rules. If the state fails to apply "specific standards" during a statewide recount that will ensure "equal application" to all votes, the lack of uniform standards is a constitutional violation (citing Bush, 531 U.S. at 106, *Erlandson* at 732: "treating similarly situated voters differently with no rational explanation … violates equal protection guarantees").[37] Here, although there was a single statutory standard for accepting absentee ballots, that standard was applied differently and inconsistently in the different counties and cities on election night, and by the trial court with its decision to strictly enforce the requirements.

The trial court found that the disparities in application of the statutory standards were the product of local jurisdictions' use of different methods to ensure compliance with the same statutory standards; that jurisdictions adopted policies they deemed necessary to ensure that absentee voting procedures would be available to their residents, in accordance with statutory requirements, given the resources available to them; and that differences in available resources, personnel, procedures, and technology necessarily affected the procedures local election officials used in reviewing absentee ballots.

Much of Coleman's evidence attempting to show the disputes between counties was excluded by the trial court. The court concluded that the disparities were not clearly demonstrated enough to warrant a change in the outcome of the election.

Although the trial court did order that an additional 351 absentee ballots be opened and counted, it took a very narrow approach in reviewing absentee ballots. It required strict compliance with all Minnesota statutory provisions and placed the burden of proof for the compliance on Coleman for any rejected ballot it proposed for counting. The trial court rejected Coleman's equal protection claim and also eschewed jurisdiction to even consider those constitutional claims. It effectively cast any equal protection issues to the U.S. Senate or Minnesota Supreme Court.[38]

Supreme Court III
Coleman's two principal contentions on appeal were that (1) similar absentee ballots were treated differently depending on the county in which they

were cast, and this disparate treatment violated voter rights under the equal protection clause; and (2) the trial court followed more strictly Minnesota statutory requirements for acceptance of absentee ballots in contrast to the practices of the county election authorities during the elections so wrongly failed to count many rejected absentee ballots.

The Minnesota Supreme Court concluded that to prevail on his equal protection claim of disparate application of a facially neutral statute, Coleman was required to prove that local jurisdictions' differences in application or the trial court's application of the requirements for absentee voting was the product of intentional discrimination. A showing that the statutory standards were applied differently with the intent to discriminate in favor of one individual or class over another was a requirement. Despite the fact that Coleman's arguments were based on *Bush v. Gore*, the Minnesota Supreme Court's equal protection analysis was based on two other cases – *Snowden v. Hughes*, 321 U.S. 1, 8 (1944), an Illinois dispute, and *Dragenosky v. Minn. Bd of Psychology*, 367 N.W.2d, 521 (MN 1985) – not *Bush v. Gore*. The Minnesota Supreme Court concluded these precedents required intentional discrimination against Coleman for a violation. This seems to be at variance with the U.S. Supreme Court admonition in *Bush v. Gore* that states have an "obligation to avoid arbitrary and disparate treatment of the members of its electorate."[39]

The Minnesota Supreme Court, like the trial court, concluded that *Bush v. Gore* was distinguishable in several important respects. In *Bush v. Gore*, the U.S. Supreme Court specifically noted that it was not addressing the question of "whether local entities, in the exercise of their expertise, may develop different systems for implementing elections" (531 U.S. at 109). The Minnesota Supreme Court's view was that *Bush v. Gore* equal protection analysis applied only to the actual counting process, not to the acceptance or rejection of unopened ballots.[40]

The essence of the equal protection problem addressed in *Bush v. Gore* was that there were no established standards under Florida statutes or provided by the state supreme court for determining voter intent; as a result, in the recount process, each county (indeed, each recount location within a county) was left to set its own standards for discerning voter intent. However, the Minnesota Supreme Court's view was that Minnesota had clear statutory standards for acceptance or rejection of absentee ballots, about which all election officials received common training.

The Minnesota Supreme Court said that Florida election officials' decisions that the U.S. Supreme Court was concerned in *Bush v. Gore* was voter intent – that is, for whom the ballot was cast – as reflected on ballots already cast in the election. In *Bush v. Gore*, officials conducting the recount were reviewing the face of the ballot itself, creating opportunities for manipulation of the decision for political purposes. At issue in Minnesota was whether to accept or reject absentee ballots return enveloped before they were opened, meaning that the actual votes on the ballots contained in the return envelopes were not known to the election officials applying the standards. Based on these factors, the Minnesota Supreme Court concluded that *Bush v. Gore* was not applicable and did not support Coleman's equal protection claims.

The Minnesota Supreme Court unanimously upheld the lower court's decision. Coleman conceded the election and Franken was sworn into the U.S. Senate on July 7, 2009.

Sarasota, Florida – 2006

The 2006 Thirteenth Florida Congressional District (Sarasota) dispute is the only House contested election since 1996[41] in which the U.S. House of Representatives did not summarily dismiss the contest without further investigation. It involved an administrative recount pursuant to state statutes with litigation in state court over that process followed by the loser filing an election contest in the U.S. House of Representatives. At its conclusion, Florida, the home of the infamous 2000 butterfly ballot, provides another lesson in bad ballot design.

The November 7, 2006, election in the Thirteenth Congressional District of Florida between Vern Buchanan (R) and Christine Jennings (D) was very close, with a mere 368-vote margin separating the candidates after the initial count.[42] Florida law provides for automatic recount in very close elections, so the Florida Election Canvassing Commission ordered a recount. On November 20, 2007, the commission certified Buchanan as the victor by 369 votes.[43]

The election night and certified recount reports of election results did have an anomalous number in Sarasota County. Almost 15 percent of Sarasota voters appeared not to have cast a vote in this congressional race.[44] This number of voters not casting a vote in the race was nearly ten times the number normally experienced in a prominent race near the top of the ballot. The Jennings campaign immediately charged that the county's voting system (iVotronic touch screen DRE) must have malfunctioned. The Buchanan campaign's initial response was that the drop off was because of the bitter nature of the primary and general election campaigns souring the electorates to both candidates. Neither candidate's explanation was correct.

In response to the widespread speculation and concern about the significant percentage of under-votes, on November 9, 2006, the Florida secretary of state directed the Florida Division of Elections, Bureau of Voting Systems Certification to conduct an audit of Sarasota's voting system and election procedures. The final audit report released by the Florida Department of State found no evidence to suggest that the official certified election results did not reflect the actual votes cast.[45] These tests confirmed what Sarasota and Florida election officials recognized: the reason for the under-vote was simple – a flawed ballot design layout. Thirteen months and 4,434 pages of report later, the U.S. House of Representatives came to the same conclusion.

For anyone unfamiliar with the system, the direct recording electronic voting system (DRE) used by Sarasota County is a machine closely resembling a common ATM machine. In elections with long, multi-race ballots, voters must go through multiscreen pages to cast their vote in all races.

In 2006, the touch screen's first page presented the voter with only the first of the federal races, the U.S. Senate, because of the large number of senate candidates. The touch screen's second page showed at its very top the other federal race, the Thirteenth District Congressional. This was followed directly below by a bright red, highly visible header for the slate of statewide races. In the first seconds after reviewing the second page image, it was clear to disinterested parties that the screen layout was the reason for the under-vote. The Thirteenth District voters are the oldest electorate of any congressional district in the nation. Any individual with impaired vision or anyone just using bifocals would have significant difficulties seeing the race on the top of the touch screen.

In other Florida counties using the DRE, similar ballot screens resulted in unusually high under-votes in races at the top of screen and followed by a larger type faced colored header.

Proceedings Involving Florida's Courts
On November 20, 2006, Jennings filed a contested election suit in Florida's Circuit Court,[46] arguing that Florida's certified vote totals excluded thousands of legal votes that were cast in Sarasota County because of malfunctioning electronic voting machines.[47] Jennings subsequently requested access to the voting hardware and software in possession of the state and county to test whether the iVotronic voting system in fact malfunctioned and caused the under-votes.[48] Jennings' discovery efforts proved fruitless, and she abandoned this litigation.

House Contest
On December 20, 2006, Jennings filed a notice of contest with the U.S. House of Representatives under the Federal Contested Election Act.[49] House procedures provide that contests are to be initially considered by the Committee on House Administration. The Committee Chairperson appointed a three-member task force to oversee matters relating to the District 13 election contest.

In Jennings's Notice of Contest, she dismissed the reliability of Florida's recount audit, arguing that merely "recounting" electronic ballots (unlike paper ballots) is inevitably a meaningless exercise because the manual "recount" consists simply of printing out the ballot image reports from the allegedly malfunctioning iVotronic systems and counting by hand the ballot images that recorded no choice for the congressional race in question.[50] Jennings argued that statistical evidence alone indicated that the large number of under-votes in Sarasota must be attributable to a malfunction of the iVotronic touch screen voting system. The percentage of under-votes recorded on electronic voting machines in Sarasota County for the congressional race was almost seven times the rate of under-votes for District 13 in the last midterm election (2.2%). In addition to this statistical evidence, Jennings submitted affidavits allegedly memorializing eyewitness accounts of Sarasota County voters having difficulties during early and election day voting on the iVotronic machines.[51]

On June 14, 2007, the task force unanimously authorized the U.S. Government Accountability Office (GAO) to test whether the voting machines contributed to the under-vote.

At a congressional hearing on February 8, 2008, the GAO reported that the results of its various tests, like the tests of Florida, did not identify any problems that would indicate the iVotronic touch screen voting system was responsible for the under-vote. The contest was dismissed.

Hamilton County, Ohio, Juvenile Court Judge Race – 2010

The fourth election dispute examined in this chapter is a 2010 dispute related to the counting of provisional ballots in a juvenile court election. This race for a minor office may at first blush seem an odd choice to examine in detail, but the explanation is not complex. In the more high-profile election disputes since the U.S. Supreme Court's *Bush v. Gore* decision, the opinion has played only a minor role or no role at all in their resolution. The continuing Hamilton County judicial election dispute, however, has a significant focus on the equal protection principles and claims enunciated in *Bush v. Gore*.[52]

The plaintiff, a candidate for the office of Hamilton County Juvenile Court judge, alleged that the Hamilton County Board of Elections:

violated the Equal Protection Clause by "refusing, without reasonable basis, to investigate whether poll worker error caused some voters to vote at the right polling place but at the wrong table while otherwise investigating similarly situated circumstances where poll worker error caused a voter to vote in the wrong precinct," and "by arbitrarily allowing some provisional voters the right to vote when the error in the ballot was caused by the poll worker, but denying other provisional voters the right to vote when the error in the ballot was caused by the poll worker."[53]

The facts of *Hunter* are convoluted. During Ohio elections, many polling locations contain multiple precincts. In such locations, voters must go to the correct precinct, that is, table, within the location. Primarily at issue in the litigation were 849 ballots that were cast by a voter in Hamilton County at the right location but the wrong precinct (i.e., at the wrong table). The board understood Ohio law to mandate that ballots cast in the wrong precinct were invalid and should not be counted unless, under a prior consent decree entered by the Ohio Secretary of State, there was poll worker error and the voter used the last four digits of his or her social security number as identification. Because the voters who cast the 849 ballots at issue did not use their social security numbers, they were not included in the consent decree terms and their ballots were disqualified.[54]

The board, however, counted a group of twenty-seven ballots that were cast at the board's headquarters in downtown Cincinnati prior to election day even though they were recorded in the wrong precinct.[55] The board found that these ballots resulted from "clear poll worker error" because an elector voting at the board's headquarters had no choice but to walk up to one person who gave them an incorrect ballot.[56]

It was the divergent rulings on these two categories of ballots that gave rise to the central theme of Hunter's case. Hunter alleged that the board counted numerous ballots that resulted from poll worker error but failed to conduct a similar investigation in other instances, including the 849 ballots primarily at issue.[57] Hunter filed a complaint and a motion for a temporary restraining order and preliminary injunction with the U.S. District Court for the Southern District of Ohio for violations of both the Equal Protection and Due Process Clauses of the U.S. Constitution. The district court granted in part the preliminary injunction the following day and ordered the board to "immediately begin an investigation into whether poll worker error contributed to the rejection of the 849 provisional ballots now in issue and to include in the recount for the Hamilton County Juvenile Court Judge any provisional ballots improperly cast for reasons attributable to poll worker error."[58]

After the district court's order, the Ohio Secretary of State provided additional guidance identifying "objective criteria for determining poll worker error."[59] At a meeting on December 28, 2010, the board rejected approximately 500 of the 849 disputed ballots, voted to unanimously count seven ballots that were miscast on account of poll worker error, and voted to count nine ballots that were determined to have been cast in the correct precinct but that had been erroneously included with those cast in the wrong precinct. The board had a 2–2 tie on whether to count 269 ballots that were cast in the correct polling location, but in the wrong precinct. As required by Ohio law, the Ohio secretary of state broke the tie by instructing the board to count some of the 269 provisional ballots, but not others based on certain boundary issues.[60]

While this lawsuit was pending, the Ohio Supreme Court issued a ruling that no provisional ballot cast in the wrong precinct should be counted and required the Secretary of State to rescind prior directives that were contrary to its decision.[61] Subsequent to the Ohio Supreme Court's ruling, the newly elected secretary of state issued a new directive requiring the board to reexamine many of the provisional ballots under the direction of the Ohio Supreme Court's recent decision.[62]

The district court, without hearing, granted in part an emergency motion by Hunter to enforce the preliminary injunction, enjoined the board from complying with the secretary of state's new directive, and required the board to count certain ballots that were investigated and found invalid because of poll worker error.[63] The district court found that the board would violate the Equal Protection Clause if it were to certify the election results as they were on November 16, 2010.[64] Both the winning candidate for the Hamilton County

Juvenile Court judgeship and the board filed an appeal of the district court's order.

The Sixth Circuit agreed that there was a "sufficiently strong likelihood of success on an equal-protection claim to weigh in favor of the district court's grant of a preliminary injunction," relying in part on *Bush v. Gore*.[65] Quoting *Bush v. Gore*, the Sixth Circuit stated: "Having once granted the right to vote on equal terms, the State may not, by later arbitrary and disparate treatment, value one person's vote over that of another."[66] Following the precedent in *Bush v. Gore*, the Sixth Circuit found that a lack of specific standards for reviewing provisional ballots could otherwise result in "unequal evaluation of ballots."[67]

The Sixth Circuit found that the twenty-seven provisional ballots cast at the board's headquarters, which were counted, and the 269 provisional ballots cast at the right polling location but the wrong precinct, which were not, are substantially similar and cannot be treated differently without raising equal protection concerns:

Despite the requirements of state law, Plaintiffs have provided evidence that, in the November election, the Board considered evidence of poll-worker error with respect to some ballots cast in the wrong precinct but not other similarly situated ballots when it evaluated which ballots to count. In doing so, the Board exercised discretion, without a uniform standard to apply, in determining whether to count provisional ballots miscast due to poll-worker error that otherwise would be invalid under state law.[68]

The Sixth Circuit concluded that "the Board's review has met the requirements of *Bush v. Gore*."[69] The newly elected secretary of state argued that the district court failed to satisfy the requirements of *Bush v. Gore* because it ordered a standard-less investigation that was not applied to the first twenty-seven ballots and that was applied inconsistently with others. The Sixth Circuit rejected that argument, finding that the previous secretary of state had issued a directive with objective criteria. Moreover, it found that the "intent of the voter" standard invalidated in *Bush v. Gore* was implemented differently by different counties for the same presidential election, but in this case, the district court's order applied to only one jurisdiction and one race.[70]

It was also argued that the district court's equal protection analysis created a broader equal protection problem because it ordered provisional ballots to be counted in Hamilton County and not the rest of Ohio.[71] The Sixth Circuit likewise rejected this argument, finding that only Hamilton County voters are eligible to vote for the Hamilton County Juvenile Court Judge, and thus, the board did not treat equally voters within its own county, which was the only equal protection concern being addressed.[72] It did recognize that "[s]tatewide equal-protection implication could arise, however, to the extent that the ballots at issue include candidates for district and statewide races that transcend county lines."[73] In sum, the Sixth Circuit found the board was "required to review all provisional ballots. In doing so, it chose to consider evidence of poll worker error for some ballots, but not others, thereby treating voters' ballots arbitrarily, in violation of the Equal Protection Clause. We therefore conclude that there is a strong likelihood of success on this equal protection claim that weighs heavily in favor of the district court's grant of a preliminary injunction."[74]

The Sixth Circuit left it to the district court, however, to apply the uniformity requirement of *Bush v. Gore* to direct the board on how to proceed with the ballots at issue. The board petitioned for a hearing *en banc*, which was denied on March 29, 2011, with no judge requesting a vote. The board then moved to have the mandate from the Sixth Circuit recalled and stayed pending *certiorari* to the U.S. Supreme Court, which was denied on April 18, 2011.

The district court held a permanent injunction hearing from July 18, 2011 through August 5, 2011 that the parties agreed should be the full and final hearing on the merits on all issues presented in the plaintiffs' complaints.[75] After a trial on the merits, the court found in favor of the plaintiffs on their claims that the board violated voters' right to equal protection under the law, but stated it could not at this time enter a judgment in favor of the plaintiffs on their claim that the board violated voters' right to due process of law.[76] Specifically, the district court held that "[t]he Hamilton County Board of Elections violated provisional voters' right to equal protection under the law when, in determining whether provisional ballots were cast in the wrong precinct because of poll-worker error, it considered evidence of the location where provisional ballots were cast for some, but not all, provisional ballots cast in the wrong precinct."[77] It proceeded to enjoin the board from (1) rejecting otherwise valid provisional ballots that were cast in the correct location but the wrong precinct, (2) rejecting nine ballots unanimously determined by the board to have been miscast because of poll worker error, and (3) rejecting the correct-location, wrong-precinct ballots under the prior consent decree. The district court did not place much reliance on *Bush v. Gore*, citing it only once in the judgment and order.[78]

DISCUSSION

Even before the *Bush v. Gore* decision, federal courts did on occasion agree to consider disputed elections. In the past, fundamental unfairness issues such as the changing of a counting process during a postelection period have spurred federal court involvement.[79] However, both pre[80] and post[81] *Bush v. Gore* the federal courts still seem to be a very limited vehicle for the resolution of recount/contest disputes.[82] In general, federal courts do not involve themselves in "garden variety" postelection disputes.[83] If, however, "the election process itself reaches the point of patent and fundamental unfairness, a violation of the Due Process Clause may be indicated and relief under § 1983 therefore is in order. Such a situation must go well beyond the ordinary dispute over the counting and marking of ballots."[84] State recount process disputes in few state elections are so shocking as to implicate due process or equal protection concerns under the Fourteenth Amendment, and thus, federal court intervention.[85]

What should be apparent from the four post–*Bush v. Gore* cases we have discussed is that the recount and contestation process in high-profile cases can be extraordinarily complex, often involving both state and federal courts, even though primarily the former. Another important lesson to glean from the four cases we have discussed is the range of issues that often arise, including disputes about provisional ballots, illegal ballots (e.g., ballots cast in the wrong precinct), lost ballots, write-in ballots, and mailed ballots. The problems reviewed included poll worker error and voter confusion, as well as issues of valid voter identification. The cases also illustrate an important point made at the beginning of this chapter, namely the need to distinguish the recount and contest phase of election disputes.

To date, the primary impact of *Bush v. Gore* on the resolution of disputed elections is not jurisprudential,[86] but legislative. The Help America Vote Act of 2002 (HAVA)[87] is most certainly a child of the disputed 2000 presidential election. How a recount is conducted is principally driven by the type of voting system used on election day and by absentee voters. HAVA led the states to replace their punch card and lever voting machines with DRE and optical scan systems, and as demonstrated elsewhere in this volume, there has been a dramatic growth in mail ballots and other forms of so-called convenience voting. However, as noted earlier in this chapter, while the adoption of DRE and optical scan systems has made recounts easier, it has not solved all the problems of recounts or subsequent contests or issues of voter confusion. It is not sufficient for a voting system to be efficient, accurate, and secure; it also must be perceived as such.[88] For example, the 2006 Sarasota Florida House contest lasted many months in large part because of distrust of the DRE system.[89]

In sum, the *Bush v. Gore* election dispute has saved election lawyers from dark and dank voting machine warehouses. The mind-numbing task of counting archaic computer punch cards is history. However, county courthouses and state courts, not federal courtrooms, remain the principal venue for disputed election resolutions.

Notes

1   The only relevant federal statute is the Federal Contested Election Act, 2 U.S.C §§ 381–91 (House); U.S. Constitution Article I, Section V, Clause 1. The U.S. House of Representatives and Senate have the express and final authority to judge the election returns and qualifications of their members, but only the House has actual rules for election contests.

2   Senate election in Alaska.

3   Although most recounts are local, many recent election cycles have had at least one statewide recount occurring somewhere in the country. Examples include 1981 NJ Gov.; 1984 IL Gov.; 1994 AL Chief Justice; 1996 HI Gov.; 1998 NV Sen.; 2000 Pres. FL/NM; 2004 WA Gov.; 2008 MN Sen.

4 *Moreau v. Tonry*, 339 S.2d 3 (LA 1976); *Lloyd v. Kechley*, 82 S.W. 2d. 739 (AR
   1985); *Berg v. Veit*, 162 N.W. 522 (MN 1917); WA 2004 Gov.
5 *Wyman v. Durkin* (U.S. Senate, 1974). *See Griffin v. Burns*, 570 F.2d 1065, 1080
   (1st Cir. 1978) (setting aside results and ordering a new election where "the closeness of the election was such that, given the retroactive invalidation of a potentially
   controlling number of the votes cast, a new primary was warranted."); *Marks v.
   Stinson*, 19 F.3d 873, 887 (3rd Cir. 1994) (remanding and authorizing remedy
   of setting aside election where illegal absentee ballots amounted to "substantial
   wrongdoing ... the effects of which are not capable of quantification but which
   render the apparent result an unreliable indicium of the will of the electorate");
   Webb v. Bowden, 124 Ark. 244 (AR 1916) (holding that illegal votes must be pre-
   sumed to account for the margin of victory where the number of votes exceeded the
   number of registered voters); *Mead v. Sheffield*, 278 Ga. 268, 273 (2004) (setting
   aside election because 481 illegal absentee ballots exceeded respondent's statewide
   lead over petitioner, which "cast in doubt" the outcome of the election); *Howell v.
   Fears*, 275 Ga. 627, 628 (GA 2002) (setting aside election where there were enough
   irregular ballots to place the result in doubt, finding it "improper and erroneous
   for courts to engage in presumptions of any kind in that exclusive area of privacy
   [i.e., voting]"; *Briscoe v. Between Consol. School District*, 156 S.E. 654, 656 (GA
   1931) (election should be voided assuming that challenged voters "had all voted
   against the result reached"); *Akizki v. Fong*, 51 Haw. 354 (1969) (invalidating election because election officials commingled nineteen invalid absentee ballots with
   valid ballots); *Adkins v. Huckabay* (LA 2000) (trial court correctly vacated and
   set aside general election decided by three votes, where five absentee ballots failed
   to substantially comply with election laws); *McCavitt v. Registrars of Voters*, 385
   Mass. 833, 849 (1982) ("[W]henever the irregularity or illegality of the election is
   such that the result of the election would be placed in doubt, then the election must
   be set aside and the judge must order a new election."); *Ippolito v. James M. Power*,
   22 N.Y. 2d 594, 598–9 (1968) (new election required where election machine
   counted sixty-eight more votes than qualified people who signed voter registration cards, even without evidence of fraud, because irregularities were sufficiently
   large in number to establish probability that the outcome would be changed by a
   shift in or invalidation of the questioned votes); *Hitt v. Tressler*, 4 Ohio St. 3d 174
   (1983) (affirming trial court's setting aside of election where voting machine malfunction failed to register votes within margin of victory); *Helm v. State Election
   Bd.*, 589 P.2d 224 (OK 1979) (election results are reasonably uncertain and thus
   must be set aside where number of voided ballots exceeds the margin of victory);
   Emery v. Robertson County Election Comm., 586 S.W.2d 103 (TN 1979) (election
   is void where evidence reveals that number of illegal ballots cast equals or exceeds
   difference between two candidates receiving most votes); *Hardeman v. Thomas*,
   208 Cal. App. 3d 153 (CA App. 1989) (ordering new election where seventeen contested votes exceeded sixteen-vote margin of victory).*Green v. Reyes*, 836 S.W.2d
   203 (TX App. 1992) (upholding trial court's voiding of election where 126 votes
   were unable to be attributed to either candidate; trial court exercised its authority
   under the election code and ordered the election void because the margin of victory was less than the number of unascertained illegal votes); *compare Noble v.
   Ada Count Elections Bd.*, Idaho 495 (2000) (evidence of ten illegal ballots, where
   margin of victory was fifty-one votes, was insufficient to show that illegal votes

changed the result of the election); cf. *Cramer v. City of Anderson,* 124 S.E. 2d 788 (SC 1962) (seventy-three illegal votes cast in special annexation election should *all* be withdrawn from the winning side, which in effect reduced affirmative vote to below the level necessary for approval of annexation).In *Gooch v. Hendrix,* 5 Cal. 4th 266, 851 P.2d 1321 (1993), an election was overturned because there were more illegal absentee ballots than the margin of victory, even though it could not be determined for whom the illegal ballots were cast.

6　Not registered, wrongly registered, or wrongly voting in the precinct (noncitizens, nonresidents, presently disqualified, and the dead), ballots improperly filled in.

7　Common reasons include printing errors or ballots for the wrong jurisdiction.

8　*McCavitt v. Registrations of Voters of Brockto,* 434 N.E.2d (MA App. 1982); *Lambert v. Levens,* 702 P.2d 320 (KS 1985).

9　Alaska: *Finkelstein v. Stout,* 774 P.2d 786 (1989); *Hammond v. Hickel,* 588 P.2d 256 (1978); Arizona: *Huggins v. Superior Court,* 163 Ariz. 348 (1990); *Clay v. Gilbert,* 160 Ariz. 335 (1989); *Grounds v. Lawe,* 67 Ariz. 176 (1948); Illinois: *In re. Durkin,* 299 Ill. App. 3 192 (1998); *O'Neal v. Shaw,* 248 Ill. App. 3d 632 (1993); *People ex rel. Ciaccio v. Martin,* 220 Ill. App. 3d 89 (1991); *Gribble v. Willeford,* 190 Ill. App. 3d 610 (1989); *Jordan v. Officer,* 170 Ill. App. 3d 776 (1988); California: *Singletary v. Kelley,* 242 Cal. App. 2d 611 (1966); *Russell v. McDowell,* 83 Cal. 70 (1890); Kansas: *Parker v. Hughe;* 64 Kan. 216 (1902); Tennessee: *Moore v. Sharp,* 98 Tenn. 491 (1896); Michigan: *Gracey v. Grosse Pointe Farms Clerk;* 182 Mich. App. 193 (1989); *Attorney General ex rel. Miller v. Miller,* 266 Mich. 127 (1934); *Ellis ex rel. Reynolds v. May,* 99 Mich. 538 (1894); Montana: *Gervais v. Rolfe;* 57 Mont. 209 (1920); *Heyfron v. Mahoney,* 9 Mont. 497 (1890); Wisconsin: *Ollmann v. Kowalewski,* 238 Wis. 574 (1941); North Dakota: *Drinkwater v. Nelson,* 48 N.D. 871 (1922).

10　A position exposed by many a high school senior following the receipt of SAT results.

11　For the secretary of state's perspective on the election dispute, see T. Heffernan, *An Election for the Ages,* WSU Press (2010).

12　RCW 29A-64.021(a).

13　This is in contrast with states that require all ballots be cast in voters' correct precinct or county.

14　RCW 29A.40.110(3) requires that the signature on an absentee ballot return envelope be "the same" as the signature in the voter registration files, as determined by the canvassing board or its designated representative, whereas WAC 434-253-047 requires a signature for a provisional ballot that "matches a voter registration record."

15　Wash. Const. Art I § 19.

16　*McDonald et al. v. Reed et al.,* 153 Wash.2d 201, 103 P.3d 722 (2004).

17　RCW 29A.04.008(1)(c),(d).

18　RCW 29A.64.139.

19　RCW 29A.64.041.

20　RCW 29A.60.110.

21　RCW 29A.60.210.

22　The "no signature" rejected absentee ballots included a ballot cast by King County Council Chairman Larry Phillips, the nominal supervisor of the King County Elections Board.

23 This seemed to conflict with *Foulke v. Hayes*, 85 Wn.2d. 629 (1975), where the election was set aside with only a number of illegal ballots exceeding the margin between the candidates, but no evidence as to how cast.

24 Individuals who have been convicted of felony offenses may have their voting rights reestablished if all sentence requirements were satisfied.

25 Jonathan Katz, California Institute of Technology; Anthony Gill, University of Washington.

26 For Gregoire's counsels' criticism of the expert testimony, see "No Guessing Allowed," *Albany Law Review*, vol. 69, pp. 561–67 (2006).

27 Cross-examination of University of Washington professor Christopher Adolph.

28 Minn. Stat. § 204C.31, subd. 2. Two justices of the Minnesota Supreme Court, two judges of district courts, chaired by the secretary of state.

29 Minn. Stat. § 204c.35, subd. 1(b)(1).

30 Another material issue involved the disappearance of a single envelope of ballots from a polling place in Minneapolis after the election night count but before the recount. The board accepted the election night count for the missing 133 ballots in the recount total. This decision was affirmed in the contest action.

31 *Coleman v. Ritchie* 758 N.W. 2d. 306 (Minn. 2008).

32 Minn. Stat. § 203B.12 (2006), or in Minn. Stat. § 203B.24 (2006) for overseas absentee ballots.

33 *Coleman v. Ritchie*, 759 N.W. 2d 47, 49 (Minnesota, 2009).

34 Minn. Stat. § 209.021.

35 Minn. Stat. § 209.045.

36 Stat. § 203B.12, subd. 2 (and § 203B.24 for overseas ballots).

37 The Minnesota Constitution "embodies principles of equal protection synonymous to the equal protection clause of the Fourteenth Amendment of the United States Constitution." *Stante v. Russell*, 477 N.W.2d 886, 889 N.3 (MN 1991). Indeed, the state constitution may require even more "stringent" review and a more robust guarantee of equal protection. Ibid. at 889.

38 *Wichelmann v. City of Grencoe*, 273 N.W. 638 (MN 1937), and *Bell v. Gannaway*, 227 N.W.2d 797 (MN 1975).

39 *Per curiam Bush v. Gore*, p. 6.

40 *Coleman v. Franken*, 767 N.W.2d 453 (2009).

41 *Robert Dornan/Loretta Sanchez*. Report of the Committee on House Oversight on H.R. 35 (February 12, 1998).

42 *Jennings*, 118, 737; *Buchanan* 119, 105.

43 *Jennings*, 118, 940; *Buchanan* 119, 309.

44 Of 123,901 ballots cast in Sarasota County, 18,000 did not have a vote in the Thirteenth District race.

45 Florida Department of State, Division of Elections Audit Report of the Elections Systems and Software, Inc.'s iVotronic Voting System in the 2006 General Election for Sarasota County, Florida: 2007.

46 Contestant filed the contested election suit in Florida's Circuit Court of the Second Judicial Circuit under Florida Election Code 102.168.

47 *Jennings v. Election Canvassing Commission of the State of Florida*, Plaintiff's Motion to Compel Expedited Discovery, November 20, 2006.

48 *ERR14*[9] *Jennings v. Election Canvassing Commission of the State of Florida*, Plaintiff's Motion to Compel Expedited Discovery, November 20, 2006.

49 2 U.S.C. §§ 381–69.

50 *Jennings v. Buchanan*, Notice of Contest Regarding the Election for Representative in the 110th Congress from Florida's Thirteenth Congressional District, December 20, 2006.

51 *Jennings v. Buchanan*, Documentation of Voting Machine Malfunction Appendix to Contestant Jennings' Memorandum Responding to the Honorable Charles A. Gonzalez's April 3, 2007 Letter Regarding the Investigation of the Election for Representative in the 110th Congress from Florida's Thirteenth Congressional District, Volume I & II, April 13, 2007.

52 *Hunter v. Hamilton County Bd. of Elections*, 635 F.3d 219 (6th Cir. 2011).

53 Ibid. at 226.

54 Ibid. at 224.

55 Ibid. at 224.

56 Ibid.

57 Ibid. at 225–26.

58 Ibid. at 226.

59 Ibid. at 227.

60 Ibid. at 227–28.

61 *State ex rel. Painter v. Brunner*, 2011-Ohio-35 at ¶23.

62 *Hunter* at 230.

63 Ibid.

64 Ibid.

65 Ibid. at 236.

66 Ibid. at 234.

67 Ibid. at 235.

68 Ibid. at 238.

69 Ibid. at 241.

70 Ibid.

71 Ibid.

72 Ibid. at 242.

73 Ibid. (citing *Bush v Gore*, 531 U.S. at 106–07).

74 Ibid. at 243.

75 *Hunter v. Hamilton County Board of Elections*, 850 F. Supp. 2d 795 (S.D. Ohio, 2012).

76 Ibid. at 801.

77 Ibid. at 847.

78 Ibid. at 839.

79 *Roe v. State of Alabama Evans*, 49 F.3d 734 (11th Cir. 1995).

80 *Bennett v. Yoshing*, 140 F.3d 1218 (9th Cir. 1998); *Hennings v. Grafton*, 523 F.2d 861 (7th Cir. 1975); *Gold v. Feinberg*, 101 F.3d 796 (2nd Cir. 1996).

81 *Spears v. Steward*, 283 F.3d 992 (9th Cir. 2002).

82 This contrasts with a significant increase in preelection litigation. Richard Hasen, "The Democracy Canon," *Stanford Law Review*, vol. 6 (2009).

83 *Curry*, 802 F.2d at 1315 (quoting *Welch v. McKenzie*, 765 F.2d 1311, 1317, vacated on other grounds and remanded, 777 F.2d 191 (5th Cir. 1985)).

84 Ibid. (quoting *Duncan v. Poythress*, 657 F.2d 691, 703 (5th Cir. Unit B 1981). cert. denied. 459 U.S. 1012, 103 S. Ct. 368, 74L.Ed.2d 504 (1982)).

85 As many scholars predicted, one scenario for *Bush v. Gore* to have a significant precedential impact is during a postelection issue related to provisional voting. Such situations have a unique similarity to the specific statewide, postelection recount addressed in *Bush v. Gore*. If anything, the Sixth Circuit's opinion in *Hunter* helps clarify that *Bush v. Gore*'s largest impact is in situations when all ballots have been cast, and a board of election, or some other administrative body, must determine which will be counted and which will not. If there are arbitrary decisions made on which ones to count, especially if such decisions are made after the ballots are already cast, there are serious equal protection concerns related to the disenfranchisement of voters.

86 Despite the application and potential expansion of the equal protection holding of *Bush v. Gore* in some lower federal and state courts, the U.S. Supreme Court has not had an opportunity to review whether and how the precedent should be expanded, and likely will not anytime in the near future. The Court will likely wait for a conflict among lower courts, which, given the relatively low number of election contests and recounts that result in litigation, could take a significant amount of time. The Court denied *certiorari* in the matter of *Wexler v. Anderson*, a case from the Eleventh Circuit that rejected an equal protection challenge to the lack of a paper record in Florida counties that use touch screens. We would also note, however, that, while *Bush v. Gore* specifically addresses equal protection concerns during postelection statewide recounts, it is possible it could eventually have a farther-reaching impact. Other cases have looked to the equal protection principles enunciated in *Bush v. Gore* for guidance in evaluating the equality of other election practices. For example, in *League of Women Voters v. Blackwell*, several Ohio voters brought claims challenging various inequities that occurred during the 2004 election presenting claims under *Bush v. Gore*. 548 F.3d 463 (6th Cir. 2008). Also see *Vanzant v. Brunner*, S.D. Ohio No. 1:10-cv-596.

87 Help America Vote Act (Pub. L. 107–252).

88 See H.R. 811, Voter Confidence and Increased Accessibility Act of 2007; U.S. House Hearing, Auditing the Vote, Subcommittee Elections, 110th Congress, First Session, March 20, 2007.

89 The DRE ballot format was especially difficult for the older voters of Sarasota, Florida in 2006. The contest in that election reinforces the importance of thoughtful consideration of ballot design – be it a butterfly or touch screen.

2

The Cites that Counted: A Decade of *Bush v. Gore* Jurisprudence

Charles Anthony Smith

INTRODUCTION

When the U.S. Supreme Court issued the opinion that resolved the 2000 presidential election in George W. Bush's favor, the five-justice coalition responsible for the decision went to great lengths to stress that the opinion should not be construed as an explication or expansion of any legal doctrine or concept. The *per curiam* opinion, presumably authored by Justice Kennedy and Justice O'Connor, specifically tried to narrow the applicability of the legal reasoning that resolved the equal protection claim by including the following passage:

The recount process, in its features here described, is inconsistent with the minimum procedures necessary to protect the fundamental right of each voter in the special instance of a statewide recount under the authority of a single state judicial officer. Our consideration is limited to the present circumstances, for the problem of equal protection in election processes generally presents many complexities. (*Bush v. Gore* 531 U.S. 98, 109 (2000))

In the immediate aftermath of the decision, the scholarly community primarily assessed either the nuanced legal arguments of the various dissenting and concurring opinions of *Bush v. Gore* or the impact the decision might have on the public regard for or institutional standing of the Court (Chemerinsky, 2001; Gibson, Caldeira, and Spence, 2003a; Gillman, 2001). Shortly after the initial round of scholarly analysis, the academy turned to questions about the more broad implications of the opinion for the doctrine of equal protection, public support of the Court, and the political preferences of the justices (Banks, Cohen, and Green, 2005; Clayton, 2002; Hasen, 2001, 2004; Levinson, 2002; Posner, 2001; Sunstein and Epstein, 2001). The Court and the opinion were criticized for a variety of defects and generally problematic legal reasoning (Dershowitz, 2003; Garrett, 2001; Gillman, 2001; Mebane, 2004). The concept of judicialization, the widely recognized phenomenon of expanded judicial activity into areas of politics and policy nominally and normally under the control of legislatures and executives, was the frame for consideration of the impact of the opinion on the other branches of government and the political process in general (Ferejohn, 2002; Hasen, 2005; Hirschl, 2002, 2004; Pildes, 2004; Shapiro and Stone Sweet, 2002; Smith and Shortell, 2007; Tate and Vallinder, 1995). The opinion opened the door to an expansion of litigation as a normal part of the campaign process and presented an example of judicialization in the context of presidential elections in the United States (Smith and Shortell, 2007). Eventually, the scholarly treatment of *Bush v. Gore* focused primarily on a consideration of the impact the decision had or could have on elections and election-related litigation (Foley, 2007; Hasen, 2005; Lowenstein, 2007; Smith and Shortell, 2007; Tokaji, 2005). Given the language limiting the scope of the opinion to the case at bar, *Bush v. Gore* had clear strategic implications for elections, but seemed at first to have been effectively limited as a precedent.

A broad scholarly meme quickly took hold that *Bush v. Gore* was designed to do nothing more than ensure George Bush rather than Al Gore became president (Dershowitz, 2003). Subsequently, the fact that the Supreme Court did not utilize the holding to cure any of a host of problems with election administration that orbit around equal protection deficiencies solidified this early assessment of the lack of precedential value of the case (Flanders, 2006; Hasen, 2006). The Supreme Court has so far completely avoided any reliance on or citation to the case. The Court has not yet cited it in any fashion, whether in any majority opinion, even one concurrence, or in any dissent. Further, despite the substantial and systematic problems with the administration of elections brought to light and emphasized by the *Bush v. Gore* litigation, overall, the implementation of reform of election administration has been modest. Indeed, because of the absence of governmental response to the opportunity for dramatic improvement of election administration presented in the aftermath of *Bush v. Gore,* the academy declared the case "dead" (Hasen, 2007). The reports of the demise of *Bush v. Gore* and the acceptance of the case as an insular event with no ongoing importance now seem, perhaps, to have been premature.

Although the U.S. Supreme Court has yet to cite *Bush v. Gore,* the balance of the judicial structure has not been so reticent to embrace and rely on the case. By March 2011, federal courts had cited *Bush v. Gore* 152 times and a host of state courts had cited it 111 times. There is no clear way to determine if the lower courts have relied on *Bush v. Gore* less frequently than they might have had the limiting language not been included. What can be seen is utilization of the case despite the limiting language and the absence of citation by the Supreme Court. After explaining the methodology used for the data collection and analysis, I show the expanse of judicial reliance on *Bush v. Gore,* consider some of the more important federal opinions that cite it, and then assess the overall impact of the ruling as well as the efficacy of the limiting language in the *per curiam* opinion. I conclude with a consideration of the implications as well as some conclusions and avenues of additional research.

DATA

To determine the extent and nature of judicial citation to *Bush v. Gore*, I used the legal citation database *Shepard's Citations* accessed through the *LexisNexis Academic* portal. *Shepard's* has two unique features that make this approach to gathering the data especially appropriate. First, *Shepard's* lists all opinions that cite any previously decided case. That is, *Shepard's* presents a comprehensive roster of every incident of citation in every opinion for every case. Second, the specific legal treatment of the previously decided case is operationalized by categorical legal concept. That is, the *Shepard's* database qualitatively distinguishes the citations so that how the case is cited is as readily apparent as whether the case was cited. The accuracy of the *Shepard's* case roster as well as the appropriateness of the categorization of the legal treatment have been rigorously tested and determined to be reliable and sound (Spriggs and Hansford, 2000).

Table 2.1 shows all citations by the federal courts of appeal to *Bush v. Gore* by circuit and opinion type. Two aspects of the citations stand out. First, all circuits but the Fourth and Seventh Circuits have cited the case. Second, the case has been cited in majority opinions thirty-five times and in dissenting opinions eleven times while being specifically followed five times including one concurrence. In short, the "opinion" is the ruling of the court. A "dissent" is written by a judge whenever that judge disagrees with the rationale or holding or both of the opinion. A judge might "concur" when the judge believes the opinion has gotten some portion of the decision correct, perhaps the outcome or the reasoning, but believes the court majority opinion has also gotten something

TABLE 2.1. *Cites to* Bush v. Gore *by Federal Courts of Appeal*

CT App.	Opinion	Dissent	Concur	Followed	Follow/C	Disting	Total
1st	6	3	1				10
2nd	4						4
3rd	1	1				1	3
4th							0
5th	5						5
6th	7	3		3	1		14
7th							0
8th	1	1					2
9th	10	2		1			13
10th						1	1
11th	1	1					2
All App	35	11	1	4	1	2	54

TABLE 2.2. *Cites to* Bush v. Gore *by Federal District Courts*

District	Opinion	Disting	Followed	Explained	Total
1st	5		1	2	8
2nd	14	2			16
3rd	7	2			9
4th	1				1
5th	2	3			5
6th	11	1	4		16
7th	4	2	2		8
8th	2	1		1	4
9th	13	4		2	19
10th	1	1			2
11th	7	1			8
DC	2				2
Total district	69	17	7	5	98

wrong or perhaps has engaged in an incomplete analysis. "Followed" refers to instances where the case is cited without comment and "followed/C" refers to instances where the case is cited without comment in a concurrence. "Disting" refers to instances where a judge has explained why the case does not apply to the present circumstances. This initial analysis suggests that the explicit effort by the Supreme Court to limit *Bush v. Gore* has not precluded the judges who sit on the various courts of appeal from at least some level of reliance on the case.

Table 2.2 shows all citations by the federal district courts to *Bush v. Gore* by district and opinion type. Here, the judges of the federal district courts have cited the case ninety-eight times and specifically followed it seven times. "Opinion" refers to the decision of the court. "Disting" refers to instances where a judge has explained why the case does not apply to the present circumstances. "Followed" refers to instances where the case is cited without comment. "Explained" refers to instances where the holding of the case is explained at some length. Like the courts of appeal, a notable feature of the roster of citations is that the citation of the case is spread across the districts.

This initial count and distribution of the citations for *Bush v. Gore* at the federal level suggests that the case has been used when and as the federal opinion writers see fit regardless of the limiting language in the *per curiam* opinion. That is, the language that specifically limited *Bush v. Gore* to the instant facts seems to have been an ineffective barrier to lower court citation of the case. When combined with the 111 state and territorial courts that have cited the case, there have been 263 citations to *Bush v. Gore* despite the declaration of the Supreme Court that the case was limited to the "present circumstances." The state supreme courts from twenty-two states from all regions of the country have cited the case. An additional twenty-five court systems beyond the state supreme courts, ranging from the Texas and Alabama Courts of Criminal Appeals to the New York and New Jersey Superior Courts, have also cited the case.

Still, although from a simple procedural standpoint, *Bush v. Gore* has indeed been cited with apparent disregard of the dicta of the limiting language, understanding the nuance of the case citation as a demonstration of precedential value or importance is largely dependent on the substantive dimension of the citations (Dear and Jessen, 2007). Accordingly, beyond the citation count, the substantive basis for the citations of *Bush v. Gore* must be determined in order to assess what, if any, jurisprudence has developed as a result of the case.

Shepard's uses editorial categories that have been developed by and taken from *LexisNexis* to explain and register the substantive manner in which a case is cited. These categories of editorial analysis are referred to as *LexisNexis Headnotes* (Dear and Jessen, 2007). The *Headnotes* represent discrete legal points made in an opinion by reference to specific passages from the cited case. The *Headnotes* are represented by a string of delimited words that narrow the range of applicable fact patterns or legal topics to which the specific *Headnote* could apply. For example, HN1, the designation for *Headnote* 1, is delimited by the phrase "*Constitutional Law > Elections, Terms & Voting > Electoral College Governments > Federal Government > Elections*" and refers to the passage and authority from the *Bush v. Gore* opinion reproduced beneath the string of key words like this:

HN 1 Constitutional Law > Elections, Terms & Voting > Electoral College

Governments > Federal Government > Elections

The individual citizen has no federal constitutional right to vote for electors for the President of the United States unless and until the state legislature chooses a statewide election as the means to implement its power to appoint members of the Electoral College. U.S. Const. art. II, § 1.

Eight distinct *Headnotes* encompass the various citations of *Bush v. Gore*. Notably, of the eight categorical *Headnotes*, numbers three through seven, inclusive, are specific explications of some dimension of federal equal protection with respect to voting while notes one, two, and eight involve dimensions of elections other than concerns about equal protection. Each one of the *Headnotes* represents a separate and specific legal point contained within the opinion. Each point contained in each *Headnote* could be cited for a specific point of legal reasoning or the rationale for some dimension of a subsequent holding or determination by a court.

The *Headnotes* that divide the *Bush v. Gore* opinion into discrete citation segments are set forth here with separate italicized short titles I have provided for rhetorical ease:

Headnote 1: *No Individual Right to Vote*

The individual citizen has no federal constitutional right to vote for electors for the President of the United States unless and until the state legislature chooses a statewide election as the means to implement its power to appoint members of the Electoral College. U.S. Const. art. II, § 1.

keyword string Constitutional Law > Elections, Terms & Voting > Electoral College

Governments > Federal Government > Elections

Headnote 2: *State has plenary power to choose electors*

The state legislature's power to select the manner for appointing electors is plenary; it may, if it so chooses, select the electors itself.

keyword string Constitutional Law > Congressional Duties & Powers > Elections > Time, Place & Manner Governments > Federal Government > Elections

Headnote 3: *Equal Protection of votes, State can take the right to vote back*

When the state legislature vests the right to vote for President of the United States in its people, the right to vote as the legislature has prescribed is fundamental; and one source of its fundamental nature lies in the equal weight accorded to each vote and the equal dignity owed to each voter. The state, of course, after granting the franchise in the special context of U.S. Const. art. II, can take back the power to appoint electors.

keyword string Governments > Federal Government > Elections

Headnote 4: *Equal Protection and vote dilution*

The right to vote is protected in more than the initial allocation of the franchise to choose electors for the President of the United States. Equal protection applies as well to the manner of its exercise. Having once granted the right to vote on equal terms, the state may not, by later arbitrary and disparate treatment, value one person's vote over that of another. It must be remembered that the right of suffrage can be denied by a debasement or dilution of the weight of a citizen's vote just as effectively as by wholly prohibiting the free exercise of the franchise.

keyword string Constitutional Law > Equal Protection > Scope of Protection

Governments > Federal Government > Elections

Headnote 5: *Equal Protection, standards*

A state supreme court's command to consider the intent of the voter in counting legally cast votes is unobjectionable as an abstract proposition and a starting principle. The problem inheres when there is an absence of specific standards to ensure its equal application. The formulation of uniform rules to determine intent based on recurring circumstances is practicable and necessary.

keyword string Constitutional Law > Equal Protection > Scope of Protection

Governments > Federal Government > Elections

Headnote 6: *Speed cannot supersede Equal Protection*

A desire for speed is not a general excuse for ignoring equal protection guarantees.

keyword string Constitutional Law > Equal Protection > Scope of Protection

Headnote 7: *Equal Protection, Statewide recounts*

When a court orders a statewide remedy, such as a statewide recount, there must be at least some assurance that the rudimentary requirements of equal treatment and fundamental fairness are satisfied.

keyword string Constitutional Law > Equal Protection > Scope of Protection

TABLE 2.3. *Headnotes and Cite Counts*

HN #	Short Description	Cites
HN 1	*No Individual Right to Vote*	42
HN 2	*State has plenary power to choose electors*	7
HN 3	*EquPr of votes, State can take rt to vote back*	50
HN 4	*Equal Protection and vote dilution*	65
HN 5	*Equal Protection, standards*	67
HN 6	*Speed cannot supersede Equal Protection*	43
HN 7	*Equal Protection, Statewide recounts*	29
HN 8	*Safe harbor date*	16
Total		319

Governments > Federal Government > Elections

Headnote 8: *Safe harbor date*

3 U.S.C.S. § 5 requires that any controversy or contest that is designed to lead to a conclusive selection of electors for President of the United States be completed by December 12.

keyword string Governments > Federal Government > Elections

Table 2.3 presents the *Headnotes* by the short title I have provided along with the citation count for each individual *Headnote*. The total of 319 specific *Headnotes* citations exceeds the total number of opinion citations because the citations in some opinions refer to more than one *Headnote*. Recall that five of the eight categories of *Headnote* are concerned with equal protection in the context of voting.

Simply sorting the citations to *Bush v. Gore* by the broad categories of "equal protection" and "other" reveals the area and focus of the development of the jurisprudence of the case. Equal protection is the explicit subject of 254 of the 319 individual citations. In other words, roughly 80 percent of all the citations by judges to *Bush v. Gore* are in the context of equal protection. The information gleaned from the *Headnotes* is even more suggestive than the mere citation count of the idea that *Bush v. Gore* has persevered beyond the intended scope of its authors. Even more telling, the context and language of the citing opinions present a compelling argument that the jurisprudence of equal protection has developed in particular ways in response to and because of the case. Accordingly, while space constraints prohibit analysis of each case, some illustrative cases taken from the federal and state courts demonstrate the point that *Bush v. Gore* has emerged as a precedential force despite the limiting language. Of course, the references to *Bush v. Gore* do not occur in a vacuum. Although citation to the case of *Bush v. Gore* is the focus here, the cases in which it has been cited have arisen in the context of a post–*Bush v. Gore* and post–Help America Vote Act (HAVA) election administration environment addressed at length elsewhere in this volume. Accordingly, although the focus here is on the citations, the great concern about election administration and the enhanced use of litigation to resolve election disputes cannot be construed solely as artifacts of *Bush v. Gore* the case. That is, the greater litigation and election administration context matters. The contestation over election administration that has occurred in the courts since *Bush v. Gore* has arisen as a result of a variety of issues. Among the most important, the election administration reform efforts at state and national levels and a greater cognition among the politically active about the potential of litigation in effecting elections have created the environment in which citations to *Bush v. Gore* have flourished. The context of these citing cases should be kept in mind even as their content is considered.

In *League of Women Voters v. Brunner*, 548 F. 3d 616 (6th Cir. Ohio 2008) (HN 3,4), the court considered the action brought by the League of Women Voters of Ohio, the League of Women Voters of Toledo-Lucas County, and some individual registered voters in Ohio. The action was based on allegations that during the November 2004 election, some citizens were arbitrarily denied the right to vote or were overly burdened in their efforts to exercise their right to vote. Specifically, the petition alleged problems with voting machines that malfunctioned, inaccurate purges of qualified and registered voters from voter registration lists, inadequately trained poll workers that were unable to resolve registration issues, instances of voters prematurely turned away from polling stations, as well as the failure of some absentee ballots to arrive at the homes of voters who requested absentee ballots before the election. The plaintiffs/appellees argued that these issues inhibited lawful voting and therefore deprived some citizens of the equal protection of the law through an arbitrary or burdensome deprivation of their right to vote based on nothing more than the idiosyncrasy of where they lived. The Sixth Circuit agreed with the plaintiffs/appellees and the lower court and affirmed that the voting system in Ohio violated the Equal Protection Clause. The court cited *Bush v. Gore* with the *Headnote* 4 quote "having once granted the right to vote on equal terms, the State may not, by later arbitrary and disparate treatment, value one person's vote over that of another." The court determined that *Bush v. Gore* at a minimum meant that equal protection requires a nonarbitrary treatment of voters. Although the court recognized that *Bush v. Gore* claimed to be limited in application, because several district courts had utilized the case in assessing challenges to voting systems, the court concluded that *Bush v. Gore* was relevant to the case at bar and was properly considered binding.

In *Stewart v. Blackwell*, 444 F. 3d 843 (6th Cir. Ohio 2006) (HN 3,4,5,6,7), the court considered the argument of some voters in Hamilton, Montgomery, Sandusky, and Summit Counties in Ohio that the use of unreliable and deficient voting equipment in these counties, but not in other counties, constituted a violation of the Equal Protection Clause. A critical dimension of the allegations was that the punch card ballots used in some of the counties were especially vulnerable to counting errors when tabulating votes. Following the logic of *Bush v. Gore*, the argument was that all the votes cast in Ohio are not counted at the same rate so they are not valued the same across the state. Although the district court ruled against the plaintiffs, as appellants, the aggrieved voters persuaded the court of appeals to reverse the ruling. The Sixth Circuit found that, because voters in some counties in Ohio are statistically significantly less likely to have their votes counted than voters in other counties, the administration of the election violated the Equal Protection Clause. Also relying on the language referenced by *Headnote 4*, the court cited *Bush v. Gore* and pointed out that the right to vote extends beyond the initial grant of the franchise and also encompasses a necessity that votes be equally weighted. Although the dissent criticized the majority for any reliance on *Bush v. Gore* given the limiting language of the opinion, the majority took the position that Supreme Court opinions all have precedential value until repudiated or overturned by the Court.

In *Black v. McGuffage*, 209 F. Supp. 2d 889 (ND Ill. 2002) (HN 3,5,7) the district court considered the claims of some Latino and African American voters in Illinois who sued members of the Illinois State Board of Elections, the Chicago Board of Election Commissioners, and various counties and county clerks alleging that the use of a punch card voting system, voting systems that had no effective way for a voter to notify the county about errors, and voting systems without adequate voter education or assistance from election judges violated the Equal Protection Clause. The court relied on *Bush v. Gore* to deny the defendants' motions to dismiss the equal protection claims. Although the court acknowledged that the Supreme Court limited its decision in *Bush v. Gore* to the circumstances presented there, the court nonetheless declared that the rationale of *Bush v. Gore* provided guidance in the case. The court determined that people in different counties in Illinois face significantly different probabilities as to whether their votes will be counted and that probability is shaped by which voting system is used by the county in which the voter happens to reside. This disparate treatment values one person's vote over another based on an arbitrary designation, which, pursuant to *Bush v. Gore* and in particular relying on the language referenced by *Headnotes* 3 and 4, violates the Equal Protection Clause.

In *Bay County Democratic Party v. Land*, 347 F. Supp. 2d 404 (E.D. Mich. 2004) (HN 3, 4), the district court considered the claim by the Bay County Democratic Party and the Michigan Democratic Party that a directive issued by the Michigan secretary of state and the director of elections to local election officials violated the Help America Vote Act of 2002. The directive at issue ordered local officials to disregard and not count any provisional ballots cast by a voter in the incorrect precinct even if that voter was otherwise in the proper jurisdiction, city, village, or township. The court found that the failure to count certain votes prevented every vote from having equal value. The court enjoined the directive and determined that eligible voters have a right to cast provisional ballots and have those ballots counted even when those votes were cast outside of the designated or proper precinct.

Two related cases from the Sixth Circuit merit particular attention because of the facts presented and the reliance of the courts on *Bush v. Gore*. First, in *State ex rel. Skaggs v. Brunner* 588 F. Supp. 2d 819 (S.D. Ohio 2008) (HN 1, 3, 4), the court embraced the role of the federal courts in resolving election disputes that might encompass equal protection claims. Before the November 4, 2008 election, two directives were established that provided guidelines for the counting of provisional ballots. Recall that provisional ballots are those cast under some procedural question such as whether the voter is at the correct precinct or is actually registered. One was issued by the secretary of state of Ohio and the other one was issued by the state court. The plaintiffs filed a complaint with the Ohio Supreme Court that argued the secretary of state had reversed an earlier interpretation of Ohio election law. As a result of a defense motion, the case was then removed to federal court in the Southern District of Ohio on November 14, 2008. The plaintiffs opposed the removal of the case from state to federal court, while the secretary of state contended that the removal was proper. The district court found that the removal was proper because the original state court complaint filed by the plaintiffs alleged a violation of a federal court order by the Ohio secretary of state and, citing *Bush v. Gore*, alleged equal protection violations by Ohio. The court, like the plaintiffs, relied on *Bush v. Gore* in assessing the legal foundation for understanding the equal protection claims, and unlike the plaintiffs, in assessing the proper venue for the case.

In the related litigation *State ex rel. Skaggs v. Brunner* 588 F. Supp. 2d 828 (S.D. Ohio 2008) (HN 1, 3, 4, 5), the court reviewed the merits of the dispute beyond the question of whether the removal was proper. The thrust of the case involved the disposition of 1,000 contested provisional ballots cast during the November 4, 2008 election in Ohio. The plaintiffs did not argue that these provisional ballots were fraudulent or had been cast by ineligible voters or suffered from any other substantive flaw. Instead, the plaintiffs claimed that these provisional ballots should not be counted because they were technically deficient in some way. That is, the provisional ballots all suffered from one of several technical flaws. The plaintiffs claimed that these provisional ballots should have been excluded from the vote count because they were missing a signature, were missing printed names, contained printed names or signatures in the wrong location on the form, or there was no proof that the voter presented proper forms of identification to obtain the ballot. The secretary of state contended that these 1,000 provisional ballots should still be counted in the vote tally because the deficiencies were due to poll worker error rather than some mistake by the various voters. All parties agreed that all of the voters who cast these 1,000 provisional votes were eligible to vote. The secretary argued that Ohio electoral law requires that all eligible voters have the right to have their votes counted equally, so as to not violate the Equal Protection Clause. Relying on *Bush v. Gore*, the court agreed with the secretary of state that all votes must be counted according to a unified criteria and law so as to ensure all votes are counted equally.

The reliance on *Bush v. Gore* has not been limited to the federal courts. Indeed, as noted earlier, state and territorial courts have cited the case more than 100 times. The Montana Supreme Court cited *Bush v. Gore* when it resolved *Big Spring v. Jore* 2005 MT 64, 326 Mont. 256 (2005) (HN 1, 5). The case arose from a dispute over the November 2, 2004 election held in Lake County, Montana. Seven ballots had markings for more than one candidate. These types of ballots are referred to as *over-votes* because the voter has chosen more than the appropriate number of candidates. The scanning machine in Lake County rejected these over-vote ballots. A county election official, upon examination of the over-vote ballots, determined that the voters actually intended to vote for the candidate Jore. The plaintiff, Anita Big Spring, an elector in Lake County, argued that counting the over-votes would violate the Equal Protection Clause because any such counting would depend on altering the standard by which all the other ballots had been counted. The court relied on *Bush v. Gore* and agreed with the plaintiff. The Montana Supreme Court ruled that the votes could not be counted or considered in determining the outcome of the election. If the votes were counted, the court reasoned, there inherently would be inconsistent standards governing the counting of all the ballots, which would undermine the equal value of each vote.

In New Hampshire, a state supreme court concurring opinion specifically followed *Bush v. Gore* while a second concurrence cited it in the *Appeal of McDonough (Ballot Law Commission)* 149 N.H. 105, 816 A. 2d 1022 (2003) (HN 5). In that case, Peter McDonough, a candidate for Hillsborough county attorney, argued that the New Hampshire Ballot Law Commission (BLC) erred in certifying his opponent as the winner. The complaint focused on 172 ballots on which voters marked their choice for straight ticket voting whereby all candidates from one party would be chosen. The ballots McDonough challenged were (1) those appropriately marked for a straight ticket Republican vote and (2) those appropriately marked to vote for some individual candidates (either Democrat or Republican); but (3) those not marked as selecting a candidate in the race for county attorney. Because the voter demonstrated the intent to vote a straight ticket for the Republican Party, the BLC ruled that those voters who failed to select a candidate in the county attorney race intended to vote to support the Republican candidate. The New Hampshire Supreme Court determined the BLC acted properly when it counted the 172 contested ballots as supporting the Republican candidate. In the concurring opinion, some justices grounded the support for the actions of the BLC in the jurisprudence of *Bush v. Gore*. In essence, because the BLC had followed uniform rules in its determination of how to count the contested 172 ballots, all votes (and voters) were treated equally.

The reach of *Bush v. Gore* even extends to the territories of the United States. In *Underwood v. Guam Election Commission* 2006 Guam 17 (HN 3, 5, 6), the Guam Supreme Court considered whether to count over-votes in the election for governor and lieutenant governor. The plaintiffs, Underwood and

Aguon (candidates for governor and lieutenant governor), contended that 504 ballots determined to be over-votes should be counted. The Guam Election Commission did not count the over-votes in accordance with the Organic Act of Guam. This resulted in the plaintiffs' opponents, Camacho and Cruz, winning the election. The Guam Supreme Court applied the analysis and guidance from *Bush v. Gore* to assess how to define a vote. The Guam Supreme Court began its reasoning with this quote from *Bush v. Gore*: "in certifying election results, the votes eligible for inclusion in the certification are the votes meeting the properly established legal requirements." *Bush v. Gore* deferred to Florida law and determined that a legal vote was one in which there was a clear indication of the intent of the voter. In the Guam election, the Guam Supreme Court ruled against the plaintiffs, specifically relied on *Bush v. Gore*, and deferred to the law of Guam, which states that over-votes are not to be counted.

EQUAL PROTECTION

Seven justices accepted that there were equal protection issues in the facts that gave rise to the *Bush v. Gore* litigation. Five justices of the "equal protection seven" voted to end the recount because Florida would not have been able to meet the "safe harbor" deadline to ensure the state's electoral votes would be counted when the Electoral College convened while two would have remanded the case to the Florida courts for recounting bound by a uniform standard. The three justices who recognized equal protection issues but declined to remand the case or otherwise provide a remedy for any equal protection issues other than a prohibition on a continuation of the recount were Chief Justice Rehnquist, Justice Scalia, and Justice Thomas. These three also asserted a rationale not grounded in equal protection that turned on the idea that the Florida Supreme Court made "new law" when it ordered the recount and thereby undermined the exclusive authority of the Florida legislature to choose the electors for the state. The two major rationales – equal protection concerns on the one hand and "new law" subverting the authority of a state legislature in a field of legislative prerogative on the other – have not proven equally robust in the decade of litigation since. While judges and litigants at almost all levels of the judiciary have presented *Bush v. Gore* in support of various equal protection claims, the premise of the "new law" objection to the actions of the Florida Supreme Court has not gained traction.

Still, the issue of whether *Bush v. Gore* has pushed the development of equal protection jurisprudence in one way or another is not obvious. As has been pointed out (Hasen, 2007), in the Ninth Circuit in *SW Voter Registration Ed. Project v. Shelley* 278 F. Supp. 2d 1131 (C.D. Cal. 2003), a conservative *en banc* panel reversed the original three-judge panel that had determined the dramatic variations in the reliability of punch card voting systems amounted to a violation of equal protection as it was framed by *Bush v. Gore*. In *Stewart v. Blackwell*, 444 F. 3d 843 (6th Cir. Ohio 2006) *superceded en banc* 473 F 3d

692 (6th Cir. Ohio 2007), the Sixth Circuit voted to hear the case *en banc* after the three-judge panel applied strict scrutiny as the level of analysis and found that a *Bush v. Gore*-grounded equal protection claim from the anticipated use of punch card ballots had merit. The vote to hear the case *en banc* vacated this pro–*Bush v. Gore* ruling automatically per Sixth Circuit Rule 35 (a).

Despite these apparent efforts by the circuits, or at least some members of the circuits, to limit *Bush v. Gore,* there is reason to believe that the case will persevere as it moves toward an established precedent of broad applicability. Specifically, even these efforts at limitation by the *en banc* panels in the Sixth and Ninth Circuits revealed some dimension of what may lie ahead. The *en banc* panel in the Ninth Circuit referred to *Bush v. Gore* as "the leading case on disputed elections" (344 F. 3d 882 (9th Cir. 2003) at p. 918) vacated *en banc* 344 F. 3d 914 (9th Cir. 2003). The vacated Sixth Circuit opinion is even more assertive. In a split opinion, Judge Martin delivered the opinion of the court, in which Judge Cole joined. Judge Gilman dissented and took the majority to task for relying on *Bush v. Gore.* In response to this critique, the majority pointed out:

Of note, *Bush v. Gore* appears to be the first case where a court recognized the developing problem with technology that we confront today. The *per curiam* opinion noted that the case "brought into sharp focus a common, if heretofore unnoticed, phenomenon" – that nationwide an "estimated 2% of ballots cast do not register a vote for President for whatever reason," and that "punchcard balloting machines can produce an unfortunate number of ballots which are not punched in a clean, complete way by the voter." *Bush,* 531 U.S. at 104, 121 S.Ct. 525. We also note that the dissent begins by criticizing our "reliance on the Supreme Court's murky decision in *Bush v. Gore.*" Dis. Op. at 880. Murky, transparent, illegitimate, right, wrong, big, tall, short or small; regardless of the adjective one might use to describe the decision, the proper noun that precedes it – "Supreme Court" – carries more weight with us. Whatever else *Bush v. Gore* may be, it is first and foremost a decision of the Supreme Court of the United States and we are bound to adhere to it.... 444 F.3d 843, 898 fn 8 (2006) superceded by 473 F 3d 692 (6th Cir. Ohio 2007) (en banc) vacating as moot 356 F. Supp 2d 791 (N.D. Ohio 2004)

In fact, the opinion seems to present a strong rebuke to any adherent of the conventional wisdom that denigrates *Bush v. Gore* or embraces a notion of the case as little more than a historical oddity:

In response to the dissent, we are of course aware that some of these cases were reviewed on the pleadings or on a motion to dismiss under Rule 12(b)(6). Coming from district courts and other circuits, they are not binding upon us (as Supreme Court decisions are). These decisions do have, however, the power to persuade, and it would be irresponsible not to consider their reasoning – both good and bad – simply because they are not binding. If we then agree with their reasoning, we ought to apply it here. If we do not agree, then we should not adopt their reasoning. This, of course, differs from Supreme Court decisions, such as *Bush v. Gore*, where we are bound to apply their reasoning regardless of whether we agree with them, find them "murky," Dis. Op. at 880, or believe that the Supreme Court issued its decision with a "lack of seriousness." Dis. Op. at 886 (quoting Richard L. Hasen, *Bush v. Gore* and the Future of Equal Protection Law in Elections, 29 Fla. St. U.L.Rev. 377, 391 (2001))

That hundreds of opinions have cited the case for some assessment of some aspect of equal protection in the context of election administration suggests that despite the limiting language and despite the apparent desire of some in the federal judiciary, *Bush v. Gore* perseveres.

Another aspect of the prospective role of *Bush v. Gore* that has been given little attention is the broad efforts of some to expand the holding beyond election litigation into criminal procedure. No court has yet embraced this expansion of the notion that equal protection as clarified by *Bush v. Gore* dictates that citizens be treated equally, even apart from voting. However, some state courts have determined that some criminal case litigants who have sought to expand *Bush v. Gore* merit an explanation embedded in opinions that explain why *Bush v. Gore* is not applicable. This wave of explanatory citations suggests that members of the judiciary take the argument seriously enough to spend time and resources distinguishing the *Bush v. Gore* equal protection analysis in the context of criminal procedure from the *Bush v. Gore* equal protection analysis in the context of election administration or claims about the right to have a vote counted.

IMPLICATIONS, CONCLUSIONS, AND ADDITIONAL RESEARCH

The straightforward implication here is that *Bush v. Gore* has begun to develop a place in the jurisprudence of equal protection despite the Supreme Court's efforts to limit its applicability. Without question, the Supreme Court has so far declined to cite the case and can be considered to have abided by the peculiar limitation contained in dicta in the *per curiam* opinion. However, federal appellate, federal district, and state and territorial courts of all levels have cited the case primarily in the context of equal protection issues in the context of litigation over election administration. *Bush v. Gore* has been the filter through which problems associated with voting technologies have been considered. Perhaps this should not be surprising. The *Bush v. Gore* analysis seemed odd in the context of the facts that gave rise to it. After all, concern over the accuracy and fairness of a vote tally might reasonably be expected to lead to a fair and accurate vote tally rather than an embrace of a clearly questionable status quo predicated on a premise that more accurate counting is an undesirable outcome in election administration. But despite the slippage between the facts upon which the *per curiam* opinion was constructed and the conclusions reached by the justices therein, the insight from the opinion in the abstract might simply present a modest extension of the logic of *Reynolds v. Sims* 377 U.S. 533 (1964) (one person one vote means districts should be about equal). If the legacy of *Bush v. Gore* is a gradual movement toward greater refinement of election processes so that more votes are actually counted in more accurate ways, then ultimately the limiting language will be, perhaps appropriately, thought of as little more than rightfully ignored partisan-driven dicta.

Of course, if every vote must be counted and political subdivisions within a state, whether counties or precincts, must count votes the same way at the same rate, then the modest logical extension of *Reynolds v. Sims* could become a significant practical alteration of the manner in which states conduct elections. Such an expansion of *Bush v. Gore* might even alter the fundamental relationship between the federal government and the states regarding election management. The early institutional choice of a home-rule approach to federal management of elections has had broad implications for the manner in which the elections are actually held (Ewald, 2009). If the counties or precincts must harmonize vote-counting behavior or the other elements of the administration of elections because of the demands of the Equal Protection Clause, there is at least some potential for a demand of cross-state harmonization as well. This could perhaps lead to a formal dismantling of home rule regarding election administration or perhaps merely an increase in the standards for acceptable election administration.

Beyond issues regarding the administration of elections, if the efforts by litigants outside of the realm of election litigation succeed in foisting *Bush v. Gore* upon a so far reluctant judiciary in nonelection litigation arenas, then the case could actually become the vehicle for widespread changes in criminal justice. For instance, if equal protection as contemplated by *Bush v. Gore* was applied to the right to a full and fair defense in death penalty cases, limitations on DNA testing might fall by the wayside. Although it seems unlikely that the judiciary will allow this expansion of the applicability of *Bush v. Gore* given the ubiquitous judicial push back against it so far, if the defense bar continues its efforts to introduce this more nuanced and expansive understanding of equal protection, successful advocacy may not be out of the question. *Bush v. Gore* might also have a substantial impact on immigration cases if a broader understanding of equal protection made its way into what is now akin to summary resolution of claims of undocumented status. Additionally, if these nonelection fields of litigation can bring a *Bush v. Gore*–driven but expanded approach to equal protection, government management of issues such as the census might also be affected.

Still, the mostly likely long-term impact of *Bush v. Gore* seems to be found in election litigation. Future research should consider the manner in which the litigants have cited the case in addition to the presentation of the case by the various courts. The arguments put forward in the briefs may reveal whether the litigation bar has settled on a robust interpretation of *Bush v. Gore* even if those on the bench continue to contest the bounds of the case. Moreover, a secondary consideration of the citations of the cases that cite *Bush v. Gore* may reveal a greater heft to the current precedential value than has been shown here. Specifically, time will reveal whether cases that affirmatively cite *Bush v. Gore* are then in turn affirmatively cited, creating a second generation of citation support for *Bush v. Gore* even if that developing body of jurisprudence avoids a direct citation to the controversial case. Second-generation citations may not generate the hostility from *en banc* panels that the Sixth and Ninth Circuits have perhaps demonstrated to direct citations of *Bush v. Gore* and could solidify the jurisprudence without a reliance on the controversial case alone. Moreover, in whatever analysis the Supreme Court might bring to bear on a case that cites a case that cited *Bush v. Gore*, the avoidance by lower courts and litigants of a potential reason to deny *certiorari*, overt dependence on a case of limited precedential value with a disfavored status among the justices, could only accrue to the benefit of the petitioner.

3

Bush v. Gore in the American Mind: Reflections and Survey Results on the Tenth Anniversary of the Decision Ending the 2000 Election Controversy

Amy Semet, Nathaniel Persily, and Stephen Ansolabehere

INTRODUCTION

Very few, if any, Supreme Court cases have captured public attention on a scale comparable to that of *Bush v. Gore*. The Supreme Court's involvement was the last scene in a political and courtroom drama that played out for more than a month on television. Even if the legal claims, let alone the holding, in the case were difficult for the public to understand, the import and consequences of the case were not: George W. Bush would be the next president. As a rare, high-salience case with understandable political consequences and clear winners and losers, *Bush v. Gore* provided a unique test of the Court's legitimacy in the public mind.

Scholars who studied the aftermath of *Bush v. Gore* found conflicting evidence of the decision's short-term effect on public attitudes toward the Court (see, e.g., Gibson, Caldeira, and Spence, 2003a, 2003b; Kritzer, 2001; Mate and Wright, 2008; Price and Romantan, 2004). A flurry of articles published between 2001 and 2004 debated whether *Bush v. Gore* indeed "wounded" the Court's legitimacy (Gibson et al., 2003a, 2003b; Kritzer, 2001; Price and Romantan, 2004; Yates and Whitford, 2002). Some researchers found that the decision altered short-term attitudes toward the Court with opinion polarized along racial and partisan lines (Kritzer, 2001; Mate and Wright, 2008; Price and Romantan, 2004; Yates and Whitford, 2002), while others found little or no effect on feelings about the Court (Gibson et al., 2003a, 2003b). All seemed to agree, however, that *Bush v. Gore* led to no long-term effects on public opinion about the Court (Gibson, 2007; Mate and Wright, 2008). Within a year, the Court appeared to recover to its pre–*Bush v. Gore* levels in public support, and the structure of support did not reveal sustained levels of racial or partisan polarization.

In the more than a decade since the Court's decision, no survey has been conducted that asks about *Bush v. Gore* or tries to link attitudes toward the decision to opinion of the Court. This chapter discusses the first survey taken on this subject since the initial fallout from the decision. In the first part, we describe the earlier literature on attitudes toward the Court and attitudes toward the decision ending the 2000 recount. Next, we look at results from our recent survey that asked respondents whether they thought the Court's decision was fair or unfair. Although a sizable share (almost 30%) of the population said they did not remember the decision, we found that the public remains polarized along racial and partisan lines in its attitudes toward the decision and that approval of the Bush presidency remains a powerful predictor of attitudes toward the decision. The last section briefly examines the effect of perceived fairness of the decision in *Bush v. Gore* on respondents' approval and confidence in the Supreme Court. Although approval of or confidence in other institutions and officeholders, such as Congress and the president, greatly determined attitudes toward the Court, attitudes concerning the decision in *Bush v. Gore* remain a statistically significant variable in predicting Court approval and confidence.

BACKGROUND

Literature on the Effect of *Bush v. Gore*

The debate surrounding *Bush v. Gore* brought to the forefront a number of issues that are often relegated to law reviews and legal symposiums. For instance, what impact do controversial decisions have on public opinion toward the Court in the short term and the long term? Do controversial decisions polarize the public along predictable lines of cleavage and if so, does public opinion about the case continue to polarize the public the same way years after the media spotlight fades? Further, do polarizing Supreme Court decisions have any impact on the public's approval of and confidence in the Supreme Court?

While there generally exists a consensus that the Supreme Court enjoys high levels of mass approval and that its "political capital" can help it generate both support and compliance with its decisions (Grosskopf and Mondak, 1998; Mondak and Smithey, 1997), scholars offer different opinions as to how and when the Supreme Court can actually move public opinion. Under the so-called legitimation hypothesis, some scholars have argued that the Supreme Court acts as a policy elite and leads opinion in a certain way (Clawson, Kegler, and Waltenburg, 2001, 2003). Individual Court cases can crystallize latent attitudes toward a controversial issue, thereby leading to polarization of the electorate as different groups take sides on the issues (Franklin and Kosaki, 1989). Salient Court decisions polarize the electorate because the discourse surrounding the case makes certain considerations more accessible in people's minds,

thereby facilitating people's ability to "make connections between their political and social predispositions and their attitudes about the issue" (Brickman
and Peterson, 2006, 107; see also Franklin and Kosaki, 1989; Johnson and
Martin, 1998; Zaller, 1992). *Roe v. Wade* provides an illustrative example.
As Franklin and Kosaki (1989) found, *Roe* further hardened the attitudes of
certain groups, such as Catholics and whites, thereby leading to greater polarization about the decision.

Research concerning the long-term effects of Court decisions on public
opinion has been even more limited, in part because of the fact that with the
exception of cases like *Brown v. Board of Education of Topeka* or *Roe*, so
few Supreme Court cases are recognizable to the American public. Further,
the Court often hears multiple cases on controversial issues, making it impossible to test the long-term impact of a single decision on public attitudes. In
their study comparing prominent abortion and death penalty cases, Johnson
and Martin (1998) argued that the Court's initial decision on a controversial
issue polarized the electorate while subsequent decisions did not. Others, like
Brickman and Peterson (2006), contend that subsequent cases can polarize
the electorate along different lines than the initial case does. For instance, they
found that abortion cases subsequent to *Roe* polarized the electorate along different lines of cleavage than the initial decision had. This can be due, in part,
to changes in the information environment and the extent to which elite cues
cement intragroup loyalty.

Scholars have also debated how controversial Court decisions impact the
public's approval and confidence in the Supreme Court in the short and long
term. On the one hand, some scholars have claimed that controversial Supreme
Court decisions have little impact on perceptions of the Court because support for the Court is largely a product of the public's commitment to a core
set of democratic values – such as commitment to social order and democratic
norms – acquired through childhood socialization into the democratic process
that remains stable over time (Caldeira, 1986; Caldeira and Gibson, 1992;
Gibson, 2007; Gibson et al., 2003a, 2003b). Under this line of reasoning,
advanced by Gibson, Caldeira, and Spence (2003a, 2003b), among others, this
long-standing loyalty to democratic norms and to the Court's place in that system is so strong and secure that short-term displeasures with specific decisions
fail to affect the primarily positive view that Americans have of the Supreme
Court. The Court's legitimacy thus functions as a "reservoir of good will"
that is rarely depleted by a particular Court decision (Gibson et al., 2003a,
365). Echoing the work of Easton (1965, 1975), Gibson and colleagues distinguish between "specific" support and "diffuse" support. "Specific" support
refers to "approval of policy outputs in the short term," while "diffuse" support denotes "fundamental loyalty to an institution over the long term" and
support that is "not contingent upon satisfaction with the immediate outputs
of the institution" (Gibson et al., 2003b, 537). While Caldeira (1986) found
that judicial action affected public attitudes toward the justices ("specific"

support), Caldeira and Gibson (1992) concluded that the same behavior of the Court had no impact on the Court's "diffuse" support, at least among the mass public.[1]

Under this line of reasoning, scholars argued that *Bush v. Gore* failed to alter public attitudes toward the Court's legitimacy (Gibson, 2007; Gibson and Caldeira, 2009a, 2009b; Gibson et al., 2003a, 2003b). Using the concept of "diffuse" support as the appropriate metric in which to assess opinions on the Court's legitimacy,[2] Gibson and colleagues, in their examination of cross-sectional data from three surveys spanning from 1987 to 2001, concluded that while opinion toward the Court may have become more polarized after *Bush v. Gore*, the 2000 election controversy did not in fact threaten the Court's legitimacy and that any effect *Bush v. Gore* had on the Court's "enduring loyalty" was "marginal indeed" (Gibson et al., 2003b, 543, 553). To the contrary, they found that the Court "enjoy[ed] at least a moderate degree of loyalty from the American people" (Gibson et al., 2003b, 545).[3] They explained this finding by reference to "positivity frames" whereby exposure to courts and "symbolic trappings of judicial power" serve to enhance judicial legitimacy, even among those unhappy with the Court's decisions (Gibson et al., 2003b, 553). Gibson and colleagues also found that while blacks as a whole were less supportive of the Court than whites, blacks nevertheless were still generally loyal to the Court as an institution – notwithstanding Court decisions that they may find unsavory – and *Bush v. Gore* failed to change "basic attachments to the institution" (Gibson et al., 2003b, 543).

Gibson (2007) reached much the same conclusion regarding the long-term effect of *Bush v. Gore*. Examining data from a 2005 survey as well as data from surveys spanning from 1987 to 2005, Gibson discovered that neither partisanship nor ideology affected "diffuse" support for the Court five years after the decision and indeed, those having strong partisan views actually expressed higher support for the Court. Consistent with Gibson and colleagues' earlier work, Gibson also concluded that the most substantively important predictor of loyalty after *Bush v. Gore* continued to be measures of democratic values – such as support for the rule of law and support for a multiparty system. Nevertheless, Gibson found the black variable to be noteworthy, indicating that after the 2000 election, blacks in fact had statistically significantly less support for the Court than nonblacks.

Contrary to Gibson and colleagues, some scholars claim that Supreme Court decisions, particularly polarizing ones, can have immediate and lasting effects on public perceptions of the Court and that the Court can indeed suffer a backlash as a result of issuing a controversial decision. Grosskopf and Mondak (1998) found that opinion on polarizing abortion and flag burning cases affected respondents' confidence in the Court. Supporting this line of work, Mondak and Smithey further concluded that the Supreme Court can regenerate support through its decisions because any support lost due to displeasure with a decision was recovered "due to public perception of a link between the Supreme Court and democratic values" (1997, 1124). Scholars have also explored the impact of group-centric forces on support for the Court.[4]

Some scholars studying the impact of *Bush v. Gore* found that it had an effect on the public's perception of the Court, at least in the short term. In his study of the 2000 election, Kritzer (2001) found that before the decision, there was no discernible relationship between partisan identification and attitudes toward the Court. By the time of the decision, however, a clear pattern became readily apparent, with feelings about *Bush v. Gore* itself being an important variable explaining the difference in the two time periods. Price and Romantan (2004) also found that confidence in the Court changed markedly after *Bush v. Gore* with divisions centering on public feelings on the decision's merits. They found that confidence in the Court rose significantly from August to December 2000, and then declined by February 2001 after the last wave of the survey. Yates and Whitford (2002) also concluded that *Bush v. Gore* polarized the electorate along partisan lines.[5] Their data indicated that while Republican support for the Court rose from 60 percent to 80 percent in the wake of the decision, Democratic support fell from 70 percent to 42 percent. Analyzing data from the 2000 National Annenberg Election Study (NAES), Mate and Wright (2008) similarly found that *Bush v. Gore* affected both "specific" and "diffuse" support for the Court, especially among partisans. They found polarization on the basis of party, ideology, and race (among other groupings) with respect to respondents' "specific" support of the Court in the aftermath of the decision. In their analysis of "diffuse" support, Mate and Wright similarly found a marked change in public attitudes before and after the decision, especially among blacks and partisans, though it was not as drastic a change as that found for "specific" support.

Yet, like Gibson (2007), scholars studying the topic found that *Bush v. Gore* led to no long-term effects on public opinion about the Court. While they believed, contrary to Gibson and colleagues, that *Bush v. Gore* had some immediate impact, Yates and Whitford agreed with them that any short-term effect declined over time and would "likely continue to fade" out (2002, 116). Mate and Wright, using the 2004 NAES, also found that the effect of *Bush v. Gore* on levels of "diffuse" support had "largely disappeared" by 2004 (2008, 346).[6] Significant, however, contrary to Gibson (2007), Mate and Wright (2008) still found ideology to be at least a statistically significant variable in predicting "diffuse" support for the questions they examined from the 2004 NAES.

To some extent, the conflict between the Gibson and colleagues' camp and the others rests on different measures used to assess public attitudes toward the Court, with each scholar using different survey questions as their dependent variable. Gibson and colleagues (2003a, 2003b) critique some scholars as improperly relying on "approval" or "confidence" questions because they contend such questions are too dependent on short-term forces and really measure "specific" support rather than "diffuse" support. Mate and Wright (2008), for instance, measured "specific" support by a question asking respondents how much confidence they had in the Supreme Court to deal fairly with the 2000 election controversy. They measured "diffuse" support by another question asking how much confidence the respondents had in the judicial branch of government, including the Supreme Court. By contrast, Gibson and colleagues (2003a, 2003b) measured "diffuse" support by constructing a variable based on respondents' answers to questions about the Supreme Court, such as whether we should do away with the Court or whether the Court can be trusted. Higher mean scores showed greater institutional loyalty to the Court. Because of the variations in question wording – that is, some scholars measuring approval or confidence and others measuring loyalty – it is impossible to compare the results directly. Both measures are important to understanding the public's feelings about the Court.

Public Opinion about the Court's Decision in *Bush v. Gore* and about the Court Itself in 2000

We first discuss the results of the 2000 NAES to see the status of public opinion on both the fairness of *Bush v. Gore* and on the Court in the immediate aftermath of the decision. The 2000 NAES is a useful and largely unanalyzed vehicle by which to test such hypotheses, because although it did not conduct a panel study around the Court's decision in *Bush v. Gore*, the survey did ask questions on the issues surrounding *Bush v. Gore* both before and after the decision's release on December 12, 2000.[7]

Responses to many questions on the 2000 NAES show just how polarized the country was in the immediate aftermath of the decision. The survey questioned respondents as to whether they felt that the Supreme Court acted fairly in declaring the Florida recount unconstitutional. Fifty-four percent said they felt the decision was fair compared to 40 percent who felt it was unfair, with an additional 5 percent saying they did not know.[8] Despite a majority of most educational groupings saying the decision was fair, only 37 percent of the least educated Americans – those without a high school diploma – felt the decision was fair. Further, while a majority of whites and Asians felt the decision was fair, only 18 percent of blacks felt similarly, with 76 percent of blacks saying the decision was unfair when questioned by NAES in the month after the decision. Democrats and liberals alike also said the decision was unfair, with less than a third of each of those groups expressing support for the Court's decision. By contrast, 85 percent of Republicans and 72 percent of conservatives said the decision was fair.[9]

Still other questions on the survey queried respondents on whether they felt that personal beliefs motivated the justices' decision making in the case. One question asked respondents whether the Supreme Court justices' personal views affected their votes in *Bush v. Gore*. The answer was surprising – opinion was split with 47 percent answering yes and 47 percent answering no.[10] Yet, when we broke down the number by how respondents actually *felt* about the decision's outcome, we saw a great deal of polarization. Of those who felt the decision was fair, 28 percent said that personal views dictated the justices' votes. By contrast, 76 percent of those who viewed the decision as unfair thought personal views motivated the justices' reasoning.

Still, despite showing polarization on many matters surrounding *Bush v. Gore*, the 2000 NAES also revealed that on some matters, public opinion heavily favored one side over the other. Consistent with Gibson and colleagues' (2003a, 2003b) argument that the public has positive opinions on the Court's legitimacy, the 2000 NAES showed that the public felt obliged to obey whatever decision the Court made. Before the decision, 88 percent said that they would accept the word of the Supreme Court as the "final word" on the Florida recount; after the decision, 73 percent expressed this view.[11] When asked whether they thought partisans would accept the Court's decision as the final word, nearly 65 percent thought they would.[12]

The 2000 NAES also asked questions that arguably can be said to measure both "specific" and "diffuse" support. With respect to "specific" support, the 2000 NAES asked: "How much confidence do you have in the U.S. Supreme Court to deal fairly with the situation surrounding the results of the election for president? A great deal, a fair amount, not too much or none at all?"[13] Before the decision, 36 percent said they had a "great deal" of confidence, 47 percent said a "fair amount," 10 percent said "not too much," 5 percent said "none," 2 percent said they did not know, and less than 1 percent did not respond. After the decision, 32 percent said a "great deal," 35 percent said a "fair amount," 18 percent said "not too much," 13 percent said "none," 2 percent said they did not know, and less than 1 percent did not answer. There were noticeable shifts in opinion along the lines of age, education, party, ideology, race, and Bush approval, among other variables, indicating at least in the immediate short term, *Bush v. Gore* had some effect on the way specific groups viewed the fairness of the decision.[14] As an example, blacks in particular exhibited a noticeable decline in confidence in the Court to decide *Bush v. Gore* fairly. Before the decision, 29 percent of blacks had a "great deal" of confidence and after the decision only 6 percent had that same opinion. Further, the percentage of blacks expressing no confidence in the Court went from 10 percent before the decision to a remarkable 35 percent after the decision.

The 2000 NAES also asked a question concerning confidence in the Court.[15] The question was: "Please tell me how much confidence you have in the Judicial Branch of government – this includes the U.S. Supreme Court. Do you have a great deal, a fair amount, not too much or none at all?"[16] Before the decision, 23 percent said they had a "great deal" of confidence, 50 percent said a "fair amount," 19 percent said "not too much," 5 percent said "none," 2 percent said they did not know, and less than 1 percent did not respond. After the decision, 21 percent of respondents said they had a "great deal" of confidence, 50 percent said a "fair amount," 21 percent said "not too much," 6 percent said "none," 2 percent said they did not know, and less than 1 percent did not respond. Looking at these numbers alone, we did not see much difference between the two periods on this measure. Although it was not as extensive as the discrepancies observed for the "specific" support measure, there still were noticeable changes in confidence in the federal judiciary as a whole before and after the decision once we looked at the data broken down by factors like race and party, among other variables. For instance, we saw a noticeable decline in the confidence that blacks had in the federal judiciary. Whereas before the decision 19 percent of blacks had a "great deal" of confidence in the judiciary, after the decision only 9 percent had that same viewpoint. We saw a similar decline among Democrats; before the decision 25 percent of Democrats expressed a "great deal" of confidence in the judiciary. This number declined to 17 percent after the decision in *Bush v. Gore* was announced.

The results of the 2000 NAES underscore the impact that the decision had in polarizing groups. Consistent with the logic of Franklin and Kosaki (1989) in their study on the impact of *Roe*, the Supreme Court's opinion in *Bush v. Gore* seemed to crystallize public attitudes, thereby intensifying the intragroup solidarity of certain groups. This resulted in polarization on the basis of race, party, and ideology, among others. As one scholar put it, such group forces "are the filters that structure and condition the Court's capacity to throw the cloak of legitimacy on a policy" (Clawson et al., 2001, 580). These particular cleavages, of course, were not unexpected. Indeed, elite discourse on *Bush v. Gore* centered on partisan cleavages. That opinion polarized on the basis of race was also of no surprise, because elite conversation heavily focused on the racial undertones of the 2000 election. Further, scholars have concluded that *Bush v. Gore* had a tangible influence on the black community. Indeed, Avery (2007) found that blacks as a whole felt that the *Bush v. Gore* decision was illegitimate and that it only reinforced their mistrust of the political system.

ATTITUDES TOWARD *BUSH V. GORE* TEN YEARS LATER

Since the initial fallout from the decision, no survey to our knowledge has specifically asked respondents their opinion of the Court's decision in *Bush v. Gore*.[17] Examining the structure of public opinion on *Bush v. Gore* ten years later is particularly important so as to see whether the initial polarization toward the decision (if not the Court) lasted beyond the contentious context in which it was delivered. Furthermore, if the structure of opinion has changed since the decision's release, perhaps we can learn larger lessons about the factors that affect retrospective attitudes toward the Court's involvement in politically charged cases.

We begin with the simple results from our question assessing the fairness of *Bush v. Gore*. We commissioned a survey called the Constitutional Attitudes Survey (CAS). The survey, conducted in June 2010,[18] asked a national random sample of 1,027 people questions on a host of topics. We structured the survey to follow what we thought was the appropriate causal structure of the variables – measuring values first, then issue positions, then approval. Regarding opinion on *Bush v. Gore*, we asked respondents the following: "You may remember that ten years ago the U.S. Supreme Court issued a decision in the case concerning the counting of ballots cast in Florida in the 2000 presidential election contest between George Bush and Al Gore. Do you think the Supreme Court decided that case fairly?" They responded as follows: 33.7 percent said the decision was decided fairly, 35.2 percent said it was not decided fairly, 28.4 percent said they did not remember, and 2.6 percent refused to answer.[19] Two conclusions immediately jumped from the responses: (1) a substantial share of the public did not remember (or did not have an opinion) about the case; and (2) those who did have an opinion were evenly split on the fairness of the decision.[20] Although Americans were less likely to have opinions about the decision than they did ten years prior, they were no less divided.

However, these simple results told us nothing as to the structure of opinion and non-opinion or as to the roots of polarization (if it exists) over the decision. We began to tackle those questions by assessing the demographic breakdown on responses to the question (see Table 3.1). We suspected (and found) that age and education strongly related to having an opinion, while race correlated with the perceived fairness of the decision – a conclusion that we later found support for in the multivariate statistical analysis. As one moved from the youngest cohort (18 to 29) to the oldest (older than 60), the share without an opinion dropped by eighteen percentage points from 42 percent to 24 percent.[21] The same pattern held as one moved from the least educated group without a high school diploma to those with a college education –the share choosing "don't remember" dropped from 44 percent to 17 percent.[22]

The racial breakdown of opinion hints at continuing racial polarization over the decision, similar to that found in the 2000 NAES. When questioned in the month after the decision in the 2000 NAES, 76 percent of blacks felt the decision to be unfair compared to only 18 percent who felt it was fair. Blacks today remain overwhelmingly of the belief that the decision was unfair – 64 percent expressing that opinion and only 10 percent saying it was fair. If we only looked at those expressing an opinion, the discrepancy was even more dramatic: 87 percent of blacks who had an opinion on the case thought that the decision reached in *Bush v. Gore* was unfair. Whites were more evenly split, with a plurality (40% compared to 31%) saying the decision was fair. As we investigated in the multivariate analysis, however, one could argue that much of these racial differences could be attributable to partisan differences among racial groups as blacks are prominently Democratic and may be more likely to disapprove of Bush.

Nevertheless, while it is difficult to make predictions both because of the sample size and the fact that our survey yielded hardly any self-described black Republicans (either weak or strong), a closer look revealed a racial effect independent of political opinions. For instance, we found that 15 percent of black moderates approved of the decision compared to 45 percent of nonblack moderates.[23] Further, even among blacks identifying themselves as any kind of

TABLE 3.1. *Age, Education, Race and Opinion on*
Bush v. Gore (%)

	Fair	Unfair	Don't Remember
Age			
18–29	27	31	42
30–44	33	37	31
45–59	35	42	23
60+	43	34	24
Education			
Less than H.S.	24	32	44
High School	35	33	32
Some College	33	37	30
College or Higher	42	41	17
Race			
White	40	31	29
Black	10	64	26
Hispanic	26	34	40
Total	35	36	29

conservative, only 30 percent felt the decision was fair compared to 84 percent of nonblack conservatives who felt it was fair. In addition, among those who "somewhat approved" of Bush, 45 percent of blacks thought the decision was fair compared to 86 percent of nonblacks.

When we examined certain political variables, such as partisanship, ideology, and Bush approval, we found the expected, substantial differences (see Table 3.2). Belief in the fairness of the Court's decision in *Bush v. Gore* began at 79 percent for strong Republicans and dropped to 7 percent for strong Democrats. Strong partisans were much more likely to have an opinion than weak partisans. Independents who lean in favor of a party were the mirror image of each other with 57 percent of those who lean Republican believing that the decision was fair and 56 percent of those who lean Democratic believing that the decision was unfair. More or less the same trend appeared for ideology, with only 14 percent of extreme liberals but 79 percent of extreme conservatives believing the decision was fair. Self-described moderates, however, were much less likely to express an opinion, as 40 percent said they did not remember the decision.

Academic commentary in the wake of the Supreme Court's decision predicted that the retrospective evaluation of *Bush v. Gore* would depend on the success of the Bush presidency. As Judge Richard Posner summarized his views, "My guess (and not only mine) is that history's verdict on *Bush v. Gore* will depend significantly, though improperly, on the success of Bush's presidency" (2001, 222). In our survey, 39 percent said that they approved of Bush and

TABLE 3.2. *Party, Ideology, Bush Job Approval, and Opinion on* Bush v. Gore (%)

	Fair	Unfair	Don't Remember
Party			
Strong Republican	79	4	17
Not Strong Republican	57	11	32
Leans Republican	57	13	29
Leans Democrat	14	56	29
Not Strong Democrat	22	45	33
Strong Democrat	7	70	23
Ideology			
Extremely Liberal	14	74	12
Liberal	16	58	26
Slightly Liberal	14	66	20
Moderate	24	36	40
Slightly Conservative	55	18	27
Conservative	66	12	22
Extremely Conservative	79	5	16
Bush Approval			
Strongly Disapprove	10	69	21
Disapprove Somewhat	26	31	43
Approve Somewhat	59	11	29
Strongly Approve	75	5	20
Total	35	36	29

61 percent said they disapproved. Among those with an opinion on *Bush v. Gore*, the correlation was quite strong ($r = 0.65$) between Bush approval and belief in the fairness of *Bush v. Gore*. Only 10 percent of those who strongly disapproved of Bush's job performance considered the decision fair, whereas 75 percent of those who strongly approved of the Bush presidency considered it fair. Among the group voicing an opinion on *Bush v. Gore*, 87 percent of those who approved of Bush thought the decision was fair compared to only 24 percent of those who disapproved of Bush.

When we controlled for all the relevant demographic and political variables, we found that, in fact, approval of the Bush presidency was the most powerful factor influencing one's attitude concerning the fairness of the *Bush v. Gore* decision – even independent of party and ideology.[24] Table 3.3 presents ordinary least squares (OLS) and logit results of the multivariate analysis limited to those in the sample who had an opinion on *Bush v. Gore* (that is, excluding those who said they did not remember). Our model fits very well – we had an R-squared of more than 0.52.[25] In addition to Bush approval, party was significant in both the OLS and logit models at the 0.01 confidence level. Race (being black) and ideology were significant at the 0.05 confidence level for the OLS

TABLE 3.3. *OLS and Logit Regressions Predicting Opinion on Fairness of the* Bush v. Gore *Decision*

	(OLS Regression)	(Logit Regression)
	Bush v. Gore Fair	*Bush v. Gore* Fair
Age	−0.013	−0.031
	0.011	0.093
	(−0.36)	(−0.33)
Least Educated to	−0.003	0.027
Most Educated	0.017	0.137
	(−0.10)	(0.20)
Black	−0.088**	−1.024*
	0.045	0.416
	(−2.98)	(−2.46)
Strong Republican to	−0.242***	−0.466***
Strong Democrat	0.015	0.116
	(−4.65)	(−4.02)
Extremely Liberal	0.143**	0.303*
to Extremely	0.014	0.122
Conservative	(3.20)	(2.49)
Bush Approval	0.419***	1.238***
	0.021	0.152
	(9.41)	(8.15)
Constant	0.364***	−0.778
	0.098	0.779
	(3.71)	(−1.00)
N	718	718
R2	0.5271	

Standardized OLS coefficients; Robust standard errors underneath for OLS regression (linearized standard errors for logit regression); t statistics in parentheses.
* $p < 0.05$, ** $p < 0.01$, *** $p < 0.001$.

model; for the logit model, they were significant at the 0.10 confidence level. In Figure 3.1, we graph the predicted probabilities showing how opinion on the fairness of the *Bush v. Gore* decision varies between those who approved of Bush versus those who disapproved of his presidency.[26]

We tested specifications of the model with other commonly used demographic variables like Southern residence, religious service attendance, gender, marital status, income, born again Christianity, knowledge, and political interest, among others.[27] Inclusion of these variables did not alter our conclusions.[28] We also estimated a regression that included measures of confidence in governmental institutions. We found that a variable that we created through principal component analysis from the questions measuring respondents' confidence

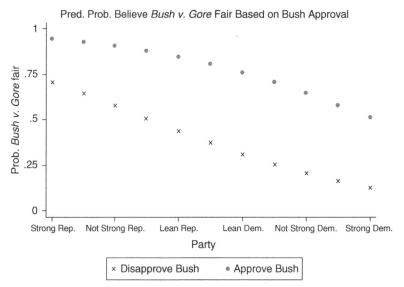

FIGURE 3.1. Predicted probabilities showing the effect of Bush approval on opinion on *Bush v. Gore.*

in the military, church, and corporations was significant.[29] Inclusion of the confidence factors did not, however, alter the significance of party, ideology, Bush approval, and race.[30]

To test the robustness of our results, we confirmed the analysis by ordered logit and multinomial logit that either included or excluded those in the survey who did not express an opinion.[31] Although our results are generally consistent, there were some minor differences. For instance, race did not reach significance in the ordered logit when using a three-stage dependent variable with the order being "fair," "don't remember," and "unfair."[32] This is probably due to the fact that the effect of race varies between respondents who expressed an opinion on the fairness of the *Bush v. Gore* decision and the respondents who said they "don't remember." Our results in the multinominal logit confirmed this. In that analysis, race was not significant for "don't remember" with "fair" or "unfair" as the reference category (or vice versa), but it was significant for "unfair" with "fair" as the reference category (or vice versa). Thus, this means that race probably does not really matter, as differentiating between respondents who "don't remember" and respondents who hold an opinion on the case's polarization along racial lines may only occur between those who hold opinions on the fairness of the decision. Of course, this result was consistent with what we found in the cross-tabulations. Our multinomial logit analysis also confirmed the fact that age and education were significant for "don't remember" with "fair" or "unfair" as the reference category but not for the "unfair" or "fair" variable. Finally, ideology was significant for the variable capturing respondents expressing an opinion on *Bush v. Gore*, but it was not significant for the variable encompassing respondents who did not remember.

The data attest to the continuing polarization in opinion over *Bush v. Gore*. Partisanship, ideology, and especially approval of President Bush's job performance all point to the same result: Democrats and liberals still find the decision unfair while Republicans and conservatives still consider the decision fair. Further, blacks felt that the decision was unfair, even more so than they did ten years prior. That the same lines of cleavage persisted ten years later is not all that surprising.[33] Consistent with Brickman and Peterson (2006), the cues that underlie the information environment today concerning opinion on *Bush v. Gore* are very similar to 2000. Further, there has been no real change in elite opinion regarding *Bush v. Gore*. Our results also lend support to the Franklin and Kosaki (1989) claim that rather than the Court being a leader on public policy, Court decisions can sometimes harden preexisting issue preferences and exacerbate long-standing intra- and intergroup differences on policy matters.

THE LINGERING EFFECT OF *BUSH V. GORE* ON APPROVAL AND CONFIDENCE IN THE SUPREME COURT

We now turn to the more controversial findings of our survey concerning the relationship between attitudes toward *Bush v. Gore* and those toward the Supreme Court today. We came to this question expecting to support the conventional wisdom that this particular decision has had no lasting effect on attitudes toward the Court. Given the upheavals of the past decade – a terrorist attack, two wars, a devastating hurricane, the Great Recession, and a historic presidential election – we expected a ten-year-old event, even if dramatically significant at the time, to fade in importance in affecting public opinion toward anything, including the Supreme Court. Add to these events the substantial turnover in the Court's membership over this period, and we expected that whatever one might have thought of the decision at the time, it should not have a continuing effect on one's assessment of the current Court. However, the data suggest that, even when controlling for partisanship and other factors, attitudes toward *Bush v. Gore* have a small effect on approval and confidence in the Supreme Court – even if the effect was relatively small.

Bush v. Gore's effect was not evident from cross-tabulations or correlations, however. To measure approval, we asked, "Do you approve of the job the U.S. Supreme Court is doing?" (The same question was also asked regarding President Obama and Congress). Of the 994 respondents who answered the question concerning job approval of the Court, 5 percent said that they "strongly approved," 56 percent said "approved somewhat," 31 percent said "disapproved somewhat," and only 8 percent said "strongly disapproved."[34] To measure confidence, we stated, "below is a list of some institutions" (including

TABLE 3.4. *Perceived Fairness of the* Bush v. Gore *Decision and Job Approval of the Court (%)*

Attitude Toward *Bush v. Gore*	Strongly Approve	Somewhat Approve	Somewhat Disapprove	Somewhat Disapprove
Fair	7	57	28	8
Unfair	4	56	31	9
Don't Remember	4	54	34	8
Total	5	56	31	8

TABLE 3.5. *Perceived Fairness of the* Bush v. Gore *decision and confidence in the Court (%)*

Attitude Toward *Bush v. Gore*	Great Deal of Confidence	Some Confidence	Hardly Any Confidence
Fair	22	61	17
Unfair	19	64	16
Don't Remember	18	64	18
Total	20	63	17

the military, the Court, Congress, church, corporations, and the president) and we asked respondents to label whether they felt a "great deal of confidence," "some confidence," or "hardly any confidence."[35] With respect to the Supreme Court, among those answering the question, 20 percent said that they had a "great deal of confidence," 63 percent said that they had "some confidence," and 17 percent said that they had "hardly any confidence."[36] Tables 3.4 and 3.5 display the uninteresting (but nevertheless revealing) cross-tabulations between opinion on *Bush v. Gore* and approval or confidence in the Court. When we look at the cross-tabulations for both sets of questions we find that regardless of one's opinion or non-opinion concerning the decision, the basic breakdown appeared to be the same. Further, the correlation was approximately zero between attitudes as to the fairness of the decision and approval and confidence in the Court. The results from the cross-tabulations and correlations caution us not to overstate the independent significance of *Bush v. Gore*. Whatever the multivariate analysis tells us, we can be confident that other variables have a stronger aggregate effect on Court approval and confidence than *Bush v. Gore*.

We turn now to our multivariate analysis to see what factors influence Court approval and confidence. We tested two dependent variables: approval of the Supreme Court and confidence in the Supreme Court. For the OLS regressions, we tested specifications using both the dichotomous and four-stage versions of the approval variable, though in Table 3.6 we report results using only the dichotomous version of the approval variable; in the logit regressions, we used the dichotomous version of the variable. We recoded the confidence variable so that 1 equaled only those respondents who expressed a "great deal of confidence" in the Supreme Court. We coded respondents who said that they had "some confidence" or "hardly any confidence" as 0.[37]

We also tested a number of independent variables that other scholars have found to be predictors of Supreme Court approval or confidence. In particular, we might expect approval of and confidence in other institutions (particularly Congress) to have a powerful effect on approval of and confidence toward the Court. We found that the correlation in the CAS between approval of the Court and that of Congress and the president is 0.36 and 0.29 respectively, and between confidence in the Court and in Congress and the president is 0.40 and 0.35 respectively, a finding consistent with the scholarly literature on the topic.[38] Specifically, we constructed indexes for the approval and confidence variables through principal component analysis. "Congress and President Approval Factor" was a factor created through principal component analysis using questions on congressional and presidential approval.[39] The principal component analysis on the confidence variables yielded two factors. "Confidence Factor 1" loaded principally on the military, churches, and corporations while "Confidence Factor 2" loaded primarily on Congress and the president.[40] In addition to confidence, we also included demographic variables commonly used in regressions. Scholars have found race to be an important predictor of attitudes toward the Court as blacks generally evince less support for the Court than nonblacks (Caldeira and Gibson, 1992; Gibson et al., 2003b). The conventional wisdom also dictates that variables like age, education, ideology, party, and congressional and presidential approval have an important impact in determining opinion toward the Court (Murphy, Tanenhaus, and Kastner, 1973). Although not reported here, we did statistical analysis on other specifications using other demographic variables and we found that our results did not differ.[41]

Most important, we also tested for the independent significance of other constitutional decisions in predicting Court approval and confidence. We were most interested, of course, in assessing the impact of *Bush v. Gore* on measuring approval and confidence in the Court ten years later. We also included a four-stage variable approval of *Roe v. Wade* to control for the fact that maybe *Bush v. Gore* only reached significance because it was serving as a proxy for the polarization of public opinion on constitutional issues.[42] In other specifications not reported here, we tested for the independent significance of other policy areas, including gun rights, the Second Amendment, gay rights, the death penalty, detainee rights, free speech, and affirmative action, among others.[43] Hardly any of these other areas showed up as significant.[44] We also tested whether respondents' knowledge of and agreement/disagreement on the outcomes of recent Supreme Court decisions mattered.[45] We created new variables based on whether respondents had knowledge of those decisions and, in turn,

if they agreed or disagreed with the Court's ruling. Depending on the specifications, some of the variables turned out to be significant, but inclusion of these
variables did not alter our general conclusion on *Bush v. Gore*.[46]

Table 3.6 reports the OLS and logit results of regressing the dichotomous
versions of the dependent variables – Supreme Court approval and Supreme
Court confidence – on the independent variables. We find that approval or confidence in other institutions, particularly that of Congress and the president,
had a very important impact on Supreme Court approval and confidence.

Most relevant to our findings is the fact that the variables measuring opinion toward *Bush v. Gore* consistently reached significance, particularly for
Supreme Court approval. Indeed, the "unfair" dummy variable was significant
to the 0.01 confidence level for the approval dependent variable. In Figures 3.2
and 3.3, we show the predicted probabilities of *Bush v. Gore* and *Roe v. Wade*,
respectively, for our dichotomous approval dependent variable for different
levels of the Congress and presidential approval variable. We constructed these
graphs using the dichotomous version of the *Bush v. Gore* and *Roe v. Wade*
variable for ease of explanation.[47] Comparing the two graphs, we see how comparatively *Bush v. Gore* appears to have a bigger relative effect than *Roe*. The
results for the confidence dependent variable are a little different if we switch
the way we measure *Bush v. Gore*. While *Bush v. Gore* was significant when we
measure it using two dummy variables ("unfair" and "don't remember" with
"fair" as the reference category), it just barely failed to reach significance if we
only used the dichotomous "fair" versus "unfair" version of the variable.

We need not debate whether "approval" and "confidence" accurately capture the notion of "diffuse" support or if it merely gauges "specific" support
over the long term. Either finding is interesting (and unexpected) for us. We
expect that the effect of the decision will fade over the long term, in any event,
as our discussion of the "don't remember" category attests. Nevertheless, attitudes toward a ten-year-old decision seem to have some lingering predictive
effect on current attitudes toward the Court.

This effect, however, was small, and our models did a mediocre job of capturing the variance in respondents' attitudes toward the Court. Even with the
many variables we included, we only captured about 20 percent of the variance
in approval or confidence in the Court. Given the robustness of models that
predict presidential and congressional approval, the inadequacy of certain fam-
ilies of variables to predict approval and confidence toward the Court is worth
noting. Not only does opinion on *Bush v. Gore* have a small effect on attitudes
toward the Court, but few variables other than generic attitudes toward other
institutions seem to carry much weight in regressions.[48] For instance, contrary
to what we found in Table 3.3 concerning the importance of race in predicting
attitudes toward *Bush v. Gore*, the race variable failed to reach significance
in the regressions predicting Supreme Court approval and confidence. This
remained the case when we tested for interaction effects, including interaction
effects between *Bush v. Gore* and race. Opinion on *Bush v. Gore* appears to

TABLE 3.6. *OLS and Logit Regressions Predicting Opinion on Approval of and Confidence in the U.S. Supreme Court*

	(1)	(2)	(3)	(4)
	OLS Regression – Supreme Court Approval	Logit Regression – Supreme Court Approval	OLS Regression – Great Deal of Confidence in Supreme Court	Logit Regression – Great Deal of Confidence in Supreme Court
Age	0.031	0.045	0.039	0.107
	0.012	0.057	0.009	0.068
	(0.79)	(0.79)	(1.06)	(1.57)
Least Educated to	0.080*	0.186*	0.032	0.176
Most Educated	0.019	0.093	0.015	0.114
	(2.06)	(2.00)	(0.84)	(1.54)
Black	0.063	0.589	−0.063	−0.653
	0.056	0.352	0.049	0.415
	(1.70)	(1.67)	(−1.63)	(−1.58)
Strong	0.078	0.113	−0.045	−0.087
Republican	0.018	0.089	0.014	0.111
to Strong	(1.26)	(1.26)	(−0.78)	(−0.78)
Democrat				
Extremely Liberal	0.069	0.112	0.035	0.043
to Extremely	0.017	0.086	0.014	0.111
Conservative	(1.29)	(1.30)	(0.65)	(0.38)
Unfair Bush v.	−0.198***	−1.041***	−0.130*	−0.864*
Gore Dummy	0.053	0.290	0.045	0.343
	(−3.82)	(−3.60)	(−2.39)	(−2.52)
Don't Remember	−0.145**	−0.813**	−0.125**	−0.950**
Bush v. Gore	0.049	0.258	0.037	0.290
Dummy	(−3.23)	(−3.15)	(−3.06)	(−3.28)
Disagree with	−0.029	−0.063	−0.095*	−0.291*
Roe v. Wade	0.018	0.091	0.016	0.128
(four–stage)	(−0.67)	(−0.69)	(−2.06)	(−2.28)
Bush Approval	0.093	0.226	−0.076	−0.230
	0.025	0.127	0.020	0.157
	(1.82)	(1.78)	(−1.54)	(−1.47)
Congress and	−0.405***	−0.964***		
President	0.020	0.117		
Approval	(−9.64)	(−8.21)		
Factor				
Confidence			0.256***	0.952***
Factor 1			0.016	0.145
			(6.46)	(6.57)
Confidence			−0.392***	−1.202***
Factor 2			0.019	0.153
			(−8.13)	(−7.86)
Constant	0.424***	−0.384	0.296**	−1.300
	0.146	0.613	0.091	0.762
	(3.45)	(−0.63)	(3.24)	(−1.71)
N	941	941	928	928
R2	0.1474		0.2133	

Standardized OLS coefficients; Robust standard errors underneath for OLS regression (linearized standard errors for logit regression); t statistics in parentheses.

* $p < 0.05$, ** $p < 0.01$, *** $p < 0.001$.

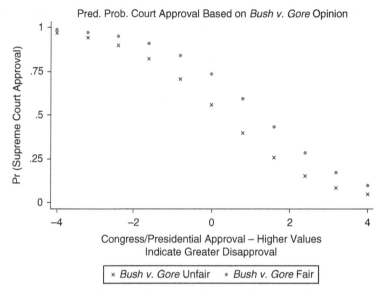

FIGURE 3.2. Predicted probabilities showing the effect of *Bush v. Gore* opinion on Supreme Court approval.

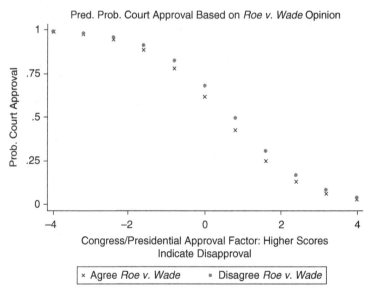

FIGURE 3.3. Predicted probabilities showing the effect of *Roe v. Wade* opinion on Supreme Court approval.

be polarized on the basis of race, but this racial divide did not carry over to blacks' approval of or confidence in the Supreme Court.

Even if the effect of attitudes toward *Bush v. Gore* were more substantial, several avenues of interpretation are possible. Perhaps the effect of the *Bush v. Gore* variable has nothing to do with the decision itself. Attitudes expressed toward the decision could merely serve as a proxy for some omitted variable that captures some version of extreme partisanship. However, we controlled for partisanship, ideology, and presidential approval in many different ways and the effect remained. Perhaps attitudes toward the decision reflect some special brand of partisanship with respect to judicial decision making, also not picked up by generic partisanship or attitudes toward other specific decisions. Although that is possible, the statistical significance of *Bush v. Gore* was not affected when we included other variables concerning the proper modes of constitutional interpretation.[49]

Of course, question wording and order can also affect results, as they do in any survey. Placing a certain question prior to another question could "cue" respondents to call to mind certain considerations that could then color their responses (Zaller, 1992). The 2010 survey first asked respondents to opine on their approval of President Obama as well as their level of confidence in various institutions, including the Supreme Court. Then, after asking a series of questions concerning their opinion on policy issues and their knowledge of recent Supreme Court decisions, the survey queried respondents on whether they approved of the Bush presidency, Congress, and the Supreme Court. Toward the end of the survey, we questioned respondents on their opinion on *Bush v. Gore*. We feel, however, that question wording and order had a minimal impact on our results. One could argue that asking respondents to opine on *Bush v. Gore* shortly after asking them about whether they approve of the Bush presidency may have caused respondents to more easily call to mind their feelings about President Bush. However, we also asked the same respondents in 2009 to rate their feelings on President Bush.[50] When we used the 2009 version of the variable in the regression predicting perceived fairness of the *Bush v. Gore* decision, we got the same results as we did using the 2010 Bush approval variable: in both, Bush approval was the most substantively important factor predicting opinion on *Bush v. Gore*. We also do not think that asking respondents their opinions on various issues altered views on institutional approval to a great extent. Ansolabehere and Jones (2010) found little evidence of simultaneity between issue placement and preferences and institutional approval. Further, we asked about institutional approval and confidence in different parts of the survey. Finally, we might add that Tourangeau, Couper, and Conrad (2004) found that in surveys conducted online, any order or context effect disappeared when questions appeared on different screens.

Finally, some have expressed to us their concern that the causal order may in fact vary; that is, respondents' approval of or confidence in the Supreme Court may determine how they react to the *Bush v. Gore* decision. Indeed, the relationship between the two is dynamic and interrelated and, as many scholars have found, it is quite difficult to disentangle the two concepts (Caldeira and Gibson, 1992; Gibson et al., 2003a, 2003b). Analyzing data in the immediate aftermath of the decision, Gibson and colleagues found in their two-stage least squares analysis that "institutional loyalty influences judgments of the fairness of the decision in *Bush v. Gore*, but not vice versa" (2003b, 551). Although we do not discuss the results here, our preliminary work doing two-stage least squares analysis indicates that causal order does not appear to be something that would seriously undercut our findings on the relationship between *Bush v. Gore* and public approval of and confidence in the Supreme Court.

CONCLUSION

More than ten years after *Bush v. Gore*, scholars still debate the wisdom of the decision and its lasting impacts. Surprisingly, however, in the nearly decade and a half since, few pollsters have surveyed public opinion on this unique episode in the Court's history. Our survey allowed us to capture American public opinion on this important decision, thereby enabling us to contribute to the debate on how the Court shapes public opinion. In a sense, our results are not all that surprising. We found that the same factors that polarized opinion on *Bush v. Gore* among the American public in 2000 – namely race, party, ideology, and Bush approval – still polarize opinion on *Bush v. Gore* today – at least among those who still share an opinion on the case. This is a result we expected to find because of the fact that the American public still views *Bush v. Gore* through the same political and racial lens. This result, of course, is also consistent with the findings by numerous scholars writing in the two or three years after *Bush v. Gore* (Gibson et al., 2003a, 2003b; Kritzer, 2001; Mate and Wright, 2008; Price and Romantan, 2004).

The lingering effect of the decision on attitudes toward the Court (if that is what we have uncovered) is still a bit of a surprise and marks a departure from the findings from the few scholars who have done any analysis of the longer-term impact of *Bush v. Gore* (Gibson et al., 2003a, 2003b; Mate and Wright, 2008). In part, the difference between our findings and those of others lies in the nature of our dependent variable. In any event, it is still important to ponder why *Bush v. Gore* seems to have at least some effect on Supreme Court approval and confidence so many years later – independent of party and ideology. Perhaps *Bush v. Gore* destroyed the faith of some in the Supreme Court and reinvigorated it for others. It still may define the institution in the minds of some share of the population. As such, it stands apart from most decisions, the salience of which quickly dissipates and produces no long-lasting effect. Indeed, *Bush v. Gore* is a unique test case precisely because, unlike cases on abortion or gay rights issues, there have been no intervening cases in the meantime by which the public can reignite its attitudes toward the controversial issue. As such, it makes it impossible to compare directly how *Bush v. Gore*'s effect differs from that of other controversial decisions.

The "long-lasting effect" we may have uncovered is probably short-lived, however. The large share of the population – particularly young people – who respond that they do not remember the decision cautions that this effect may be generationally specific. In ten more years we should expect an even smaller share of the population to remember and have opinions on the case. When we reassess attitudes on *Bush v. Gore* another decade from now, it will have faded further in the memory of those who focused on it in 2000 and will be a curiosity of history for the generation that learns about it for the first time.

Notes

1   Caldeira and Gibson did not totally discount that changes in "diffuse" support could occur; rather, they ascribe any dissonance to a "wholesale shift in style" of the Court rather than "short-term disagreements with the Court's policy" (1992, 659). This could occur, for instance, during periods of upheaval or when the Supreme Court bases its decision on the "pursuit of policy objectives" rather than legal principles. Further, Caldeira and Gibson found that opinion leaders – in contrast to the mass public – tend "to link support for the Supreme Court to the satisfaction of specific policy preferences" (1992, 636).

2   Specifically, Gibson and colleagues (2003b) measured "diffuse" support through a series of questions concerning the Supreme Court, such as whether respondents trust the Court, whether they think we should do away with the Court, and so forth. Higher scores indicated greater institutional loyalty toward the Court.

3   In a regression with a factor comprising "loyalty to the Supreme Court" as the dependent variable, Gibson and colleagues (2003b) found variables that reflected various democratic norms, affect for Bush, awareness of the Court, knowledge of the Court, and race to be statistically significant.

4   For instance, scholars have concluded that public support for the Court varies on the basis of attributes like race (Caldeira and Gibson, 1992); partisanship/ideology (Dolbeare and Hammond, 1968; Murphy, Tanenhaus, and Kastner, 1973); issue positions (Murphy and Tanenhaus, 1968); political activism (Adamany and Grossman, 1983); political sophistication and attentiveness (Caldeira and Gibson, 1992); status as an elite (Beiser, 1972); religion (Franklin and Kosaki, 1989); education (Casey, 1974); age (Kessel, 1966; Murphy and Tanenhaus, 1968); social status (Casey, 1974); attitudes toward other governmental institutions (Caldeira and Gibson, 1992); or even how the decision was framed in the first place (Nicholson and Howard, 2003).

5   Likewise, Nicholson and Howard (2003) found that *Bush v. Gore* polarized public opinion concerning confidence in the justices themselves. They also found that "diffuse" support erodes if a decision is framed in such a way so as to make clear the decision's ramifications.

6   Specifically, Mate and Wright found that while blacks still were more likely than whites to think that the decision was unfair, the "extra negativity engendered by the decision" in 2000 had all but evaporated by 2004 (2008, 346). They also found that the role of partisan identification and ideology had unexpectedly reversed with

Democrats and liberals actually being more supportive of the Court in 2004 than they were prior to the *Bush v. Gore* decision.

7 Specifically, it employed a rolling cross-sectional design that ran from December 1999 through mid-January 2001, including interviews with more than 58,000 respondents. There was sufficient variation in both periods to allow us to make comparisons, but because it was not a panel study there could be some differences between the two groups that our analysis might not capture.

8 Less than 1 percent did not answer (NAES, Question CS24, December 13, 2000–January 19, 2001). All numbers given for the NAES survey are rounded to the nearest whole number.

9 Another question asked respondents if they approved of the decision "stopping and reviewing [the] Florida recount." Of those who answered, about 36 percent "strongly approved," 17 percent "somewhat approved," 13 percent "somewhat disapproved," and 30 percent "strongly disapproved" (NAES, Question CS16, December 11–19, 2000). A similar question with slightly different wording asked only after the decision queried respondents whether they approved of the Court's action declaring the Florida recount unconstitutional. Thirty-six percent said they "strongly approved," 15 percent said they "somewhat approved," 11 percent said they "somewhat disapproved," and 34 percent said they "strongly disapproved" (NAES, Question CS20, December 13, 2000–January 19, 2001).

10 Another 6 percent answered that they did not know (NAES, Question CS23, December 11–19, 2000).

11 The wording was a bit different for both of these questions. NAES, Question CS17, asked on December 11–12, 2000, gave respondents more choices, as it allowed respondents to answer "very likely," "somewhat likely," "not too likely," and "not likely," whereas NAES, Question CS21, asked December 13, 2000–January 19, 2001, asked respondents to answer yes or no to whether they would accept the Supreme Court decision on the recount as the final word. Further, for NAES, Question CS17, 2 percent did not know and 1 percent did not answer. For NAES, Question CS21, 3 percent did not know and less than 1 percent did not answer.

12 NAES, Question CS18, December 11–12, 2000.

13 The question, NAES, Question CS22, was phrased this way from November 29–December 12, 2000. After the decision was announced (thus from December 13, 2000 to January 19, 2001), the first part of the question was reworded: "How much confidence do you have that the U.S. Supreme Court dealt fairly…"

14 Although not reported here, we did cross-tabulations of many of the NAES questions to see how opinion changed before and after the decision.

15 Similarly, Brady (2000) looked at data from the 2000 National Election Study. One question asked respondents to rank the Supreme Court on a "feeling thermometer" from 1 to 1000. During the first twelve days in December 2000 before the opinion was announced, Brady found that the respondents' feeling on the Court "dropped sharply by about five points," with a noticeable 7.5 percent decline among Democrats, a 5.7 percent drop among Independents, but a 4.3 percent increase among Republicans.

16 NAES, Question CM04, November 28, 2000–January 19, 2001.

17 Nor to our knowledge have there been any surveys that allow researchers to assess *both* "specific" and "diffuse" support.

18   We also commissioned a Constitutional Attitudes Survey in July 2009 of 1,677 participants, but the questions on that survey did not ask about *Bush v. Gore*. For the 2010 survey, we queried 1,198 of the respondents from the 2009 survey. Knowledge Networks conducted both surveys. The codebook is available at http://www.law.columbia.edu/null?&exclusive=filemgr.download&file_id=55737&rtcontentdisposition=filename%3DPersily%20codebook.pdf. Among other topics, the survey measured opinion about President Barack Obama's job performance, general knowledge and attitudes about American courts and other institutions, and attitudes about various policy and constitutional issues. The survey's findings on originalism were studied in another article published in the *Columbia Law Review* (see Greene, Ansolabehere, and Persily, 2011).

19   Question 604_2010. For the remainder of this chapter we exclude those who refused to answer the question unless otherwise stated. As such, the percentages in the cross-tabulation tables were calculated excluding the small number of people who did not answer the respective questions.

20   These results differ from the results of the 2000 NAES where 54 percent said they felt the decision was fair, 40 percent said they felt the decision was unfair, 5 percent said they did not know, and less than 1 percent did not respond (NAES, Question CS24, December 13, 2000–January 19, 2001). Our results also differ from the conclusions of Gibson and colleagues (2003b), who in a poll taken in early 2001 found results consistent with the 2000 NAES that a majority (56.2%) thought the decision was fair, with 41.9 percent feeling it was unfair. They also found that 97.2 percent of respondents offered an opinion on the issue – a far cry from the close to 30 percent of respondents in the CAS survey who responded they "don't remember" or refused to answer.

21   By contrast, in 2000, it was actually the oldest cohort of Americans older than age sixty who were less likely to offer an opinion. According to the 2000 NAES, about 9 percent of respondents aged sixty and older answered "don't know" to the question concerning the fairness of the *Bush v. Gore* decision (NAES, Question CS 24, December 13, 2000–January 19, 2001). This contrasts with the 4–5 percent of respondents in the other age cohorts who answered "don't know."

22   Again, we saw a similar pattern in the 2000 NAES but the numbers were not as dramatic. About 13 percent of those with less than a high school education answered "don't know" to the question concerning *Bush v. Gore*'s fairness compared with the 4–6 percent who answered that way in higher categories of education.

23   All of the percentages in this paragraph are only of people expressing an opinion on *Bush v. Gore*.

24   There was a high correlation between and among party, ideology, and Bush approval. Between party and ideology, the correlation was -0.63, between ideology and Bush approval it was 0.47, and between party and Bush approval it was -0.63. We thus looked at the variance inflation factors (VIF) to see whether multicollinearity clouded our results. All of the VIF values were less than three, with party, ideology, and Bush approval predictably having the highest values of 2.51, 1.85, and 1.77, respectively.

25   We also tested this model with various ways of measuring each of the independent variables. For instance, in the model we include in Table 3.3, race was measured as a dummy variable with black being 1 and nonblack being 0. We tested a specification where we included a dummy variable with white being 1 and nonwhite being

o. The same variables remained significant, though; as expected, the coefficient on the race variable was smaller when we used the white dummy variable instead of the black dummy variable. The survey we conducted in 2010 also had a unique way of measuring partisanship. Respondents were first asked whether they were Democrat, Independent, or Republican (Question 7_2010). Those who expressed a party preference were then asked whether they were strong or not strong partisans (Question 8_2010, Question 9_2010). The remaining individuals – those saying that they were Independent as well as those who said they were some other party, no party, or did not answer – were then asked whether they leaned toward the Democrats or Republicans (Question 10_2010). From this data, we constructed a six-point scale going from strong Republican to strong Democrat. In 2009, we measured party differently because the question itself asked respondents to place themselves on a seven-point scale (Question partyid7). The correlation between the two measures of party was 0.89. We tried regressions using both measures and came out with consistent results.

26 For ease of explanation, we used the dichotomous version of the Bush approval variable (Question 599_2010) in estimating the regression that is the basis for this graph.

27 Our 2009 and 2010 surveys had a number of knowledge questions. Questions 301–05 from the 2009 survey and Questions 520_2010–523_2010 from the 2010 survey inquired into respondents' knowledge of various recent decisions of the Court. We constructed several knowledge variables adding up the responses to the questions and we also did principal component analysis of the knowledge questions. No matter how we tested it, we did not find knowledge to be significant in the *Bush v. Gore* regressions.

28 We also tested various interactions, including interactions between and among party, ideology, Bush approval, and race. Generally, it remained the case that the same values stayed significant, though there were some differences. For instance, when we put in an interaction term for black and party, black no longer remained significant, most likely because the effect of race was somehow intertwined with party. This of course was not unexpected. In our logit results, black also did not reach significance when we included an interaction between black and Bush approval. Further, although the same variables remained significant, we noticed slight changes in the substantive values of the variables when the insignificant interaction term was included in the regression. The R-squared remained generally in the 0.52–0.53 range whenever any interaction term was included. We also tested an interaction between age and education and found no difference in the results.

29 If instead we put in just the question on confidence in the military, church, or corporations individually, we found that confidence in church and corporations – but not the military – reached significance.

30 However, it did increase the R-squared from 0.5271 to 0.5457, and likelihood ratio tests done on unweighted regressions indicated that inclusion of the confidence variables yielded a better model fit.

31 To do this, we created a dependent variable that was ordered "fair," "don't remember," and "unfair." Although it was not strictly a linear progression going from each category to the next, to create a continuum it seemed most logical to put the "don't remember" response in the middle.

32 Black was also not significant in the ordered logit when we included interaction terms between and among party, ideology, black, and Bush approval.

33 Indeed, our regression results do not differ markedly from those of Gibson and colleagues (2003b) when they regressed various independent variables on opinion regarding fairness of the *Bush v. Gore* decision asked of 2001 respondents. Similar to our analysis, they found party, affect for Bush, and race to be statistically significant variables; they also found that awareness, variables that measured "perception of who won the national election," and "perception of who won the Florida election" – variables not included in our survey – to be significant.

34 Question 601_2010.

35 Question 501_2_2010.

36 About 5 percent and 2 percent of respondents, respectively, declined to give an answer to the questions on Supreme Court approval and confidence. In our 2009 survey, we asked respondents to opine whether they felt that the Supreme Court was "too conservative, too liberal or about right" (Question 8). Twenty-two percent said "too conservative," 29 percent said "too liberal," and 48 percent said "about right."

37 We also tried the regressions using the three-stage variable as well as a variable where we recoded "hardly any confidence" as 1 and a "great deal of confidence" or "some confidence" as 0. Further, we tested specifications using as the dependent variable several approval/confidence variables created through principal component analysis. *Bush v. Gore* was significant in these other variations, except that it was not significant if the "hardly any" dummy variable served as the dependent variable.

38 Indeed, Caldeira (1986) and Price and Romantan (2004) found a positive linkage between confidence in the Court and confidence in other institutions. There are a number of reasons we might expect to see such a linkage. Some citizens might perceive the Court as part of the monolithic entity that is the federal government, viewing it as a single "governing coalition" (Caldeira and Gibson, 1992, 645). Approval and confidence may also reflect respondents' attitudes toward the incumbents holding power in the other branches as well as be correlative of respondents' general level of trust in institutions (Price and Romantan, 2004).

39 Specifically, we created the "Congress and President Approval Factor" using Questions 500_2010 and 600_2010.

40 We created "Confidence Factor 1" through a principal component analysis using Questions 501_1_2010, 501_4_2010, and 501_5_2010, measuring confidence in the military, church, and corporations, respectively; and we created "Confidence Factor 2" using Questions 501_3_2010 and 501_6_2010, measuring confidence in Congress and the president, respectively. Although we would like to derive measures of "generic" and "partisan" confidence, both factors probably point to latent partisan or ideological variables. To put the matter more specifically, confidence in the military, churches, and corporations probably points to ideological affinity with the Republican Party while confidence in the president and Congress probably points to latent attitudes toward the Democrats. In addition to a confidence factor, we used principal component analysis to create a variable of the two questions asking respondents whether they approved of the job that Congress and the president were doing. We used this "approval" factor as an alternative to the

"confidence" factor in some specifications when Supreme Court approval served as the dependent variable.

41 As we did with the *Bush v. Gore* regressions, we tested the independent significance of Southern residence, religious services attendance, gender, marital status, income, born again Christianity, and political interest, among others.

42 Question 510_2010.

43 Questions 201–18; Questions 511a–511f_2010; Questions 512a–512f_2010; Question 515_2010; Questions 517_1–517_4_2010; Question 519_2010.

44 None of the other policy areas reached significance for the confidence dependent variable. For the approval dependent variable, questions concerning the death penalty, free speech, and gay rights reached significance.

45 As noted before, our survey asked a number of different questions in both 2009 and 2010 relating to respondents' knowledge of recent Supreme Court decisions concerning eminent domain, the death penalty, detainee rights, gun rights, gay rights, free speech, criminal law, and governmental power. These were Questions 301–305 from the 2009 survey and Questions 520_2010–524_2010 from the 2010 survey.

46 For example, opinions on gun rights, the power of the Environmental Protection Agency to limit carbon omissions, and the power of the government to limit corporate free speech showed up as significant in some of the regressions with approval as the dependent variable.

47 For ease of explanation, we reestimated the logit regression in Table 3.3 using a dichotomous version of the *Bush v. Gore* and *Roe v. Wade* variables. The dichotomous version of the *Bush v. Gore* variable was coded o for "unfair" and 1 for "fair"; respondents answering "don't remember" were not included. The regression results were consistent using either the dichotomous or dummy variables; we wanted to do a simple comparison graphically showing the larger perceived impact *Bush v. Gore* had on Court approval than *Roe* had and using the non-dichotomous versions of the variables would be too confusing. In addition to estimating the results using a dichotomous version of *Bush v. Gore*, we also tried specifications using different versions of dummy variables relating to the *Bush v. Gore* variable. For instance, we tried other specifications where we used "unfair" or "don't remember" as the reference category, respectively.

48 We also tried some regressions that included variables created through principal component analysis based on questions measuring respondents' attitudes on moral traditionalism (Questions 4a–4d), equalitarianism (Questions 3a–3f), and libertarianism (Questions pair a, pair b, pair c). Except for one of our egalitarian factors barely reaching significance, none of these variables proved important in our analysis.

49 We also included, in both factor form and as individual questions, variables that relate to respondents' view of what it takes for a person to be a good Supreme Court justice (Questions 102a–102h), a battery of questions that Gibson and colleagues created themselves and that he found strongly correlates with institutional loyalty (Gibson and Caldeira, 2009a). We asked respondents to rate whether they felt that justices should 1) Strictly follow the law no matter what people in the country may want; 2) Feel empathy for the people involved in a case; 3) Protect people without power from people and groups with power; 4) Respect the will of the majority of people in the United States; 5) Stay entirely independent of the president and

Congress; 6) Follow his or her conscience or sense of morality; 7) Respect existing Supreme Court decisions by changing the law as little as possible; and 8) Uphold the values of those who wrote our constitution 200 years ago. While a few of these showed up as significant in some of the regressions, inclusion of these variables did not distract from our finding on the significance of *Bush v. Gore*.

50 In the 2009 survey, we asked respondents to rate their feelings on President Bush using a four-stage scale: "favorable," "somewhat favorable," "somewhat unfavorable," or "unfavorable" (Question pa0002).

PART II

WHAT HAS CHANGED SINCE *BUSH V. GORE?*

4

What Hath HAVA Wrought? Consequences, Intended and Not, of the Post-*Bush v. Gore* Reforms

Charles Stewart III

The Help America Vote Act (HAVA)[1] was the most important direct federal response to the 2000 electoral fiasco in Florida. HAVA has many provisions, some directly inspired by the controversy, others that came along for the ride. In addition to mandating certain changes in how states conducted federal elections, HAVA appropriated $3 billion for the improvement of voting systems, most of which went to purchase new voting machines.[2]

It is natural to ask whether this was money well spent. Are elections better administered in the United States than before? Have the shortcomings targeted by HAVA improved? It is the purpose of this chapter to address these questions.

But first, we must try to understand what problems HAVA aimed to address and how they were identified as problems in the first place. The Florida recount controversy featured shortcomings of the election system in Florida that almost everyone agreed presented problems, such as inconsistent recount criteria, malfunctioning voting machines, and poorly designed ballots. Specific features of HAVA address these precise problems. At the same time, other issues that did not feature prominently in the Florida drama, such as the difficulty that visually impaired voters had in casting ballots independently, are also addressed by HAVA. Where did these provisions come from, and what does their presence say about the policy process in the realm of election administration?

Finally, major moments of lawmaking often provide the nucleus for new political movements to arise, in ways unanticipated by the lawmakers

An earlier version of this chapter was presented at the conference "*Bush v. Gore*, Ten Years Later: Election Administration in the United States," Center for the Study of Democracy, University of California, Irvine, April 16–17, 2011. I would like to thank participants at that conference along with participants at a faculty workshop at the Moritz College of Law of the Ohio State University for comments that helped improve the argument. Special thanks go to Ned Foley for carefully reading that earlier draft and making helpful suggestions. The remaining errors are all my own.

themselves. Examples in the recent history of election reform include concern about the use of computers in casting and counting ballots and efforts to require voters to produce photo identification to vote. HAVA seems to be implicated in movements such as these. How did this occur? Did it happen *because* of provisions of HAVA, or despite them?

The core of this chapter is a data-driven attempt to assess the consequences of the Help America Vote Act. In assessing the consequences of a piece of legislation, it is useful if something approaching legislative intent can be divined. However, like most complex legislation, assessing the goals and impact of HAVA is problematic. To help gain some traction in discerning the goals behind HAVA, I begin with a relatively narrow focus, asking what *Bush v. Gore* revealed about problems with Florida's election system. I next turn to an account of HAVA's passage, to see how the concerns that were framed in the Florida context fared once they entered a larger national policy-making arena.

In the consideration of both Florida's reform process and the congressional process that produced HAVA, we see other issues imported into the policy debate. The design of HAVA was affected by new issues; some of these new policy concerns ended up overshadowing the particular problems HAVA was intended to address.

After discussing how two major reform processes digested the election problems that were presented to them, I turn to the evidence about how HAVA made a difference in American election administration. I first examine the evidence, to the degree it exists, about the improvement of election administration along four domains that were clearly addressed in HAVA – voting machine accuracy, voter registration quality, access to voting by the disabled, and election fraud. I then examine two important unintended consequences of HAVA, namely the controversies over electronic voting and the movement to require photo identification at the polls. The conclusion provides an overall assessment of the achievements of HAVA while also questioning HAVA's continued relevance, in light of the rise of absentee voting, attacks on the Election Assistance Commission (EAC), and the current climate of fiscal austerity.

FLORIDA AND HAVA

How did contemporary observers initially diagnose the problems that were revealed in Florida? How did the political process transform those diagnoses into policy recommendations and law? What have been the consequences of these laws? To answer these questions, we begin with a brief summary of the reform efforts that followed close on the heels of the Florida controversy, one that focused on the Sunshine State itself, and the other that led to the passage of national legislation, the Help America Vote Act of 2002 (HAVA).

The story of how Florida responded to the recount controversy is an important place to start, because the Sunshine State was ground zero of election breakdowns. Even after the controversy receded, the whole world continued to watch. Policy makers in the state, therefore, not only had reasons to act, but they also had reasons to appear responsive to identifiable problems. The political ambitions of Florida's governor, Jeb Bush, along with his desire to redeem a reputation besmirched by the controversy, boded well for pursuing a technocratic reform path.

HAVA, on the other hand, is a natural vehicle to examine if we want to see how national politics processed the problems presented first by Florida. HAVA's passage involved national interests, and its most important deliberations occurred in a legislative setting, although members of Congress also had the benefit of the research undertaken by national reform commissions, most notably the National Commission on Federal Election Reform, sometimes termed the Carter-Ford Commission (National Commission on Federal Election Reform, 2001a, 2001b). HAVA was a convenient place for interest groups to aim their efforts. Although reform groups such as the League of Women Voters, Common Cause, and the NAACP tried to influence state reform efforts, the process that led to the passage of HAVA provided groups such as these with a forum to press their cases about election reform. Therefore, if the Florida process was tailor-made for a technocratic approach to election reform, the process leading to HAVA was well suited for the expansion of the scope of conflict (Schattschneider, 1960) and the incorporation of issues that were not prominent in Florida.

Florida

Bush v. Gore itself focused on the recount in Florida, and in particular, on whether the manner of the recount was constitutional; if it was unconstitutional, the question then became whether a remedy was possible within the Electoral College timetable set by Congress. These were the most politically charged of the issues that arose in Florida. Despite the political hot potato these issues presented, no federal legislation has been passed to address questions such as recounts and electoral disputes (see Colvin and Foley, 2010).

Even if the *Bush v. Gore* episode did not lead to major legal changes in how disputed presidential elections are decided, it was still about a recount, and prominent recounts often produce policy change. Recounts reveal the imperfections of election administration and provide rare opportunities to correct them (Weiner, 2010). In the particular case of Florida, the problems that were revealed were disproportionately technological. Machines failed, demonstrated by the presence of "pregnant chad" (Jones, 2000). Even when they seemed to work properly, some machines found more invalid ballots than others (Governor's Select Task Force on Election Procedures, 2001, chart 4). Poor ballot design led to confusion, votes for the wrong candidates, and over-votes (Mebane, 2004; Wand et al., 2001). A disconcerting aspect of these problems is that voters could do precisely what they were instructed to do, and still some votes would simply not be counted.

As an immediate response to the recount controversy, Governor Jeb Bush appointed a task force on "election procedures, standards, and technology," which was charged with reviewing these topics and making recommendations about how policies and laws should be changed to improve Florida's elections.[3] Although some elements of the task force report revealed a desire on the part of some commission members to lay most of the blame for the recount controversy at the feet of voters who could not follow instructions, the commission could not deny the hard evidence of voting machine failure. Following on this evidence was a series of recommendations intended to centralize and improve the performance standards of voting systems used in the state, decertify older voting systems, appropriate funds for new voting systems, institute a process for continuous improvement in voting systems, and provide for state review of ballot designs.

It is instructive to consider where the governor's task force focused its energies in making recommendations to address the problems that had emerged in 2000. Of the thirty-five reform recommendations, more than one-third were in the areas that the Bush-Gore drama highlighted most, the recount process and voting technologies (Stewart, 2011b, table 10). Another large set of recommendations pertained to the political status of the various supervisory figures in the Florida drama, such as the county supervisors of elections and the county canvassing boards.

A few recommendations were snuck in to address problems that were only tangentially related to the recount controversy. A good example was the issue of uniform poll closing times, one that had long vexed the state because of its straddling two time zones, but only relevant in 2000, to the degree that some believed that reporting on results from the Eastern time zone depressed turnout in parts of the state in the Central time zone.

Bearing in mind subsequent developments, it is notable how the task force treated issues pertaining to voter registration. First, heeding evidence that a large number of registered voters had gone to the polls on election day only to find their names not on the registration lists, the commission recommended that the state develop a real-time, centralized computer system for managing voter registration. Second, in light of subsequent controversies over requiring photo IDs to vote, it is interesting that the task force actually recommended *abolishing* the state's voter identification card in favor of redoubling efforts to provide voters with better information about where and how to vote. One measure of the low priority placed on voter identification is that in a public opinion poll about reform proposals commissioned by the Collins Center when the task force was wrapping up its work, voter identification was not one of the fourteen reform ideas respondents were asked about.[4]

Third, as a remedy to registration problems on election day, the Select Task Force recommended that the state consider provisional ballots to deal with both administrative errors and angry citizens, despite the fact that testimony concerning the topic "revealed confusion" about how provisional ballots were used in other states and how they might be implemented in Florida.

Another topic that bears mentioning is the treatment of absentee ballots, or convenience voting, in the task force report. Like registration problems, the use of absentee ballots became a minor character in the recount saga. At the time, Florida was a "for cause" absentee ballot state, meaning that voters had to certify they were out of town or incapacitated on election day in order to vote absentee. In the heightened scrutiny of Florida's electoral environment, it was revealed that some counties were more lenient than others in enforcing the for-cause provisions. It was clear that the campaigns, particularly Republican campaigns, were using absentee ballots to lock down their supporters' votes ahead of election day, sometimes with the cooperation of supervisors of elections (Cooper, 2000). To level the strategic playing field, the task force recommended changing Florida's approach to early and absentee voting, removing the for-cause requirement, reducing the amount of information required on absentee ballot applications, and generally prohibiting challenges to absentee ballots after they had been opened.

Two aspects of these recommendations are particularly notable. First, the task force made them despite acknowledging that liberalizing the use of vote-by-mail would exacerbate the problems of over-voting and under-voting. Second, absentee ballot liberalization provided a significant dose of partisan balance to the task force recommendations, insofar as most of the other high-profile recommendations tacitly endorsed Democrats' criticisms of Florida's electoral practices in 2000.[5]

Despite initial worries that the Select Task Force's recommendations would languish in the 2001 legislative session, most of its proposals were adopted. After 2001, election reform in the Sunshine State reverted to partisan form.[6] Because of the subsequent history of election reform in Florida and the rest of the nation, the serious efforts at bipartisan consensus and technocratic matching of problems to solutions stand out. The process was only slightly distracted by extraneous issues, and earnestly focused on ending Florida's reputation as only a few feet shy of a banana republic.

HAVA

The 107th Congress convened only two weeks following the *Bush v. Gore* decision and Gore's subsequent concession. Therefore, it was natural for a flurry of bills to be introduced to address the issues the recount controversy raised. At least thirty-five House and Senate bills were filed in early 2001 pertaining to voting machines, sixty-three to voter registration, and seventy-five to election administration.[7] Although Florida representatives and senators cosponsored some of this legislation, none of the bills that attained a high profile was introduced by representatives from Florida or any of the other states that had come across the radar screen as having problems related to voting, such as Georgia and Nevada. The bills that attracted a significant number of cosponsors in the House and Senate were generally introduced by members who held institutional positions that placed them naturally front and center as leaders in any effort to change election laws.[8]

The general approaches in the two chambers reflected the partisan majorities that controlled each – Republicans in the House and, after Sen. Jim Jeffords (VT) abandoned the Republican Party to become an Independent on May 24, 2001, Democrats in the Senate.[9] The House eventually passed a bipartisan bill by the end of the first session (2001); the Senate's efforts wavered between partisan and bipartisan before an initial bill was passed in the second session. The House vehicle (H.R. 3295) generally set lower performance standards, provided weaker enforcement, provided for a less powerful election commission, and authorized lower spending for new technology than the Senate bill (S. 565).

House negotiations over the contours of an election reform bill ensued over six months, in an effort to work out the bipartisan compromise that finally became H.R. 3295. The only point of contention in committee consideration of the bill was an amendment offered by Steny Hoyer (D-MD) to add additional voting system accessibility requirements for the disabled and those with limited proficiency in English, which failed on a four-to-five party-line vote (H.Rpt. 107–329, p. 56).

The issues of accessibility and limited English proficiency recurred when the Rules Committee considered H.Res. 311, to bring H.R. 3295 to the floor.

The most direct attempt to add stronger accessibility provisions came in a motion by Alcee Hastings (D-FL) to allow an amendment that would condition HAVA funds on states meeting minimum standards concerning the "full accessibility to polling places, as well as full accessibility to technology, for people with disabilities." This motion, too, went down to a defeat, on a three-to-seven party-line vote (H.Rpt. 107–331, pp. 2–3). This left in place a "manager's amendment," which passed the House, merely requiring states to *consider* the use of accessible machines. H.R. 3295, the Ney-Hoyer bill, passed on a 362–63 vote on December 12, on the first anniversary of the *Bush v. Gore* ruling.

The Senate bill was also negotiated over a months-long period, but with an ever-shifting set of coalition configurations. Initially, the competing bills were Christopher Dodd's (D-CT) S. 565, which called for strict, detailed national standards for voting machines as part of a federal program to help states purchase new voting equipment, and Mitch McConnell's (R-KY) S. 953, which avoided federal mandates. Initially, S. 953 was a joint effort with two Democrats, Chuck Schumer (NY) and Robert Torricelli (NJ), and the list of sponsors was much more bipartisan than Dodd's efforts, which attracted no Republican cosponsors.

As Senate Rules Committee deliberations proceeded, McConnell's attempts at bipartisanship broke down, however. He eventually urged Republicans to boycott the meeting that marked up S. 379; Schumer and Torricelli, Rules Committee members, abandoned McConnell at this point in favor of Dodd. Unlike in the House, the Senate effort had become partisan.

Bipartisanship was restored at the end of the year, when negotiations between Dodd and McConnell were renewed. Now, however, Christopher Bond (R-MO) became part of the principal negotiating team. The three – Dodd, McConnell, and Bond – eventually worked out a compromise that was more aggressive than the House bill on most points. However, it also added new provisions concerning voter fraud and a requirement that first time voters who had registered through the mails show identification when they voted. Although negotiations finished up before the end of the year, Dodd's bill, S. 565, which had become the Senate vehicle, was not formally considered by the Senate until the second session.

When the Senate finally took up S. 565, floor deliberations became stalled over the antifraud/voter ID provisions that Bond had insisted on as his price for agreeing to the bill. Schumer introduced an amendment to strip the bill of the voter ID requirement; a motion by Bond to table it failed 46 to 51. Then, Bond threatened a filibuster so long as the Schumer amendment was viable. After two unsuccessful cloture attempts, Democrats agreed to Bond's antifraud provisions. The bill passed on April 11, 2002 on a 99–1 vote, sending it to conference.

The antifraud provisions of the Senate bill also caused delay in the conference proceedings. Knowing his Republican Senate colleagues would support him, Bond held firm. In the end, the conference report maintained the Senate's antifraud provisions. The conference report on H.R. 3295 passed the House, 357 to 48, on October 10, the Senate, 92 to 2, on October 16.

As finally passed, HAVA had something for everyone to love and something for a few to hate. For those who wished to increase voter convenience and "make every vote count," the law mandated that states use voting equipment that notified voters if they under-voted or over-voted, add provisional ballot provisions to their state laws, and develop a centralized, computer-based voter registration file. For those worried about federal intrusion into state affairs, the EAC was established to be a clearinghouse and keeper of voluntary voting machine standards, not a regulator or enforcer of federal law. For those convinced that inattentive voters, not bad machines, caused voting problems, HAVA provided funding and programs to improve the quality of voter education and poll worker performance. Finally, for those worried about the parlous financial state of election administration, the law provided more than $3 billion to assist the states in improving elections, from technology to polling place practices.

Press accounts have emphasized the left's dissatisfaction with HAVA, due to the inclusion of the identification requirement and the wide berth given to states to implement the act. However, the roll call record casts doubt on this characterization. One can see this in the House roll call votes to originally pass H.R. 3295 in late 2001, and then to accept the conference report, with the various changes from the Senate, in 2002. Table 4.1 reports the results of probit analysis of these roll call votes, in which the independent variable is each

TABLE 4.1. *Votes on H.R. 3294, 107th Congress. (Standard Errors in Parentheses)*

	Passage		Conf. report	
	Rep.	Dem.	Rep.	Dem.
DW-NOMINATE	−5.18	1.91	−	3.41
	(1.06)	(0.60)	4.15	(1.32)
			(0.83)	
Intercept	4.32	1.59	3.22	3.09
	(0.66)	(0.27)	(0.49)	(0.64)
N	216	209	209	196
Pseudo R2	.25	.05	.16	.10
Llf	−	−	−	−
	50.13	101.06	82.21	38.32

Passage vote: House roll call 428, Dec. 12, 2001.
Conference report vote: House roll call 462, Oct. 10, 2002.

member's first-dimension DW-NOMINATE score, to measure the ideological placement of senators.[10] To help tease out differences due to differential whipping by the two parties, I run the estimation separately for each.

The coefficients describe an ends-against-the-middle voting pattern on both the initial passage and the final conference votes. Liberal Democrats *and* conservative Republicans were less supportive than were more centrist members of their parties.

This pattern is further illustrated in Figure 4.1, which graphs the estimated probabilities of voting yea, as a function of DW-NOMINATE scores. A couple of other points are apparent upon examining these graphs. First, although support for HAVA dropped off at both ends of the ideological spectrum, it dropped off faster on the conservative end. Second, the net effect of changes to the bill, from the initial passage to the conference, was to *increase* support for HAVA on the left and *decrease* it on the right. Therefore, while liberal House Democrats were certainly dissatisfied with the identification requirements that were imported into HAVA from the Senate, this dissatisfaction was more than outweighed by the addition of the stronger reform provisions on other dimensions that were strengthened by the Senate.

It was widely acknowledged that the source of the energy within Congress for adding a provision concerning accessibility was Dodd, who stated he had a special interest in the issue because of his sister, who was blind.[11] The provision was not originally included in the McConnell-Schumer-Torricelli bill (S. 953), and as we have seen, the Rule that brought HAVA to the House floor precluded a vote on the issue. Therefore, it is easy to imagine that if Sen. Jeffords had not switched parties, making Dodd the chair of the Senate Rules and Administration Committee, the requirement that every precinct have at

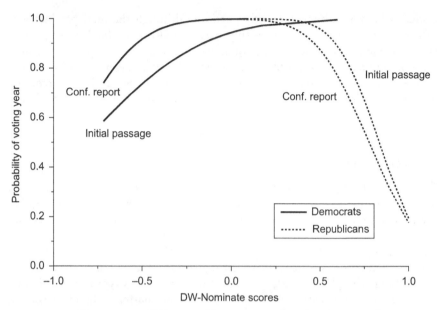

FIGURE 4.1. Votes to pass H.R. 3295 (Dec. 12, 2001) and approve conference report (Oct. 10, 2002), as a function of DW-Nominate scores.

Note: Graphs based on coefficients reported in Table 4.1.

least one machine that allowed disabled voters to vote independently and in secret would not have passed.

The origin of the voter ID requirement was clearly Sen. Bond, who had established a high profile as a crusader against voter fraud, following another 2000 election controversy, this one involving the U.S. Senate election in Missouri. That election pitted the incumbent senator John Ashcroft (R) against Gov. Mel Carnahan (D), who died in a plane crash in the midst of the campaign.[12] The new governor, Roger Wilson (D), had announced that if the deceased Carnahan won the election, he would appoint Carnahan's widow, Jean, to the seat. The episode that drew Bond's ire was an order by a local circuit judge in St. Louis to hold open polls in the city an additional three hours because of long lines, an order that was quickly overturned on appeal as contrary to state law. Bond charged that the attempt to hold the polls open longer was the product of a "criminal enterprise," although later Justice Department investigations revealed that the polling place chaos that prompted the original order was due, in fact, to overzealous attempts by the local board of elections to purge the voting rolls.[13]

The process that led to the passage of HAVA shared an important characteristic with the process that led to the reform recommendations in Florida – it produced centrist recommendations that focused on the problems that had been highlighted in the recount controversy. Unlike in Florida, the process that produced HAVA was more overtly partisan, although the final product was sufficiently inclusive that partisanship was muted on the final passage vote. Also unlike in Florida, the presence of issues that were only tangentially related to the widely recognized problems in Florida played a bigger role with HAVA. Voter fraud was not a major issue with the governor's Select Task Force. The issue of disability access was acknowledged in Florida, but deferred to future study.

CONSEQUENCES INTENDED

The process through which provisions were accreted onto the Help America Vote Act, from the initial appearance of problems in Florida to the signing ceremony on October 29, 2002, should give one pause in trying to discern an overarching intent or logic to the Act. The legislative process is a good one for reminding us that Congress is a "they," not an "it" (Shepsle, 1992), that policy making often consists of solutions looking for a problem (Cohen, March, and Olsen, 1972; Kingdon, 1984), and that policy making is typically dominated by narrow interests with intense attention to the matter at hand (Freeman, 1955; Lowi, 1964). That said, it is clear that the Florida controversy was a necessary condition for the passage of HAVA and that HAVA's aim was to mitigate a series of deficiencies in American elections the controversy uncovered.

Even controlling for the inevitable hyperbole that surrounded statements in support of HAVA, the bill's supporters inside and outside of Congress expected voting machines to get better and for registration problems to diminish. Supporters of the disability provisions expected access to the polls among the disabled to increase. Supporters of the voter identification provisions expected fraud to decline. Therefore, it is natural to ask whether the impact of the bill can be measured, and if elections have been improved in these ways since its implementation.

The purpose of this section is to review the evidence on each of these issues – voting machines, registration, accessibility, and fraud. These topics are listed in the order in which data are available, before and after the passage of HAVA, to assess improvements in election administration nationwide.

As a general matter, data to assess the quality of election administration is poor, if it exists at all, a fact related to V. O. Key's assessment of election administration in the mid-twentieth century as the most "neglected and primitive" branch of public administration (Key, 1949, 443).[14] However, the data are not uniformly bad. At the "good" end of the spectrum, measures of voting machine performance and voter registration quality have existed since before the 2000 election, which can be utilized directly to assess whether things have improved since 2000. At the other end of the spectrum, data to assess how accessible voting was before and after 2000 is virtually nonexistent. Many argue that what data do exist disprove that voter fraud is common.

Voting Machines

The common metric used to assess the quality of voting machines after the Florida controversy is the residual vote rate, which is defined as:
(Turnout$_t$ −Votes cast$_{t,o}$)/Turnout$_t$, for election t and office o.[15] The office o is usually the top-of-the-ticket race, either the president in on years or the governor or U.S. senator in off years. Because it is a highly visible office for which voters infrequently abstain to vote, most studies that use the residual vote rate to assess the quality of voting machines stick to presidential elections.

Using data from before and including the 2000 presidential election, Ansolabehere and Stewart (2005) showed that optical scanning voting machines generally produced lower residual vote rates than punch cards, a finding that helped support the machine trade-in provisions of HAVA, and a requirement that the EAC regularly report residual vote rates in its assessments of American elections. Using data from 2000 and 2004, Stewart (2006) showed that the HAVA-induced changes to voting technologies had resulted in roughly one million votes being "recovered" in 2004. Had localities not abandoned mechanical lever machines and punch cards after 2000, there would have been one million more under-votes and over-votes than actually occurred in 2004.

Bringing this research even further up to date by including election returns from 2008 confirms these earlier findings, with two important amendments.[16] First, it now appears that localities that abandoned mechanical lever machines in favor of optical scanning have not benefited from a reduction in the residual vote rate, although the definitive evidence will only be available once New York's experience with optical scanning has reached equilibrium.

Second, residual vote rates have fallen nationwide, even in local jurisdictions that did not change voting machines. Controlling for other factors, the residual vote rate fell roughly 0.5 percentage points in 2004 and 2008, compared to 2000. Expressed in terms of voters, this amounts to roughly 710,000 fewer residual votes in 2008, *even before we take into account voting machine changes*. Why the residual vote rate declined so much, independent of voting machine changes, is open to speculation. The heightened partisan competitiveness across the decade certainly had something to do with it. However, the size of the effect is too large to be accounted for by fewer voters simply abstaining when they vote for president.[17] Therefore, it is reasonable to attribute at least part of the reduction of the residual vote rate since 2000 to other changes in election administration, such as greater attention to quality control in canvassing.

In summary, the HAVA-mandated abandonment of punch cards clearly improved the accuracy of voting machines that were used throughout the United States; findings concerning the mandated abandonment of mechanical lever machines are less consistent. Overall, voting machine performance, measured by the residual vote rate, has improved nationwide, even in jurisdictions that kept their old optical scanners. There are multiple, complementary explanations for why this was so, but it seems fair to allocate some of the credit to HAVA's role in focusing attention on the overall quality of election administration in the United States.

Voter Registration

A second important theme that arose during the Florida recount controversy was problems with voter registration. Two types of complaints were prominent. The first consisted of reports from those who believed they were registered to vote, but who were not on the voting list at the precinct where they appeared on election day.[18] The second consisted of reports that the state Division of Elections had pressed a private contractor that it hired to conduct list maintenance of the central voter file to adopt a name-matching strategy that was guaranteed to increase the number of "false positive" matches by removing a large number of qualified voters because they were mistaken for former felons (Stuart, 2004).

One effect of the recount controversy was an increase in the salience of restoring voting rights to former felons (Manza and Uggen, 2004). Despite increasing the salience of former felons' voting rights, the controversy failed to produce many direct changes in law or regulation on this topic. In Florida, for instance, the governor's Select Task Force simply recommended that the legislature review the issue of restoring voting rights to felons who had completed their sentences (Governor's Select Task Force on Election Procedures, 2001, 69). In the Senate, Harry Reid (D-NV), Russell Feingold (D-WS), and Arlen Specter (R-PA) proposed amending HAVA to restore the voting rights of felons who had served their sentences, which went down to defeat, 31 to 63.[19]

However, greater attention to the general problem of voter registration was present in two ways in HAVA. The first was the requirement that states adopt provisional ballots as a "fail safe" device to deal with registration problems on election day. The second was through the requirement that each state implement "in a uniform and non-discriminatory manner a single, uniform, official, centralized, interactive computerized statewide voter registration list defined, maintained and administered at the state level."

At first blush, it appears that states have complied with the requirement to implement provisional ballots, although the practices employed, as written into law, vary considerably (Whitaker and Traldi, 2009). Most states also appear to be at least moving toward full compliance with the centralized voter registry requirement, with the notable exception of California.

However, the implementation of these requirements has varied significantly from state to state, and even from county to county within states. The centralized voter registry was supposed to improve the quality of the data included in these files – guard against typographical errors, ensure that addresses were valid, and so forth – but Ansolabehere and Hersh (2010) have shown numerous clerical errors in the state files. Nationwide, of 185 million registration records in the United States, 16 million were estimated to be invalid. The percentage of registered voters identified as deceased ranged from around 0.1 percent in Florida to more than 2.5 percent in Washington, DC and Ohio. In Arkansas, roughly 20 percent of registration records were judged either to have an undeliverable address or to be deadwood, or both, compared to only about 2 percent in Washington, DC and California.

The implementation of provisional ballots has likewise been variable. As the Florida Select Task Force indicated in its 2001 report, when HAVA was being considered and adopted, there was no consensus about what provisional ballots were. States that had never used provisional ballots were left wondering how to marry their creaky voter registration lists to a policy that, at its extreme, might allow voters to show up virtually anywhere and vote at least a partial ballot. Add to this the fact that states without provisional ballot provisions in 2000 probably had different attitudes toward facilitating voting, compared to states that did not, and the situation was ripe for significant implementation disparities (Stewart, 2009, 2011b).

Despite a rocky start to some of the state centralized voter files and the disparate implementation of provisional ballots across states and counties, it is still possible that registration problems have diminished since 2000, and that at least part of this improvement is due to efforts associated with HAVA. We can see evidence of improvement by examining responses that registered voters have given in the Current Population Study's Voting and Registration Supplement (VRS), conducted by the Census Bureau every two years.

The most widely cited statistic about the prevalence of registration problems following the 2000 presidential election came from the Caltech/MIT Voting Technology Project report (2001), which projected that 3 million votes were lost in 2000 because of registration problems. This estimate was based on an extrapolation from answers to the question asked in the VRS about why nonvoters said they failed to vote.

According to the data in the VRS, the percentage of registered voters failing to vote because of a registration problem has dropped each year since 2000. The rate was 0.92 percent in 2000, falling to 0.74 percent in 2004 and 0.57 percent in 2008. However, the drop in voter registration problems has not eliminated the large degree of variability across states in the prevalence of voter registration problems. States were just as variable in 2010 as they were in 2000 (Stewart, 2011b, 25–29).

On the whole, then, registration problems appear to have declined since 2000, although it is impossible to peg this improvement on any particular change induced by HAVA. States still vary considerably in how frequently registration problems beset their voters – a degree of variation that overwhelms the estimated degree of improvement nationwide.

Accessibility

The accessibility of voting machines and polling places to disabled voters occupied little attention in the early news accounts of the problems that surfaced in Florida or elsewhere around the country. However, advocates for the disabled, who had worked persistently over the previous decade to reduce the barriers that hindered independent voting among this population, were immediately drawn to the post–*Bush v. Gore* policy-making process as a perfect opportunity to extend their earlier gains.

As we saw in the previous section, until Sen. Bond changed reform dynamics by introducing the issue of voter fraud into the mix, the one recurring issue that divided Congress in the consideration of HAVA was the extent to which access to the polls for the disabled should be a priority.[20] In the end, the accessibility provisions were added to HAVA. These provisions virtually guaranteed that every election jurisdiction would buy at least one DRE for each precinct. For local election officials worried about the confusion that would arise by having multiple voting technologies in each precinct, the path of least resistance was simply to migrate entirely to DREs. Because of the monetary costs of this requirement, and the significant political backlash its implementation provoked, it is natural to ask whether HAVA has helped improve access to independent voting by the disabled.

Perhaps underscoring the elusive nature of information about the accessibility of voting to the disabled, there are no studies that allow us to assess directly how access to voting to the disabled changed after HAVA, particularly as it relates to the use of voting machines.[21] The only longitudinal data pertaining to voting that can address the subject again comes from the VRS, but the data are of limited utility. Unfortunately, the Current Population Survey, which is the core instrument on which the VRS travels, did not include disability status in its monthly release of microdata until 2009.[22] Therefore, the only nationwide longitudinal data about voting barriers faced by the physically disabled pertain to the experience of the disabled who are unemployed, which is far from representative. Of the limited data available about the experience of disabled voters, the best are cross-sectional in nature, and therefore cannot document improvement or retrogression.

With these caveats in mind, the best available data can establish three general findings that link the goals of HAVA to the accessibility of voting to those who are disabled. First, data from the Survey of the Performance of American Elections (SPAE) establish that the main problems that kept disabled individuals from voting, compared to the nondisabled, were transportation problems getting to the polls and problems getting absentee ballots.[23] Second, the same dataset also establishes that among those who actually voted, disabled voters had a slightly more difficult time finding their polling place, were more likely to state they had difficulty using the voting equipment, and were more likely to report receiving help filling out their ballots. Third, overall, disabled voters were only slightly less likely to state that they were "very confident" their vote was counted as cast, compared to nondisabled voters – 68 percent versus 71 percent.

One final piece of evidence concerning the increased ability of disabled voters to vote without assistance comes from examining the use of touch screen voting machines that were provided for the use of disabled voters. As far as one can tell, only Florida reports the number of votes cast on these machines, separate from the others. In 2008, 6,921 votes in Florida were cast on touch screen terminals (out of 8.5 million votes cast), which is less than the number of precincts in the state. Based on results from the 2009 American Community Survey, it appears that 2.8 percent of Florida's voting age population is visually disabled. Considering that only 0.07 percent of Florida's votes in 2008 were cast on electronic touch screens, it is clear that the so-called accessibility machines are not being used as extensively as they might be.

Thus, what little evidence we have about the experience of the disabled in voting suggests that major barriers continue in the realm of getting to the polls or acquiring absentee ballots, matters that were not central to HAVA. Within the realm of HAVA, the scant evidence we have from Florida indicates that electronic machines are not being widely used for their intended purpose. Disabled citizens still have problems voting; there is little evidence that much has changed since 2000. In that sense, HAVA has not been an especially effective vehicle for granting to disabled individuals richer access to the ballot box.

Fraud

It is indisputable that voter fraud was the least systematically documented problem that HAVA eventually addressed. Alongside careful (if preliminary) attempts to quantify the number of lost votes due to machine malfunctions, polling place problems, and registration snafus, the best evidence of a comparable problem with voter fraud consisted of a few anecdotes, most of which dissolved as cases of *fraud* – as opposed to mistakes – upon close examination.

Of course, absence of evidence is not evidence of absence. Measuring directly the incidence of any crime is generally difficult to impossible, particularly when the victim does not directly encounter the perpetrator. The difficulty of measuring the incidence of voter fraud has led to a number of ingenious efforts to assess whether fraud has occurred. Much of this research has unfolded in the comparative context, particularly in research about developing countries, where various types of electoral shenanigans are said to be common (Alvarez, Hall, and Hyde, 2008; Hyde, 2007; Mebane, 2006).

One of the EAC's first major controversies came about from its attempt to respond to calls to move the matter of measuring voter fraud from the anecdotal to the systematic. When the EAC received a draft report about the prevalence of fraud from a bipartisan team of contractors, Job Serebrov and Tova Wang, the commission edited the report to downplay the lack of evidence about fraud and to intimate that fraud was indeed regarded as a common problem.[24]

Although the data necessary to assess whether the other areas targeted by HAVA for improvement – voting machines, registration, and accessibility – are often of poor quality and incomplete, some evidence does exist, and efforts continue apace to improve the quality of data necessary to assess performance on these dimensions. There is not only a lack of data to assess whether HAVA helped to reduce election fraud, there is little agreement on how to start.

CONSEQUENCES UNINTENDED

The evidence presented in the previous section suggests that HAVA improved elections. Of course, it is impossible to disentangle entirely improvements to elections that occurred because of specific provisions of HAVA, such as the mandate to improve election machines, from the fact that election administrators became more careful in the aftermath of the Florida fiasco. Attributing improvements in voting machines and election administration specifically to HAVA, rather than to a general interest in making elections better, probably gives too much credit to the act itself.[25]

Still, to the degree that HAVA had a direct effect on improving the quality of elections in the United States, it seems appropriate to call these *intended* consequences of HAVA. Similarly, it seems appropriate to identify a set of *unintended* consequences of HAVA, even though we know that they may have occurred without HAVA having ever passed. The two unintended consequences I wish to draw attention to are, first, the controversy over the use of electronic voting machines, and second, the growing controversy over voter fraud, and in particular, the movement to mandate the use of photo identification at the polls.

Electronic Voting Controversy

The most important unintended consequence of HAVA was to revive an earlier controversy over the use of computers to cast and record votes. The use of computers to cast and count ballots was controversial before 2000. A classic *New Yorker* article in 1988 addressed charges that the software was prone to manipulation (Dugger, 1988), making reference to reports by Roy Saltman that gained new life after Florida (Saltman, 1975, 1988).

Despite these earlier concerns, DRE use grew during the 1990s, easily outpacing the growth in the size of the electorate.[26] During the same decade, the use of optical scanners grew, too, while the number of voters using mechanical lever machines and hand-counted paper ballots fell significantly and punch card ballot use remained flat.

For understanding how HAVA helped reignite controversy over the use of computers in elections, it is important to recognize that growth in DRE usage during the 1990s occurred primarily in towns and counties that were abandoning mechanical lever machines. Of the counties that switched to DREs during the 1990s, 89 percent had previously used mechanical lever machines. This was in stark contrast with counties that transitioned to optical scanning during the same period, 75 percent of which had previously used other forms of paper ballots, either optical scanning or punch cards. Thus, the technology upgrade path before HAVA was one of two sorts: either (mechanical) machine to (electronic) machine or (old-fashioned) paper to (modern) paper.

HAVA changed the pattern of voting machine use, and in particular, altered dramatically the path of technology upgrades among localities that had used older systems. In particular, communities that had been traveling along the paper upgrade path were pushed over onto the machine path. Thus, before HAVA, only 11 percent of communities adopting DREs had previously used paper ballots; after HAVA, 60 percent of new DRE purchases came in areas that had previously voted on paper.

If HAVA had not been adopted, would the rush to DREs during the 2000s have been so rapid? The answer is clearly no. As Ansolabehere and Stewart (2008) argue, the reason is that, left to their own devices, states and localities had spent a century establishing equilibria between voting technologies and the laws, rules, and cultures associated with their use. As localities moved to automation in the 1980s and 1990s, they chose a technology upgrade path that was consistent with these equilibria.

Thus, the mandate for jurisdictions that were comfortable with paper-based voting systems to move over to an electronic system was ripe for the creation of political controversy. This time, the political system was more attentive to the types of alarms that had originally been sounded in 1988. Opposition to the use of computers in elections was aimed in two directions. The first was a heightened attack on Internet voting, which mainly focused its effort on stopping plans to use computer networks to transmit ballots to and from overseas military voters (Alvarez and Hall, 2004, 2008). The other was a more general effort, which was spearheaded by a wide variety of computer scientists, to stop the spread of DREs.[27]

It is unclear how deep in the psyche of public opinion this activism has sunk, because no nationwide polls probing the attitudes of voters about different types of voting machines have been taken. Polls taken in three states – California, New Jersey, and Virginia – are consistent with the Ansolabehere-Stewart equilibrium story, to the degree that voters are most comfortable with the voting equipment they have long used, whether it be machines or paper. Regardless of where public opinion stands, it is likely that any local official considering the new deployment of DREs knows that he or she is in for a fight. This fact has had consequences for more recent trends in the adoption of voting equipment, as DRE usage has actually shrunk for the first time.[28]

Perhaps just as important for the future of the voting machine industry, the presence of the DRE controversy has provided a convenient meme for the left to question the legitimacy of the outcomes of closely fought elections. The public opinion data on the subject shows that opposition to DREs rises steeply as voters become more liberal. The blogosphere was full of accusations that hacked DREs had lost the 2004 election in Ohio for Kerry, despite a repudiation of this charge by the Democratic National Committee (cf. Kennedy, 2006; Democratic National Committee, 2005). Because distrust of electronic voting machines resides overwhelmingly among the left, the results of the 2008 and 2012 presidential elections muted the volume of this concern.[29] The next test of this argument will come in 2016, should the Democratic candidate lose by a small margin.

The Voter Fraud Controversy

While it may not have been a causal *consequence* of HAVA, the second unexpected feature of the act was that it became the opening salvo over Republican concerns with election fraud and the movement to require voters to show photo identification at the polls.

It is unknown whether interest in voter fraud was organized around ideological and partisan lines before 2000, but the public opinion evidence since then demonstrates that it certainly is now. For instance, when asked in the 2008 SPAE how often voter fraud occurred in their communities, 55 percent of "very liberal" respondents answered, "it almost never happens," compared to 28 percent of respondents who self-identified as very conservative.

Stories of the sort told by Sen. Bond in 2001 and 2002, on the way to adding the identification requirement to HAVA, have resonated with the public. Again, it is impossible to tell whether support for voter identification requirements has grown since 2000, but by 2008, support had risen to very high levels. Indeed, among the seven reform items asked about in the 2008 SPAE, requiring identification at the polls was by far the most popular, being supported by 76 percent of respondents, including 65 percent of Democrats. The next most popular reform proposal was making election day a holiday, at 58 percent support.

Although majorities of both Republican and Democratic voters support photo identification laws, Republican legislators have championed efforts to enact them.[30] The rush in many states during the 2011 state legislative season to enact photo identification laws was not only an indicator of the popularity of the reform among Republican lawmakers, but an acknowledgment that if another electoral backlash occurred in these states in 2012, their opportunities to pass photo ID laws would vanish.

Interestingly enough, it is possible to trace a path from the current attention to voter fraud and voter ID laws back to HAVA and its attention to improving voter registration lists. It is quite easy to argue that many of the examples of voter fraud that conservative politicians highlighted are, at most, registration fraud, if not an error of some sort. When registration fraud occurs, it is often because of the overzealousness of third-party registration canvassers. To some on the right, this is an invitation to advocate for legislation that prohibits third-party groups from soliciting voter registrations. Another avenue is simply to have the state initiate voter registration, using data it already has about potential voters in databases such as driver license files. It is not a large step from complying with HAVA's requirement that voter registration files be integrated with driver's license databases to making that linkage happen in real time – one could get a driver's license and register to vote in the same transition, seamlessly. This is a strategy most successfully implemented in Delaware, which is a model to other states.[31] Therefore, conservative attention to the poor quality of voter registration lists may lead to real efforts to improve them, to the benefit of a large number of voters, especially if the Delaware technology is extended to social service agencies.[32]

CONCLUSION: THE FUTURE RELEVANCE OF HAVA

A central topic of this chapter has been whether HAVA has had measurable effects on the conduct of American elections. The narrow policy question is whether HAVA has improved election administration. A fair answer to this question is yes – it has led to fewer votes being lost by voting machines and election day administrative breakdowns, and to fewer voters being turned away because of registration problems. Still, it is unclear whether the provisions added to encourage greater accessibility to voting machines among the disabled has made much of a difference. In addition, HAVA, either the provisions contained therein or the political process it fostered, played an important role in stoking paranoia[33] about elections being stolen, either because of hacked voting machines or fraudulent voting. Concern over fraudulent voting may have occurred without HAVA ever passing, but it is hard to imagine the anti-DRE movement being so active and successful without HAVA's accessibility requirements.

In assessing the role that HAVA played in improving elections in America, it is natural to ask what role it will play in the coming years, as the problems that beset Palm Beach County recede into the background. In answering this question, it is important to ask what parts of the voting equation HAVA overlooked. Most obviously, it overlooked absentee ballots and voting by mail, a phenomenon that has increased fourfold since 1972 and by roughly 60 percent since 2000. Insofar as HAVA failed to address voting by mail at all, it is unlikely to have much of an influence on the fastest-growing part of the electoral ecosystem. Stewart (2010) shows that the vote-by-mail pipeline is significantly "leakier" that the one for voting in person. Similarly, Alvarez, Beckett, and Stewart (2011) show that although California has reduced its residual vote rate over the past two decades by upgrading voting machines, the rise in the residual vote rate due to an increase in voting by mail has essentially wiped out these voting machine gains.

Because many election administrators regard voting by mail as cheaper than maintaining voting precincts, it is likely that the use of the mails will only

increase in the coming years, causing growth in "lost votes." If the past is any
guide to the future, federal attention to problems inherent in voting by mail
will only occur if there is a catastrophe in a presidential election involving
absentee ballots.

Another major factor affecting the continued relevance of HAVA is the
state of the economy and the future viability of the EAC. The dislike of the
EAC by the secretaries of state is well known; the 2010 election of Indiana's
former secretary of state, Todd Rokita, to the House and his appointment to
the House Administration Committee have given new energy to efforts to
abolish the EAC. In addition, unexpended funds that were part of the EAC's
election administration improvement program were zeroed out under the FY
2011 continuing resolution (H.J.Res. 44) passed in early March 2011. This
is the last of the new money poured into election administration improvement because of HAVA. Consequently, the most primitive and underfunded
of public administration is ending the decade of election reform even more
underfunded than before.

The real gains since 2000 should not be undersold. However, if there is one
lesson to be learned from the *Bush v. Gore* saga and its aftermath, it is that
well-run elections are hard to pull off. New attention and money have helped
improve elections in America. Let us hope we are not moving into a new era of
inattention and penury in election administration.

Notes

1 Pub. L. No. 107–252, 116 Stat. 1666 (2002).
2 The effective mandate to replace machines was achieved in two ways, through
   a program in Section 102 that funded the replacement of punch card and lever
   machines, and through restrictions in Section 301 that set standards for voting
   machines used in federal elections. Although Section 301(c) allowed states to ret-
   rofit existing equipment to meet the new standards, all states with punch cards and
   lever machines accepted Section 102 funding.
3 See http://www.collinscenter.org/page/voting_home.
4 Source: A telephone survey of a random sample of adults aged eighteen and older,
   conducted April 3–8, 2001 by Schroth & Associates for The Collins Center for
   Public Policy, Inc. and the James Madison Institute, http://www.sayfiereview.
   com/sayfie-review-featured-columnists1c.php?authid=2008091617034226&coli
   d=2010110107291012.
5 Subsequent experience with more liberalized absentee voting laws in Florida have
   confirmed that this mode tends to be favored by Republicans. However, in 2004
   Florida also introduced early voting, which has been a mode favored by Democrats.
   See Florida Senate, Committee on Ethics and Elections, "The Effect of Early Voting
   on Turnout in Florida Elections: 2010 Update," October 2010, http://www.flsen-
   ate.gov/Committees/InterimReports/2011/2011-118ee.pdf.
6 For example, see James L. Rosica, "Fla. Legislature OKs Election-Law Overhaul,"
   Miami Herald, May 5, 2011, http://www.miamiherald.com/2011/05/05/2203413/
   fla-legislature-oks-elections.html.

7 These bills were discovered by searching the database of congressional bills at thomas.loc.gov. These bills, of course, overlapped somewhat.

8 The bills that attracted more than 10 percent of chamber members as cosponsors were H.R. 775, Voting Improvement Act (Steny Hoyer [D-MD], ranking members, House Administration Committee, 70 cosponsors); H.R. 1170, Equal Protection of Voting Rights Act of 2001 (John Conyers [D-MI], ranking member, Judiciary Committee, 168 cosponsors); H.R. 3295, Help America Vote Act of 2002 (Robert Nye [R-OH], chair, House Administration Committee and majority whip, 172 cosponsors); S. 218, Election Reform Act of 2001 (Mitch McConnell [R-KY], chair/ranking member, Rules and Administration Committee, 14 cosponsors); S. 379, Federal Election Modernization Act of 2001 (Chuck Schumer [D-NY], member, Rules and Administration Committee, 12 cosponsors); S. 565, Martin Luther King, Jr. Equal Protection of Voting Rights Act of 2002 (Christopher Dodd [D-CT], ranking member/chair, Rules and Administration Committee, 50 cosponsors); and S. 953, Bipartisan Federal Election Reform Act of 2001 (Mitch McConnell [R-KY], chair/ranking member, Rules and Administration Committee, 70 cosponsors).

9 This account is drawn primarily from "Election Overhaul on Hold." In *CQ Almanac* 2001, 57th ed., 15–3–15–6. Washington, DC: *Congressional Quarterly*, 2002. http://library.cqpress.com/cqalmanac/cqal01–106–24134–1079453 and "New Voting Standards Enacted." In *CQ Almanac* 2002, 58th ed., 14–3–14–5. Washington, DC: *Congressional Quarterly*, 2003. http://library.cqpress.com/cqalmanac/cqal02–236–10367–664151.

10 The particular file with DW-NOMINATE scores used was hl011111e21_pres. dta. I thank Keith Poole for so kindly sharing his data with the profession. DW-NOMINATE scores in this context can be thought of as measures of the ideological location of senators arrayed along a scale that goes from -1, for the most liberal representatives, to +1 for the most conservative.

11 See, for instance, the comments of Sen. Dodd in support of S. 565, *Congressional Record*, 107th Cong., 2nd sess., p. S1146.

12 A good summary of this election and the controversy that followed can be found in Fountain (2000).

13 Online NewsHour, Bond Alleges Voter Fraud in Missouri, November 9, 2000, http://www.pbs.org/newshour/updates/november00/carnahan_11–9.html; "Stipulation of Facts and Consent Order," *U.S.A. v. Bd of Elec. Commn. for St. Louis City*, 4:2002cv01235 (E.D. Mo.), filed August 14, 2002, http://www.clearinghouse.net/chDocs/public/VR-MO-0025–0001.pdf.

14 The following deal with the sorry state of affairs in the availability of data to assess the performance of election administration in the United States: Gerken (2009); Ansolabehere and Persily (2010); Gronke and Stewart (2008); Alvarez, Ansolabehere, and Stewart (2005); Stewart (2008b).

15 Studies that use the residual vote rate to assess the performance of voting machines include Ansolabehere and Stewart (2005); Caltech/MIT Voting Technology Project (2001); Garner and Spolaore (2005); Kimball and Kropf (2005, 2008); Knack and Kropf (2003a, bEM1_9781107048638.doc – CIT000161); Miller (2005); Stewart (2006). For a discussion of assessing voting technology more generally, see Stewart (2011a).

16 The statistical analysis on which this and the following paragraphs are based may be found at Stewart (2011b, 20–23).

17 A number of studies have found an abstention rate in presidential elections of around 0.5 percent.

18 Chapter 2 of the U.S. Civil Rights Commission's report, "Voting Irregularities in Florida during the 2000 Presidential Election," contains an account of many of the reports of voters who were denied access to the ballot because of voter registration problems. The report is available at the following URL: http://www.usccr.gov/pubs/pubsndx.htm.

19 *Congressional Record*, 107th Cong., 2nd sess., Feb. 14, 2002, p. S809.

20 Prior to HAVA, the main laws governing access to polling places for the disabled were the Voting Accessibility for the Elderly and Handicapped Act (VAEHA), passed in 1984, and the Americans with Disabilities Act, passed in 1990. The 1965 Voting Rights Act also guarantees the right of blind voters to receive assistance in voting. For a discussion of the laws and their implementation as of 2002, see U.S. General Accounting Office (2001). The primary thrust of post–*Bush v. Gore* advocacy emphasized the ability of disabled voters to vote independently, without assistance.

21 The most recent published scientific study of access of the disabled to the polls appears to be Kruse and colleagues (1999).

22 Bureau of Labor Statistics, "Frequently Asked Questions about Disability Data," http://www.bls.gov/cps/cpsdisability_faq.htm.

23 The Survey of the Performance of American Elections is an Internet-based survey of 10,000 registered voters – 200 from each state – conducted during the week immediately following the 2008 presidential election. The focus of the survey was on the voting experience. The survey was supported by the Pew Center on the States, under the Make Voting Work Initiative, along with the JEHT Foundation and the AARP. Registered voters were asked whether they voted in 2008. If they did not, they were asked a series of questions to probe why not. If they did vote, respondents were asked the mode of voting they used (in person on election day, in-person early voting, or absentee/mail voting) and then received a series of questions about their experience, depending on the mode. Data and the final report may be downloaded at the following site: http://dspace.mit.edu/handle/1721.1/49847.

24 The original report may be found in Wang and Serebrov (2007). The report as released by the EAC may be found at http://www.eac.gov/research/other_reports.aspx. See Urbina (2007) for a news account of this episode.

25 A similar argument is made in Stewart (2004) concerning the move in Georgia to mandate the use of a single DRE beginning in 2002.

26 Information about the use of voting technologies before 2000 was provided by Election Data Services. Data after 2000 were gathered by the author.

27 For a review of this literature, see Stewart (2011a).

28 Election Data Services, "Nation Sees Drop in Use of Electronic Voting Equipment for 2008 Election – a First," http://www.electiondataservices.com/images/stories/File/NR_VoteEquip_Nov-2008wAppendix2.pdf.

29 For an extended variant of the argument being made here, see Stewart (2008a).

30 The obsession among Republican leaders with rooting out voter fraud also played a large role in the scandal that received national attention in early 2007 over the firing of seven U.S. Attorneys nationwide. Among the reasons given for these firings was a complaint among Republican campaign operatives, such as Karl Rove, that they had not been aggressive enough in pursuing reports of voter fraud. See Driesen

(2008) for a comprehensive review of the scandal, including citations to newspaper accounts linking the firings to the perceived inattention to voter fraud cases, among other political and electoral considerations.

31 See Nhu-Y Ngo, "Delaware Inspires Maryland to Modernize Its Voter Registration System," Brennan Center for Justice, March 28, 2011, http://www.brennancenter. org/blog/archives/delaware_inspires_maryland_vrm/.

32 Of course, by tying voter registration closely to the driver's license database, one risks the possibility of disenfranchising voters who do not have driver's licenses, which is the major concern of photo ID opponents. However, as the evidence from Maryland cited in Ngo (2011) reveals, a large number of voters *with* driver's licenses may now be disenfranchised because of poor procedures.

33 I use this word advisedly, in the same sense of Hofstadter's classic essay (Hofstadter, 1965).

5

Voter Confidence in 2010: Local, State, and National Factors

Lonna Rae Atkeson

BACKGROUND

Since the election controversies of 2000, scholars of American politics have invested research time and effort into the study of election administration and election performance. These include studies on residual vote analysis (Ansolabehere and Stewart, 2005; Mebane, 2004; Wand et al., 2001), election auditing (Alvarez, Atkeson and Hall 2012; Atkeson et al., 2008), the role of poll workers (Alvarez and Hall, 2006; Atkeson, Alvarez, and Hall., 2009b; Claassen et al., 2008; Hall, Monson, and Patterson, 2009), the role of technology (Alvarez and Hall, 2004; Kimball and Kropf, 2005, 2008; Knack and Kropf, 2003b; Stein et al., 2008; Tomz and Van Howling, 2003), provisional votes (Alvarez and Hall, 2009; Atkeson, Alvarez, and Hall, 2009a; Kimball and Foley, 2009; Kimball, Kropf, and Battles, 2006; Pitts and Neumann, 2009), voter identification (Ansolabehere, 2009; Atkeson, et al., 2010; Cobb, et al., 2012; Pitts and Neumann, 2009), and voter confidence (Alvarez, Hall, and Llewellyn, 2008a; Atkeson and Saunders, 2007; Bullock, Hood, and Clark, 2005; Claassen et al., 2008; Murphy, Johnson, and Bowler, 2011), among others. These studies have been in direct response to the presidential election meltdown in 2000, which for the public focused largely on Florida, but was also seen in other states, especially those where the race was very close, including New Mexico and Ohio (Caltech/MIT Voting Technology Project, 2001). This work has been highly productive, creating new linkages between political scientists, local election officials, and legal professionals to create a data-driven approach to election reform and a push to improve and modernize the local election systems across the nation (Alvarez et al., 2009; Atkeson, Alvarez, and Hall 2010; Atkeson et al., 2011; Gerken, 2009; Liebshutz and Palazzolo, 2005).

Understanding the factors that contribute to voter confidence is an important component of the election performance literature. The interest in voter confidence stems from very visible problems in the election process observed since 2000 (Atkeson et al., 2010; Hall et al., 2009; Sinclair and Alvarez, 2004; Tomz and Van Houweling, 2003; Wand et al., 2001), attention by the mass media to the possibility that voting machines may not be counting the votes correctly, weak computer security in many systems that allows for break-ins (Kohno et al., 2004), the specter of voter fraud by citizens (Griffin and Johnston, 2008), and procedural manipulations by election officials to potentially change turnout (Kennedy, 2006; Koppelman, 2010). These potential problems heightened interest in election administration and led scholars to consider how voters evaluate the election process.

The perception that citizens and voters have about the integrity of their vote and the election process more generally is critical because elections are the link between citizens and their elected officials. If voters do not have faith in this most fundamental aspect of a democratic society – the outcome of elections and the correct counting of votes – then the legitimacy of representative government might be at risk.[1] In addition, legislators, Supreme Court justices, and citizen activists have repeatedly connected voter fraud issues with voter confidence, thus voter confidence has become an important theoretical link in policy debates on election reform. For example, the Commission on Federal Election Reform noted the importance of voter confidence in its report, "Building Confidence in U.S. Elections," when it stated:

> The vigor of American democracy rests on the vote of each citizen. Only when citizens can freely and privately exercise their right to vote and have their vote recorded correctly can they hold their leaders accountable. Democracy is endangered when people believe that their votes do not matter or are not counted correctly. (p. 9)

Given its perceived importance by policy makers, legislators, the courts, and local election officials, it is not surprising that political scientists have also focused on understanding this question. Therefore, over the past decade and a half, scholars have worked to develop and analyze a new measure of trust in the voting process: voter confidence. These studies have largely focused on demographic differences, the effects of winning and losing, voter technology, and voters' experience at the polls (though see Gronke and Hicks, 2009b). Given the prominent role that fraud has played in the debates surrounding voter confidence as well as policy measures like voter identification that have been linked to voter confidence, I extend the analysis of voter confidence by including the role of attitudes toward fraud and the current voter identification law. I also consider the changing electoral context, including the job performance of the president. In addition, I consider how perception of voter confidence changes from an individual vote being counted correctly to confidence in all the votes in the county or state being counted correctly. To examine this question, I use New Mexico voter survey data from a post-2010 general election poll. New Mexico offers an interesting place to examine this question, given that it has been at the center of electoral attention as a battleground state since the 2000 election, during which it had the closest election in the country with only a few hundred votes separating Bush and Gore (Atkeson and Tafoya, 2008a). In addition, New Mexico offers an environment with largely weak voter identification laws and a uniform voting system statewide (optical scan) preventing voting technology issues from playing a role in voter confidence.

WHY VOTER CONFIDENCE?

Voter confidence has emerged as a critical feature of election reform efforts. Policy makers, legislators, and activists, for example, have framed the debate around voter identification, postelection audits, and, most recently, election day registration as important issues that relate to protecting the system against fraud and ensuring voter confidence (Alvarez, 2011; Atkeson et al., 2008). Nowhere is this more clearly seen than in the recent U.S. Supreme Court case *Crawford v. Marion County* that ruled on the legitimacy of a rather strict voter identification law in Indiana. According to the state of Indiana, there are four reasons the state has a compelling interest to create a voter identification law. These include: (1) deterring and detecting voter fraud, (2) the modernization of election procedures, (3) administrative problems in Indiana's voter registration rolls that include dead people and people who are no longer residents, and (4) safeguarding voter confidence in the election process. On the voter fraud and voter confidence claims, which are clearly related, the state argues that, "The Voter ID Law serves two purposes. First and foremost, it helps with deterring and detecting in-person voter fraud, a long-recognized compelling interest of the state (*Marston v. Lewis*, 410 US 679, 681 (1973)). Second, it helps to safeguard voter confidence in the legitimacy of election results, an interest the Court has repeatedly deemed compelling. Further, the means to vindicate these interests is so well tailored the voter ID Law stands up to any level of scrutiny" (Indiana State Brief: 44).

The plurality opinion written by Justice Stevens and joined by Justice Kennedy and Chief Justice Roberts asked whether the state's interests in these factors outweigh the additional burdens placed on the voting citizens in the state of Indiana and ruled in favor of the state's voter identification law.[2] This framework uses the flexible balancing tests between interests outlined in *Anderson v. Celebrezze*, 460 U.S. 780, 789 (1983). The additional burdens placed on some voters were not seen as severe enough, given the evidence provided, to trigger the need for civil rights protections. Specifically with regard to voter confidence, the justices in the plurality opinion argued, "While that interest is closely related to the State's interest in preventing voter fraud, public confidence in the integrity of the electoral process has independent significance, because it encourages citizen participation in the democratic process" (553 U.S. 2008: 13).

In addition, the voter confidence argument is used to favor voter technologies that provide a verifiable vote record. For example, in 2004, reported problems with new DRE machines in New Mexico led the state to abandon the new technologies it had purchased with initial Help America Vote Act (HAVA) monies to move to a statewide system that used optical scan bubble paper ballots that provided a vote record independent of the voting machine (Atkeson and Saunders, 2007). Other states, including Florida[3] and Ohio,[4] have followed suit. Many states also have instituted postelection ballot audits that check the voting systems against the paper voting trail to determine that the machines are functioning correctly and that the votes are counted accurately. Perceptions about these factors affect the legitimacy of the election outcomes (Traugott and Conrad, 2012). All of these measures and reforms are justified, in part, because of a desire to maintain voter confidence, and although research is mixed on the role voting technology plays in voter confidence, there does seem to be some support for this linkage (Alvarez et al., 2008a; Atkeson and Saunders, 2007; Conrad et al., 2009; Herrnson et al., 2008a, 2008b; Murphy et al., 2011). Thus, voter confidence in the perceived legitimacy of election outcomes and the election process is an important policy matter and provides one reason public opinion on voter confidence should receive close scrutiny.

While political science has long been attentive to broad measures of diffuse system support such as trust in government (Citrin and Luks, 2001; Hetherington, 1998), government responsiveness or external efficacy (Atkeson and Carrillo, 2007; Banducci and Karp, 2003; Craig, Niemi, and Silver, 1990), political alienation (Aberbach, 1969), and confidence in governmental institutions (Cook and Gronke, 2005), we have spent much less time examining citizen beliefs in government processes. Voter confidence represents an undertaking into this important question through a focus on the electoral process, and research suggests that it is distinct from other measures of system-level support (Atkeson, Alvarez, and Hall, 2009a; Gronke and Hicks, 2009b), which tend to test the evaluation of elected leaders in government (Citrin and Luks, 2001), and an accumulation of grievances and disappointments within and across administrations (Miller, 1974).

Theoretically, focusing on the process of democracy is important because process is fundamental to the way a democratic society functions. If voters do not have confidence that their vote is counted correctly or that the system of elections is free, fair, and accurate, then the most fundamental aspect of representative democracy, the direct election of its leaders, is in doubt. Simply put, if citizens do not believe in the election process, then the entire system of republican government becomes a questionable enterprise. Although a voter may not trust the current sitting government – perhaps because the voter supports a different political party or a different set of political candidates – this does not necessarily mean that those leaders do not have legitimate standing to make decisions on behalf of the majority or plurality of the electorate who supported them. However, if a voter does not trust that those leaders hold their seats legitimately – if the voter does not have confidence that the election was administered fairly and that all the votes were counted accurately – then the reason

TABLE 5.1. *Percentage Voter Confidence Across Levels of Vote Aggregation*

	Individual Voter Confidence	County Confidence	State Confidence
Not at all confident	2	2	4
Not too confident	5	10	13
Somewhat confident	39	43	43
Very confident	54	45	40
Mean	3.45	3.32	3.18
N	776	761	758

for voter distrust is more fundamental and may have greater consequences to system-level conditions.

Voter confidence has mostly been examined at the level of the individual voter, but system-level confidence is also important (but see Atkeson et al., 2009b). Just because a voter believes that his ballot is counted correctly, does not mean that he believes that ballots within the larger electoral process at the jurisdiction or county level or across jurisdictions at the state level are counted correctly. Yet policy makers and political scientists move easily between contexts in their discussions and we do not know how these more global measures of voter confidence perform. In 2010, the New Mexico Election Administration Survey asked about voter confidence at the level of the individual, precinct, county, and state. Table 5.1 presents the results for individual, county, and state for the following question: How confident are you that your vote and all the votes at the following administrative levels were counted as the voter(s) intended? The response categories are (1) not at all confident, (2) not too confident, (3) somewhat confident, and (4) very confident. The category of "precinct" is excluded because the frequency or marginal results are nearly identical with the individual voter confidence variable. The data show a high degree of voter confidence at all institutional levels. Interestingly, the results show that as voters move from the individual to larger system levels that voter confidence declines (paired t-test, p < .001, two-tailed test). More than a majority of voters (54%) indicated that they were very confident at the individual voter level, but only two in five (40%) indicated they were very confident at the state level, a difference of 15 percent.

FACTORS THAT INFLUENCE VOTER CONFIDENCE?

Similar to models of trust and efficacy, factors that explain voter confidence display both short- and long-term characteristics and are social and political in nature. Short-term factors include aspects of voters' personal experiences at the polls and the local and national election context (Atkeson and Saunders, 2007; Claassen et al., 2008; Hall et al., 2009). The local factor in essence is the objective experience voters have with the voting process and focuses on external attributions in understanding voter confidence and includes their experience with the ballot and their experience at the polls. When voters have problems voting, for example, because they find the ballot confusing, find poll workers unhelpful, wait in long lines, are unsure whether their absentee ballot arrived, or made a mistake on a ballot and had to get a new one, they are likely to feel less confident that their vote will be counted. Thus, I expect a poor voting experience to be negatively related to voter confidence.

Over the past decade and a half, the chatter about potential voter fraud and voter irregularities has continuously led to changes in voting methods. These include the move away from lever voting machines, election verification policies including postelection audits, and the move by many states to require stricter voter identification policies. In addition, elites at various levels have fueled the fires of this debate by focusing on procedural irregularities and manipulation of voter processes. For example, in Florida in 2000 this focused on the purging of the voter roles, and in 2004 in Ohio this focused on a number of administrative rules and procedures that appeared designed to disenfranchise certain types of voters (Kennedy, 2006; Palast, 2000). Voter confidence may not be immune to the national debate or events on the ground; indeed these factors may be important in understanding voter confidence (see Gronke and Hicks, 2009b). Voters may feel disenfranchised when their vote is diluted by the participation of ineligible voters, and such feeling may reduce their confidence. Voters may also feel less confident when they believe that they have seen voter fraud. Such observations may lead them to question the integrity and manipulability of the electoral process, decreasing their belief in its objective administration. Similarly, voter attitudes toward their state law may also matter if they are incorporating the larger national debate into their opinions. Because weak voter identification laws are assumed to encourage fraudulent voting, voters who perceive their law as not meeting the fraud standard may be less confident. Although a number of these factors have not been considered before, they are considered here to expand our understanding of voter confidence and how it may differ across levels of voter confidence abstraction (personal, county, and state).

Two other factors that may be related to the voter experience are whether the voter is a first time voter or whether the voter was asked for a photo identification for authentication, an issue related to voter fraud. First time voters are new to the system and are required to show identification if they were registered by a third party. Their inexperience with the process may create more doubt or enthusiasm for their actions, resulting in a decrease or increase in voter confidence. Being asked for photo identification may also matter. Certainly one of the primary arguments for voter identification is to protect the system against fraud as discussed earlier. But voter identification proponents also argue that the policy establishes safeguards that create the perception of security, ultimately enhancing voter confidence. We know from previous studies that, broadly speaking, a higher-quality polling place with better-trained poll workers presents a good voting experience that enhances voter confidence (Atkeson and Saunders, 2007; Claassen et al., 2008; Hall et al., 2009). If security represents another aspect of the polling place experience, then ensuring voter eligibility through strict identification policies may have a similar and positive effect. New Mexico has relatively loose laws for voter identification, making the identification method the choice of the voter (§ 1–1-24 NMSA 1978). However, implementation of this policy is very mixed, with poll workers sometimes taking the lead and requesting stricter forms of voter identification, including a photo ID, and many other times voters just opting to show a photo identification without being asked (Atkeson, Alvarez, and Hall 2009; Atkeson et al., 2010, 2011a, forthcoming). In the New Mexico data, 22 percent of in-person voters indicated they were asked to show a photo identification. Given the variation in implementation, it is possible to test how being asked to show a physical form of identification influences voter confidence. This variable is coded one for those who showed a photo ID and zero for everyone else.

The way voters choose to execute their vote is also an important factor. In New Mexico, voters can choose to vote absentee by mail, early in person, or on election day.[5] Absentee voters, in particular, experience a different election process than in-person voters. Absentee voters have to request a ballot, receive it, fill it out, and return it in time to be counted. Absentee voters do not have the opportunity to insert their ballot into the counting machine or observe that the machine appeared to function properly. Therefore, absentee voters are further removed from the election process than in-person early or election day voters and may feel less confident that their ballot is likely to be counted. Voters engaging in absentee voting, for example, may feel that their ballot is less likely to be counted because they may believe that these ballots only get counted if the race is close or may worry about their ballot arriving on time to be counted because they must have trust in both the U.S. postal service and in the local jurisdiction's process. Several studies suggest that absentee voters had significantly less voter confidence, a finding that supports this hypothesis (Alvarez, Hall, and Llewellyn, 2009; Atkeson and Saunders, 2007; Bryant, 2010).

A short-term political characteristic is the positive relationship between support for the winning candidate and voter confidence (Alvarez et al., 2009; Atkeson and Saunders, 2007; Bullock et al., 2005). This is similar to findings in the trust in government and political efficacy literatures, which consistently show a party winner effect (Anderson and LoTempio, 2002; Anderson and Tverdova, 2003; Banducci and Karp, 2003; Clarke and Acock, 1989; Craig et al., 1990; Ginsberg and Weissberg, 1978). Early studies on voter confidence in the first half of the past decade found that Democrats were less confident than Republicans, and it was believed that this was linked to the fact that they lost in both the 2000 and 2004 presidential elections (Alvarez et al., 2008a; Atkeson and Saunders, 2007; Bullock et al., 2005; Hall, Monson, and Patterson, 2007). In 2008, however, the Democrats won and research shows that partisan voter confidence reversed with Democrats displaying greater voter confidence than

Republicans and Obama voters in particular showing greater voter confidence than McCain voters (Alvarez et al., 2009; Atkeson et al., 2009b). In addition, research shows that after the 2006 election, in which Democrats took control of the U.S. House of Representatives, there was a national-level increase in voter confidence for Democrats (Alvarez et al., 2009). Later studies confirm the theoretical expectation of a winner effect and this has been largely linked to the most immediate election context with no studies showing a relationship between presidential support and voter confidence (Atkeson et al., 2009b). However, there may be a national component. Given that in 2004 Republicans controlled the White House and the legislature, the variables tapping winning would likely be highly correlated with presidential approval and therefore may wash out. In 2010, however, the House of Representatives changed hands, but of course, the president remains in office, giving us a different governing context, divided government, where attitudes toward the nation's leader may influence voter confidence. Therefore, I expect winners to have greater levels of system support than losers in all three models and test the role of national actors, particularly the president.

Finally demographics are potentially always important for understanding attitudes. Although theoretically with the exception of African Americans, who have a long history of disenfranchisement, there is no a priori reason to expect to see differences here, nevertheless because of their general importance we control for them. Research suggests that education may (Alvarez, Hall and Llewellyn, 2008a; Murphy, Johnson, Bowler, 2010) or may not (Atkeson and Saunders, 2007; Hall, Monson and Patterson, 2008; Bullock, Hood and Clark, 2005) be related to voter confidence (Alvarez et al., 2008a; Atkeson and Saunders, 2007; Bullock et al., 2005; Hall, Monson, and Patterson, 2008; Murphy et al., 2011). Race has been shown to matter for blacks in terms of voter confidence prior to 2008 (Alvarez et al., 2008a; Bullock et al., 2005; but see Gronke and Hicks, 2009b), but perhaps not surprisingly, given that an African American won the election, it did not matter for blacks in 2008 (Alvarez et al., 2009). However, research shows consistently that it has not mattered for Hispanics (Atkeson et al., 2010; Atkeson et al., 2011a; Atkeson and Saunders, 2007; Stein et al., 2008). Gender sometimes matters (Alvarez et al., 2009; Alvarez et al., 2008; Hall, 2008; Murphy et al., 2011) and sometimes it does not (Atkeson and Saunders, 2007; Hall et al., 2009. Age largely appears to not matter (Atkeson and Saunders, 2007; Hall et al., 2009; Magleby, Monson, and Patterson, 2008; Stein et al., 2008), except for one study of California voters (Murphy et al., 2011). The weight of evidence, especially when the administrative unit is held constant, suggests that demographics or predispositions should have little influence in explaining voter confidence.

DATA AND METHODS

I use the 2010 New Mexico Voter Election Administration Survey for our analysis. This mixed mode voter survey was based on a random sample of registered voters in the state of New Mexico. A few days after election day, sample members were sent a postcard asking them to participate in our online survey or request a mail survey with a self-addressed stamped envelope. Registered voters who did not respond were contacted a total of three times. The second postcard was sent November 15; the third was sent December 1. In addition, as part of a mode response test, we sent out only a mail survey to a small subset of voters and only allowed a small subset of voters to respond online. The response rate was about 17.7 percent (n = 813) using Response Rate 2 (RR2) as defined by the American Association for Public Opinion Research (AAPOR, 2008). Note that this is the minimum response rate and includes all voters we tried to contact, regardless of whether we were able to contact them. More than seven in ten respondents (71%) chose the Internet option and not quite three in ten (29%) chose the mail option. Postelection analysis of the sample showed it accurately reflected many sample population characteristics and the election outcome, suggesting the response rate did not produce a biased sample (data not shown).[6]

Dependent Variables

We focus on three dependent variables that capture voter confidence at the voter, county, and state levels. The frequency of these variables and their associated means are shown in Table 5.1. For these questions the voter was presented with a grid and asked, "How confident are you that your vote and all the votes at the following administrative levels were counted as the voter(s) intended?" The administrative units include your vote, your precinct, your county, and your state. Response categories included very confident, somewhat confident, not too confident, and not at all confident. Voter confidence was the sixth question in the survey and was only preceded by one independent model variable, first time voter. Because of the small number of individuals who indicated that they were not at all confident, these variables were collapsed into three categories: very confident, somewhat confident, and not too confident and not at all confident combined.

Given the ordinal nature of our dependent variables we test our models using ordered probit with STATA MP 11.0.

Independent Variables

Four types of indicators are included in the analysis. The first type is the voter experience. These include the voting method. Two dummy variables are included, one for absentee voters and one for early voters, with election day voters included, making them the point of comparison. Given previous research, I expect that absentee voters will have lower levels of confidence than early or election day voters. I also include a dummy variable for first time voters, but have no specific expectation for this variable because theoretically it could be positive or negative or make no difference. I also include a dummy variable for a poor voting experience. This represents a truncated count of the number of problems voters had during their election experience. Any problem a voter had placed them in the poor experience category.[7] Problems in voting included: whether a mistake was made on the ballot and the respondent had to obtain a new ballot, rating the poll workers only fair or poor, if it was somewhat or very hard to find their polling location, if absentee ballot instructions were very hard or somewhat hard to follow, or if an absentee voter was very or somewhat concerned that their ballot would not arrive in time to be counted. The last element of the voting experience is a dummy variable coded one if the voter was asked for a photo ID and zero otherwise.

The second set of variables focuses on whether the respondent was a political winner or loser. Here voter partisanship is included, as dummy variables. The variable Democrat is scored one for any Democratic identification and zero otherwise. The variable Independent is scored one for a self-identified independent and zero otherwise. This leaves self-identified Republicans as the comparison group. We also controlled for whether the voter voted for the gubernatorial winner, Republican candidate Susana Martinez. This was an open race and a competitive contest. However, it is important to note that there were high-profile House races also going on in the state. Two of New Mexico's recently elected freshmen House incumbents were returned, but one incumbent, Democrat Harry Teague, was defeated by Steve Pearce, who had resigned the seat in 2008 to run for an open U.S. Senate seat. Thus, winning and losing was complicated by multiple election contests (Alvarez, Hall, and Llewellyn, 2008). Finally, we included a measure of approval for President Obama. This was measured on a four-point scale along with a series of individuals and institutions. The questions asked, "We are interested in whether you strongly approve, approve, disapprove, or strongly disapprove of how the following are handling their jobs." For Obama the frequency was 32 percent strongly disapprove, 18 percent disapprove, 35 percent approve, and 15 percent strongly approve, with a mean approval of 2.34.

The third type of indicator involves attitudes toward fraud and the voter identification process in the state because that has been a major reason for enacting voter identification laws and a variety of other electoral reforms. I look at three separate variables to tap into voters' perceptions of fraud and election processes. The first is a question that asked, "In the last ten years, in how many elections did you witness what you believed to be election fraud?" Twenty-nine percent of respondents reported none, while 21 percent provided the number of elections in which they observed fraud, with a range of twenty (0 minimum, 20 maximum) with most responses clustering around one, two, or three elections. The mean number of fraudulent elections was 1.2. That leaves 50 percent of respondents who indicated they did not know. On all of the measures of fraud there is a large number of respondents opting for the "don't know" response. Given the difficult nature of the question "don't know" represents a viable answer. Therefore to control for these individuals I created two dummy variables, the first capturing those who responded that they had witnessed fraud and the second capturing those who answered "don't know." The first dummy variable scores a one if a respondent witnessed fraud; all others score zero. The second dummy variable scores a one if a respondent indicated they didn't know if they witnessed fraud; all others score zero. I expect those who have witnessed fraud to have lower levels of voter confidence than those who have not, thus I expect a negative relationship with voter confidence. Given that "don't know" is a response of uncertainty whereas the answer "none" represents certainty on this issue, I hypothesize that the effect of not knowing about fraud on voter confidence is more likely to be negative than positive.

For those respondents who indicated they had seen fraud, they were asked a follow up open ended question that asked them to "describe the experience." Interestingly, voters' definitions of fraud are much broader than those in the legal, academic, or activist community. Table 5.2 shows the breakdown of the answers to the open-ended question and shows that more than three in five (61%) incidents of observed fraud relate to the 2000 presidential election in Florida and the 2004 presidential election in Ohio. Overall, 61 percent of voters believe that election fraud is a function of the manipulation of voter processes by especially political elites, including the Supreme Court's *Bush v. Gore* ruling in 2000 that was explicitly referenced by voters. This suggests that the mantle of fraud, as understood by voters, is largely a product of the battle among elites to control processes and disenfranchise voters selectively. However, it is important to note that 20 percent of responses mentioned election administration issues such as "miscounts," "found ballots," "poll workers," and so forth. A rather paltry 7 percent by comparison mentioned illegal voting by noncitizens and filling out absentee ballots at senior homes despite the enormous amount of press surrounding these issues and the state legislative activity for voter identification policies. In addition, ACORN voter registration fraud activities in 2008 represent an additional 4 percent.

The second fraud variable is a truncated index of four variables that tap voters' perceptions of types of fraud that might be occurring in the polling place.[8] The question was, "Below is a list of possible illegal election activities that may or may not take place in YOUR COMMUNITY. Please tell me whether you think each event occurs all or most of the time, some of the time, not much of the time or never: A voter casts more than one ballot, tampering with ballots to change votes, someone pretends to be another person and casts a vote for them, a non–U.S. citizen votes."[9] We took the mean of these four variables and then truncated them so that everyone who had a mean score above two on a four-point scale, representing an answer of "all or most of the time" or "some of the time," was scored a one (36%), while everyone else, including those who responded "don't know" scored a zero (don't knows represented 23%

TABLE 5.2. *Open-Ended Responses to Explanation for Witnessing Fraud*

Reason	Percentage
2000 Bush Gore Election/Supreme Court/Florida	39
2000 or/and 2004 election/Florida/Ohio	22
Election Administration Problems	20
Individual Fraud, Illegal Voters	7
ACORN	5
Unspecified	5
Obama 2008	2

of voters across these measures).[10] A dummy variable for those who indicated "don't know" across all four measures was created, scoring them a one and everyone else a zero.

Last in this category, I used a measure that tapped into how voters feel about New Mexico's voter identification law. The survey asked, "New Mexico's voter ID law requires voters to identify themselves. The minimum identification is to state their address, name, and birth year. Do you think the minimum identification is too strict (.3%), just right (39%), or not strict enough (61%)?" Given the frequency, we coded all those who indicated just right or too strict a zero and everyone who indicated it was not strict enough a one.

The last category is demographics. The models include a variable for gender (female equals one, male equals zero), age (continuous), a four-point ordinal variable of education (high school or less, some college, college graduate, and advanced degree), and two variables for race and ethnicity (one representing Hispanics and one representing other minorities). I also included a dummy variable for survey mode (one for Internet, zero for mail) in case survey mode influenced attitudes.

RESULTS

Table 5.3 shows the results of the multivariate model. I begin by focusing on the fraud and voter identification variables because they extend previous analysis on the question of voter confidence and show consistent effects across all three levels we examine. The variable witnessing fraud, uncertainty about fraud, and perceptions of fraud in the polling place are important to voter confidence at all levels. The uncertainty effect is particularly prominent at the individual voter confidence level. Voters who indicated they had "witnessed" fraud had a much lower probability (17%) of being very confident, from 64 percent to 81 percent, and that uncertainty regarding fraud led to a probability difference of 11 percent (from 70% to 81%). Perceptions of fraud create even a larger change in the probability of being very confident at 23 percent (from 58% to 81%), and for uncertain voters on this dimension their change in the probability of being very confident is much smaller at only 11 percent (from 70% to 81%). At the county level, the results are roughly similar with "witnessing" fraud leading to a change in probabilities of 20 percent (from 48% to 68%) for very confident voters and uncertainty leading to a rather small change of 6 percent (from 62% to 68%). Similar to the individual-level model, there is a large effect for perception of fraud, with a 22 percent change in probability in being very confident (from 46% to 68%). At the state level, both the witnessing of fraud and the perception of fraud variables perform identically, with a 22 percent difference in the likelihood of being very confident (33% when the variable is low and 55% when it is high). Voters who were uncertain also had a lower voter confidence of about 10 percent, from 44 percent to 54 percent. Uncertainty suggests a state of risk and, thus, voters who are unsure are somewhat less confident than voters who are certain that fraud does not exist at all.

The voter identification law has no influence on individual-level or county-level voter confidence and only a marginal (p < .097) significance at the state level. This is reflected in the change in probabilities, which is fairly small at only 7 percent (from 60 percent when the rather weak voter identification laws are considered just right to 53 percent when it is seen as not strict enough). This suggests at best a marginal and very modest roles for state laws influencing voter confidence.

There is no difference between voting modes; absentee voters have a negative coefficient, but it does not reach even marginal definitions of statistical significance. It is important to note that the model may have picked up problems with absentee voting through the voter experience variable that included concerns that an absentee voter's ballot would not arrive in time to be counted. Thus, the lack of a direct effect of the absentee voting variable, may be due, in part, to the fact that the model picks up the hypothesized reason for lower voter confidence among absentee voters more directly in the poor voting experience variable, which does show a negative and significant relationship across all three levels of confidence. Thus, consistent with previous studies, what happens during the voting experience is an important predictor, and, perhaps more importantly, those experiences inform attitudes about confidence at other levels. Thus, voters infer from their poor experience at the polls that there are larger problems with voting at the county and state levels. The probability of a voter being very confident that her ballot was counted as intended when a voter had a bad experience at the polls is reduced by 9 percent, from 81 percent to 72 percent. The probability of a voter being very confident that all the ballots were counted as intended at the county level reduced the likelihood of a very confident response by about 14 percent, from 69 percent to 55 percent, and at the state level by about 11 percent, from 53 percent to 42 percent.

TABLE 5.3. *Ordered Probits of Voter Confidence at Multiple Levels*

	Voter Confidence	County Voter Confidence	State Voter Confidence
Voting Experience			
Vote by Mail	−.062	.031	.087
	(.144)	(.141)	(.140)
Vote Early	.037	−.013	.011
	(.108)	(.104)	(.103)
First Vote	−.767*	−.514	−.296
	(.460)	(.455)	(.452)
Poor Voting Experience	−.307**	−.357**	−.291*
	(.154)	(.153)	(.153)
Asked for ID	.264**	.140	.132
	(.135)	(.128)	(.126)
Winning and Losing			
Democrat	−.447**	−.398**	−.372**
	(.176)	(.171)	(.169)
Independent	−.410**	−.169	.019
	(.187)	(.181)	(.180)
Martinez Vote	.232+	.156	.079
	(.160)	(.156)	(.153)
Approval of Obama	.218***	.233***	.286****
	(.072)	(.069)	(.068)
Attitudes			
Witness fraud	−.524****	−.530****	−.525****
	(.140)	(.134)	(.132)
Witness Fraud DK	−.347**	−.295***	−.228**
	(.116)	(.112)	(.109)
Likelihood of Fraudulent Voting	−.685****	−.584****	−.525****
	(.119)	(.114)	(.112)
Likelihood of Fraudulent Voting DK	−.381***	−.186	−.100
	(.131)	(.126)	(.124)
Law Not Strict Enough	−.141	−.154	−.181*
	(.116)	(.111)	(.109)
Demographics			
Gender (female)	−.086	−.041	−.131
	(.096)	(.093)	(.092)
Age	−.003	−.006	−.003
	(.003)	(.003)	(.003)
Education	.056	−.012	−.021
	(.049)	(.048)	(.048)
Hispanic	.078	−.005	.055
	(.128)	(.124)	(.122)
Other Minority	.291	−.070	−.059
	(.261)	(.247)	(.243)

(continued)

TABLE 5.3. *(cont.)*

	Voter Confidence	County Voter Confidence	State Voter Confidence
Survey Mode (mail)	.008	−.003	.039
	(.112)	(.109)	(.108)
μ_1	−2.022	−1.93****	−1.28****
	(.378)	(.369)	(.386)
μ_2	−.456	−.463****	.006
	(.371)	(.363)	(.356)
LR Chi–Square	104.11****	91.67****	103.92****
N	674	663	661

Note: + p < .15, * p < .10 **, p < .05, *** p < .01, **** p < .001, two – tailed tests.

First time voters also had a lower level of confidence, but this was only consequential in the first model that focused on voters' ballots being counted as intended. The change in probability for this group of voters is fairly high, with 81 percent of repeat voters likely to indicate they are very confident versus only 55 percent of first time voters. More research on new voters and their experiences needs to be conducted.

I also find that voters who were asked for identification were more confident than those who were not asked for identification, but this only influenced attitudes at the individual voter confidence level and not at higher levels of confidence. Although significant, the effect is fairly small, moving only 6 percent for those very confident, from 81 percent when a voter was not asked to present photo identification to 87 percent for those asked to present a photo ID.

Consistent with other studies we find support that winning and losing matters to voter confidence. Given that it was a Republican year, with Republicans taking over the U.S. House of Representatives and a majority of governorships, it is not surprising to find that Democrats were once again less confident at all three levels than Republicans. We also find that Independents were also less confident at the individual level. The effect was roughly the same for each group, 14 percent for Democrats and 13 percent for Independents. Thus the probability of being very confident was about 81 percent for non-Democrats, and on average 67 percent for Democrats and 68 percent for Independents.

We see an extremely marginal effect for voters who supported GOP gubernatorial winner Susana Martinez (p < .15, two tailed test), suggesting that voting for her increased individual confidence slightly, but did not influence confidence at other levels. Perhaps most interesting here is that there is a strong effect for approval of President Obama at all levels of confidence, something we have not seen previously. Reported models in 2006 in New Mexico and Colorado (Atkeson and Saunders, 2007) did not include a presidential approval variable because it was insignificant, a 2008 examination of voter confidence in New Mexico showed no effect of lame duck President George

Bush on voter confidence at any level (Atkeson et al., 2009b), and Gronke and Hicks (2009b) included a similar measure in their study, but it drops out when election day experiences and perceptions of fraud are included in the model. However, in 2010, with a very similar model the results show a strong and consistent finding for presidential approval on voter confidence. The likelihood of being very confident at the individual level with the lowest opinion of Obama's performance is 75 percent, but it is 90 percent for those with the highest opinion of his performance. At the county level the change in probabilities is slightly higher at 22 percent, with a change from 60 percent to 82 percent, and even higher at the state level, with a change in probabilities of 32 percent, from 42 percent to 74 percent. Perhaps the 2010 election was more of a referendum on Obama than is usually the case. Or perhaps Democrats took solace in an election won the last time, but lost this time, given they maintained control of the presidency and the U.S. Senate. Future research on voter confidence should examine when presidential approval matters and when it does not and develop theoretical explanations for why.

Demographics, as expected, do not help us understand voter confidence. There are no differences between whites and Hispanics or other minorities, males and females, voters with different levels of education, or across different age levels.

CONCLUSION

This study demonstrates that there is an interesting story about voter confidence that considers the larger electoral context. As previous studies have shown, I find that short-term effects regarding voters' experience with the voting process and winning and losing are important to voter confidence levels. We also find that in 2010 attitudes toward the president's general job performance contributed significantly to all levels of voter confidence. This is something that has not been seen before and raises questions about how winning, losing, and control of government matter to voter confidence. For example, it could be that winning is about individual candidates and power in government, creating both dyadic and collective representation explanations for voter confidence. This is something that needs to be examined in future research both theoretically and empirically.

Voter identification policies appear to have little effect in these models. The results show that voters who were asked to show a photo ID were more likely to be confident in their individual vote, but this did not carry over into higher levels of confidence. Moreover voters who thought the current law was not strict enough did not display lower levels of confidence, except a very marginal effect at the state level.[11]

However attitudes and perceptions about fraud matter quite a bit. Both perceptions of fraudulent activities such as vote tampering and noncitizen voting and the belief that fraud has happened in recent elections are negatively associated with voter confidence. Interestingly, the models that perceptions of fraud are mainly driven by media exposure to the 2000 and 2004 presidential elections. More than a majority of voters who had seen fraud saw it not up close and personal, but lived it vicariously through the media information storm that was presented in postelection spins from elites (e.g., Kennedy, 2006), and an HBO movie (*Recount*)). This is an interesting finding because political elites would not see manipulation of the process through rules and procedures as election fraud, but for voters any nefarious activity that appeared to disenfranchise voters was problematic.

This suggests that fraud is seen at both ends of the spectrum and election reforms need to consider that some voters are more worried about fraud from the bottom up and others are more concerned from a top-down perspective. The two variables are positively related, but only weakly so ($r = .12$), suggesting two different types of concerns are relevant to fraud. Voters who perceive a higher likelihood of fraudulent activities taking place by individuals acting against the rules of the game is problematic as well as elites manipulating the process. So far, most election reforms have focused on defeating voter fraud at the individual level and the use of the hand counts to ensure the accuracy of election outcomes, but have not focused on fundamental changes in the process that would eliminate partisan run elections and elite manipulation of processes. Such actions may be very popular (Alvarez, Hall, and Llewellyn, 2008b) and provide an interesting counterpoint to current measures.

Thus, the 2000 presidential election and the *Bush v. Gore* court decision have had a profound influence on the election landscape. Over the past decade and a half, new policies have been implemented as a direct result of the irregularities seen there. Moreover, the influence of both the 2000 and 2004 presidential election contests on citizens' perceptions of the election process has been quite large as shown by the fraud measure that was examined here. Activities of elites are consequential to opinion formation and have played an important role in their maturation. As we move forward, we should focus on a data-driven and less partisan approach to election reform.

Notes

1   Though more recently, scholars have also asked if such changes in government support represent a maturation of the public that expresses a healthy but critical electorate (Norris, 1999).
2   Justices Scalia, Thomas, and Alito's concurring opinion, however, argued that there was no discrimination because all voters were treated equally.
3   See the February 2008 electionline.org briefing "Back to Paper: A Case Study" at http://www.pewcenteronthestates.org/uploadedFiles/EB21Brief.pdf. See also Ian Urbina, "Influx of Voters Expected to Test New Technology," *New York Times*, July 21, 2008, A1.
4   See Directive 2008–01 at: http://www.sos.state.oh.us/SOS/Upload/elections/directives/2008/Dir2008–01.pdf.

5 New Mexico allows for no-excuse absentee voting.

6 See Atkeson and Tafoya (2008) and Atkeson et al. (2011b) as previous examples of tests on the representativeness of our sample.

7 A truncated index was used because most voter complaints were very limited, leaving a distribution that would not lend itself to different types of problems. In addition, this allowed us to combine experiences of absentee and in-person voters, otherwise missing data problems across voting modes would have limited the analysis to one type of voter.

8 This variable is truncated, in part, because of the large number of respondents answering don't know and because of the theoretical importance of a don't know response. A truncated measure provides a way of keeping these individuals in the model by placing them into the zero category.

9 The Cronbach's alpha for this scale is .883, suggesting that combining them into one index is an acceptable statistical strategy. An exploratory factor analysis also delivers only one factor.

10 Voters who answered a single one of the four fraud questions were included in the index mean score.

11 However, it is important to note that if we remove the variable that measures perceptions of fraud in the polling place, the variable that captures attitudes toward the law becomes negative and significant for each model. Thus, model specification is an important consideration. An examination of the probabilities suggests, however, that the effect of this variable is, relatively speaking, rather small at 8 percent (from 70% to 78%) compared to what is seen for the perception of fraud measure.

6

Early Voting after *Bush v. Gore*

Paul Gronke

The Supreme Court's decision in *Bush v. Gore* was explicitly limited in its judicial scope: it awarded the 2000 election to George W. Bush – and nothing more. But the aftermath was a different matter: in the years following, the "case and controversy from which it arose gave rise to a new wave of legislative and judicial attention to the mechanics of elections" (Lowenstein, Hasen, and Tokaji, 2008, 82).[1] A sea change in media coverage and extensive legal commentary shone a light on every aspect of America's election system.[2] In this chapter, we concern ourselves with just one of these: early voting.

Early (or "convenience") voting[3] is a family of related methods by which citizens cast ballots at a time and place other than on election day at the precinct. Expanding outward from its modest beginnings in a small number of reformist Western states (California, Oregon, and Washington) joined by one Midwestern (Iowa) and two Southern (Texas, Tennessee) pioneers, early voting has become a regular fixture of American elections. In the 2008 presidential contest, nearly one-third of votes were cast at a place and time other than the precinct on election day.[4]

On the face of it, nothing about the *Bush v. Gore* decision turned on the mode by which the ballots had been cast. Unlike some legal, administrative, and technological changes that can be traced almost directly to *Bush v. Gore*, early voting has a more complex origin. Major reforms were already under way well before 2000 – beginning as early as 1978 in California – and no single piece of legislation or rule making can be pointed to as a catalyst. However, in the decade following the disputed election, early voting was caught up in the reform fervor that pervaded the election ecosystem. Most notably, the federal government passed landmark legislation, including the 2002 Help America Vote Act (HAVA), which laid down new standards in voting technology and

The author thanks the Election Initiatives at the Pew Center on the States for their generous funding, and Reed College for providing administrative support to EVIC. All analysis and conclusions are the responsibility of the author.

accessibility. HAVA also provided significant financial support for changes in voting technology that, we argue in this chapter, made the adoption and extension of early in-person (EIP) voting far easier. In addition, some states, such as Florida, added new modes of voting as an explicit response to the controversies surrounding the 2000 contest. *Bush v. Gore*, we find, did not give birth to the contemporary machinery of early and absentee voting laws, but in the aftermath of the election, the process of reform ran more quickly, accelerating and broadening the pace of change.

We explore *Bush v. Gore* and a decade of election reform through the lens of early voting, progressively sharpening our focus from aggregate and national to state and region and finally to the individual voter. Each level of analysis adds insight into early voting over the past decade and a half, showing how (and whether) the 2000 presidential election changed the environment for this mode of balloting. We ask:

- Did rates of early voting change after 2000?
- Were the developments in early voting spread uniformly across the country, or can we identify salient regional differences?
- Did the post-2000 reforms affect the composition of the early voting electorate?

A BRIEF HISTORY OF EARLY VOTING

Absentee voting was first established for soldiers during the Civil War, and became available in many states between the First and Second World Wars, primarily as an extension of absentee balloting for members of the military serving overseas.[5] Guidelines typically required a voter to have specific reasons for not being able to vote on election day. Throughout the following decades, states expanded their absentee laws to include additional qualifying excuses; the 1955 Federal Voting Assistance Act added citizens living overseas, and the 1970 Voting Rights Act firmly established ideals of short residency requirements and absentee provisions for voters who had moved close to the time of an election, reflecting a trend in state election law reform in the 1960s. By the mid-1970s, voting laws had been expanded to include eighteen-year-olds and citizens living overseas, increasing the demand for non-precinct balloting.

In 1978, shortly after the passage of 1975's Overseas Citizens Voting Rights Act, California became the first state to offer no-excuse absentee balloting. Oregon and Washington followed suit, adopting no-excuse absentee voting by the 1980s. Since then, twenty-nine additional states have adopted early voting in one form or another. There is almost no uniformity in early voting schemes among the thirty-two states that currently allow voting before election day.[6] The periods and methods of balloting vary significantly, as do the number and distribution of voting centers and the oversight of ballot casting. For example, in the 2010 election, Kentucky was the first state to send out its domestic absentee ballots on September 14, forty-nine days prior to election day on November 2. The first official early in-person voting began in Georgia's county election offices on September 21, forty-two days prior to election day (not to be confused with *advance voting*, a term that the state reserves for early in-person voting available at several locations in each county for a week prior to the election). Compare these extended periods to the highly truncated schedule offered by the State of Oklahoma, which provided for only four days of early in-person voting, from October 29 to November 1. Heterogeneity in early voting methods is largely attributed to the various circumstances under which states adopted early voting, although the passage of the MOVE Act has encouraged, for better or for worse, states to move their domestic absentee ballot mailing deadline forty-five days prior to election day in order to correspond to the mandated ballot transmission period for UOCAVA ballots.[7]

THE NATION: THE GROWTH OF THE EARLY ELECTORATE

As we have seen, early voting laws were in place well before the 2000 contest. Perhaps, however, the seismic shock of that election was reflected in the frequency with which voters turned to alternative methods of balloting. Certainly, the early voting landscape has experienced clear changes since that pivotal election, with growth in availability of early voting in jurisdictions across the United States. Coverage of long and inconvenient lines may have encouraged some citizens to cast a ballot at a time of their own choosing – avoiding the elections office altogether and sending the ballot through the mail.

There is no doubt that Americans have embraced early voting in increasing numbers. The proportion of ballots cast at locations other than at the precinct grew by approximately 50 percent in each presidential election from 2000 to 2008 (with slight downturns in the midterms). According to the Associated Press, 44 million voters – 34 percent of the electorate – cast an early ballot in 2008, compared to just 16.6 million – 16 percent of the electorate – in 2000.[8]

The Current Population Survey's (CPS) Voting and Registration Supplement provides further insight into the growth in early voting. Starting in 1972, some forward-looking member of the census added "voted absentee" to an item that asked about the time that the ballot was cast. Unfortunately, a specific question about alternative voting methods was not added until 1996. From thereon, the CPS is the best long-term comparative record of how many early votes were cast and what kinds of citizens cast them.[9]

Since 1996, as shown in Figure 6.1, the decline in precinct voting has been slow but steady, decreasing from nine in ten voters to fewer than seven in ten today. Use of the absentee by-mail ballot has typically exceeded early in-person voting, which appeared later on the scene and remains far less popular in Western states (see later in this chapter for more detailed regional breakdowns). Early in-person voting, however, has risen in popularity rapidly, and 2008 marked the first time that voting by mail and early in person were

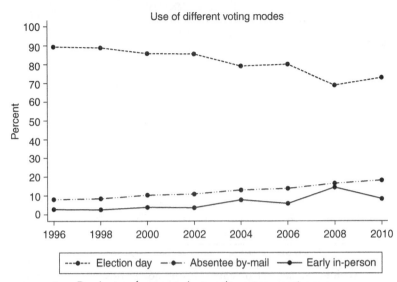

FIGURE 6.1. Precinct and non-precinct voting rates, 1996–2010.
Source: Current Population Survey Voting and Registration Supplement.

roughly equal in terms of votes cast. The higher year-to-year variation in early in-person voting is not surprising; as we show in our final section, the early in-person electorate is more similar to the election day electorate than to those who vote absentee, and are consequently more responsive to election-specific forces that increase or depress turnout.

By any measure, the growth in non-precinct voting since the early 1990s has been dramatic. However, there is little clear evidence that the 2000 contest altered this trajectory. Focusing on turnout, however, may disguise other more subtle changes in the election system that did respond to *Bush v. Gore*.

An alternative lens through which we can examine early voting is that of *availability*. After all, a citizen cannot cast an early vote if the option is not available. If we turn our gaze to state election laws, shown in Figure 6.2, we find that over the past quarter century many states have relaxed requirements for absentee ballots (most frequently removing the requirement for an excuse), legalized early in-person voting, and extended the length of time and number of locations provided for early in-person voting. In all, thirty-two states now offer some form of no-excuse early voting (whether by mail, in person, or both).

The aggregate view, however, once again reveals no notable spike on or around 2000. In fact, we see a slight decrease in the growth rate of states with no-excuse absentee balloting. It is true that some high-profile states, including Colorado, Florida, Georgia, Illinois, New Jersey, and Ohio, changed their laws during the past decade and a half. However, it is extremely difficult to tease out systematic causes to account for the pattern of growth. Geographically, early adopter states tended to be in the West (California,

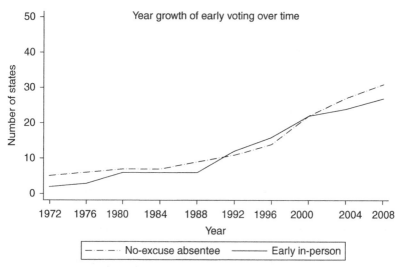

FIGURE 6.2. Growth in the number of states offering no-excuse and early in-person voting.
Source: Cemenska et al., 2009.

Oregon, Washington) – though there are exceptions, such as Iowa, which has allowed no-excuse absentee voting since 1990, and Tennessee, which provided for early in-person voting in 1994 (most of the final holdouts, allowing nothing beyond excuse-required absentee balloting, are in the Northeast). As we have shown elsewhere, the political and policy background of adoption reveals at least three patterns: states that adopted because of a tradition of populism and citizen activism (California, Oregon); states that adopted after an election crisis (Florida, Ohio); and states for which we could find very little public debate over the adoption of early voting, but these findings were mostly suggestive and far from systematic (Gronke and Galanes-Rosenbaum, 2008).

There is one additional possibility: perhaps the rate at which legislative proposals were made increased after *Bush v. Gore*, but for various reasons, proposals were not passed into law.[10] Figure 6.3 displays the number of proposed laws and the number of states that considered early voting legislation from 2000 to 2009. There has been substantial activity in state legislatures (top panel of Figure 6.3), as we would expect given an area of policy that, even five years after HAVA, had "changed dramatically" (Pew Center on the States, 2007). It's less clear that this is a wave sweeping across the country; the total number of states considering proposals varies year to year but does not show systematic growth (bottom panel of Figure 6.3). Many more proposals were made regarding early voting than "vote by mail" (VBM) (this category includes no-excuse absentee voting) and the number of proposals for permanent absentee status spiked late in the decade. Because absentee voting was already in place in so many states, it

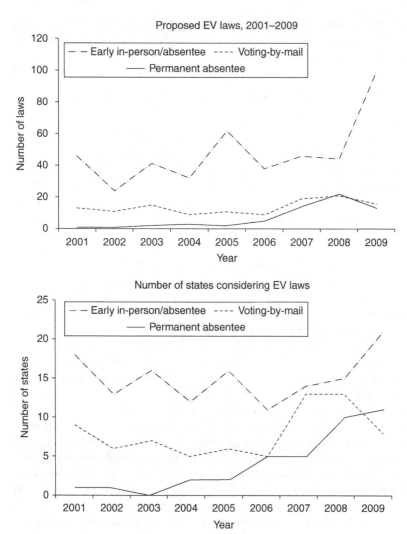

FIGURE 6.3. Early voting proposals in the states, 2001–2009.
Source: National Conference on State Legislatures.

is once again not surprising to see less activity on this front. If we can discern any pattern from these data, it is that more state legislatures tend to consider more election reform proposals after an election – the number of proposed bills spiked after the 2004 and 2008 presidential contests. This suggests that, even if we had pre-2000 data, we might easily conflate election seasonality – legislators propose rule changes immediately after major elections – with a *Bush v. Gore* effect.

Our first lens on early voting after *Bush v. Gore* focused on the aggregate levels of voting and of legislative proposals. When viewed through this lens,

there is little evidence of a substantial change in the rate of balloting or the
level of legislative activity. Early voting reforms were well in place prior to
2000 and continued apace afterward.

THE STATES: THE EMERGENCE OF FOUR EARLY VOTING REGIMES

It may be that national trends in early voting are too blunt an instrument for
uncovering the effects of *Bush v. Gore*. America has a remarkably decentralized system of election administration, and the passage of HAVA is unlikely to
change these deeply embedded institutional patterns (Ewald, 2009). We move
to a more detailed level of analysis, probing beneath the surface of the national
figures, considering how the effects of a national controversy and major federal legislation are mediated by a decentralized election administration regime.
Indeed, the national figures turn out to obscure substantial variation across the
fifty states and the District of Columbia. A key result of the past decade and a
half, we argue, has been the emergence of four distinct patterns of early voting
across the United States. While *Bush v. Gore* may not have caused this shift, it
arguably accelerated it by prompting the passage of HAVA and by encouraging
more states to reform their election systems.

Figure 6.4 displays the *variability* in statewide "advance" voting rates since
2000.[11] We are encouraged that the trend in the median level of advance voting across the fifty states and DC tracks the CPS figures closely, giving us some
comfort that respondents recall correctly how they cast their ballot. However,
the medians are less interesting than the variability. In 2000, states clustered
into a fairly tight range; 50 percent of statewide advance voting rates were
between 5 percent and 19 percent with another quarter between 3.4 percent
and 5 percent. In the 2008 election, the bottom quartile ranged from 4 percent
to 10 percent and the interquartile range was thirty-five percentage points –
two and a half times as large as it was just two presidential elections before. If
HAVA was supposed to lead to some amount of uniformity in election administration across the United States, the result with respect to early voting has
been quite the opposite. The trend has been toward higher rates of early voting,
but also substantially greater variability across states.

These changes have been far from random. Some level of regional uniformity
has underpinned national heterogeneity, to a point where we would argue that
four distinct early voting regimes have emerged in the United States. Figure 6.5
plots CPS turnout rates using early in-person (top panel) and absentee by mail
(bottom panel) across regions. As is immediately apparent, early in-person ballots are cast by a quarter to half of all voters in the South. The regional leaders in this respect are Texas and Tennessee, both of which have allowed early
in-person voting for more than fifteen years. However, the region shifted as a
whole after 2000, when Florida and Georgia legalized both no-excuse absentee
and early in-person voting, followed by North Carolina's hybrid "one-stop"

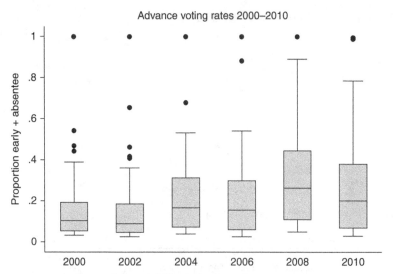

FIGURE 6.4. Increasing variability in early voting rates across states.

system. In 2008, more than a quarter of the CPS respondents reported that they cast early in-person ballots. Other regions have seen significant upticks in early in-person voting, but nothing comparable to the South. This change was particularly pronounced among African American voters in the region, who flocked in great numbers in 2008 to cast early in-person ballots for Barack Obama (Gronke and Hicks, 2009).

Contrast this with the trend line for absentee balloting. With Oregon and Washington leading the pack (98% and 85% respectively), followed by Colorado (59%) and California (40% absentee), the region as a whole is nearing half of all ballots cast absentee. These large states dominate the regional figures and disguise some underlying diversity. Nevada is primarily an early in-person voting state (61% of ballots); Utah, Arizona, and Hawaii have mixed systems; more than 75 percent of voters from Wyoming and Alaska report that they voted at the precinct. Nonetheless, the Western region, overall, is a region that votes by mail.

The Northeast remains remarkably immune to these transformations. Only Vermont and Maine allow early in-person and no-excuse voting. In the rest of the Northeast, and much of the Midwest (save Iowa and Ohio), citizens must either provide an excuse for casting an absentee ballot or show up at the precinct on election day – and most do the latter.

Why would these patterns obtain? We have already proposed the "low-hanging fruit" hypothesis: populist, primarily Western states were early adopters of no-excuse absentee voting. We have speculated elsewhere that this could be attributed to the political culture in this region – the same culture that supports an active initiative and referendum system (Gronke and Galanes-Rosenbaum, 2008). While it is extremely difficult to determine the precise causal effects of

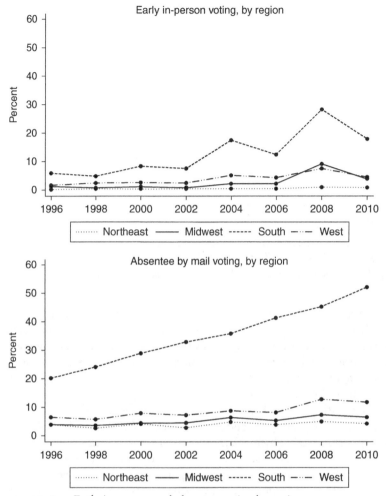

FIGURE 6.5. Early in-person and absentee voting by region.

Bush v. Gore, it is plausible to support that the passage of HAVA (and therefore, indirectly, the 2000 election) provoked or encouraged reform in states that had been balking. Still, why the Southeast and not the Northeast? Is this really all about Florida? While it is only a single state, it is one that exemplifies the trajectory of early voting (and election) reform since *Bush v. Gore*.

SPOTLIGHTING FLORIDA: ADMINISTRATIVE INNOVATION IN RESPONSE TO *BUSH V. GORE*

In response to the chaos of the 2000 general election, Florida adopted legislation aimed at ridding the election system of its problems. Elections officials looked to early voting as a way to increase turnout while also alleviating much of the 2000 mess: lines would be shorter; those who needed individual assistance could be attended to; there would be fewer disputes; and ambiguity issues with ballots and laws would be resolved or never occur at all. Beginning in 2002, county elections supervisors could choose to offer early voting, but it was not uniformly required or implemented across the state until 2004. In an editorial supporting the adoption of statewide early voting, the *Palm Beach Post* claimed, "early voting would help lessen the election-day strain on facilities and systems and would diminish the demand for absentee ballots. Elderly voters who require more time would have it. Elections officials could trouble-shoot potential technical problems and fix them before the mass turnout." Citing the 2000 "election day meltdown," the article continues, "if Floridians have learned anything about voting since 2000 it's that [Florida] cannot run elections on the cheap and that the more safeguards built into the system, the better" (*Palm Beach Post*, 2004).

By 2004, the state legislature defined early voting as "casting a ballot prior to election day at a location designated by the supervisor of elections," and "passed legislation which standardizes early voting throughout the state."[12] The passage of this legislation, designed to fix certain problems and improve voting for Floridians overall, had several problems of its own. Under pressure to fix the problems from 2000 as quickly as possible, especially before the next presidential election, the Florida state legislature neglected to include voter protection provisions that would have mirrored the protections in other voting laws. According to Florida law, campaign supporters cannot solicit voters within fifty feet of the entrance to a polling place on the day of "any election"; however, Secretary of State Glenda Hood "decided that the early voting sites were exempt from the 50-foot barrier because they are in local government buildings to which the public must have access" (Kam and Keller, 2004). Furthermore, although elections supervisors in each county are allowed to open additional early voting sites, the only sites they are *required* to have are the single sites at their elections offices. This meant that, potentially, some citizens would have considerably greater or less access to early voting than others, simply based on how populous their county was or how easy it was for them to get to the elections office.

Unfortunately, the optimism that accompanied the state's adoption of early voting for 2004 evaporated within the first few hours of actual balloting. Reports of an elected official receiving only half of a ballot when she asked for a paper copy instead of using the touch screen machines came in around 10 A.M. Subsequent hours and days yielded reports of harassment and intimidation, very long waits, and people leaving discouraged (Suarez, 2004b; Word, 2004). One of the most high-profile reports of early voting problems in Florida came from Palm Beach County, where "One worker wearing her identification badge around her neck was throttled by an irate person 'who tried to choke her with it'" (Kam and Keller, 2004). By the time election day rolled around, the media circus surrounding early voting made it seem like a complete failure.

Concerns about the lack of the fifty-foot non-solicitation zone in the legislation proved prudent, as many voters reported campaign supporters harassing, intimidating, or simply annoying them. Poll workers themselves complained to elections supervisors about campaigners from both major parties, and some quit because of the stress this caused. As Kam and Keller reported, "The early voting problems reveal yet another facet lawmakers failed to consider in their sweeping election reform package passed in the wake of the 2000 fiasco – the establishment of early voting sites without the same protections given to precinct locales on Election Day"(Kam and Keller, 2004, page 1B). In some counties, early voting was nearly shut down: early voting required considerably more staffing than traditional precinct voting.

One oft-cited problem was the number of sites available to voters. Generally, too few machines led to long lines and extended waits. More specifically, however, there was heavy criticism from many interest groups and minority communities about the lack of early voting sites in areas where black, Latino, and low-income residents could vote. When William E. Scheu replaced John Stafford as Duval County election supervisor, he quickly added sites at four regional libraries in Jacksonville, "including one on the city's northwest side, a predominantly black area," in response to the outcry. This and other areas in urban Florida had a history of elections issues affecting minority groups as happened in 2000, when "27,000 ballots were mismarked and thrown out because of misleading instructions" (Word, 2004).

Even at sites with an adequate total number of machines, long waits ensued because of technological limits. In Miami Dade County, for instance, twenty sites were open for early voting. County residents were allowed to vote at any of the twenty sites. However, because machines lacked enough memory to store all the ballot forms needed to address each of the different local issues, only half of the machines at any one site could be used for ballots appropriate for local residents. The remaining machines, which largely went unused, were dedicated to ballots other than those facing the local community. As a result local residents faced long waits while about half the machines in each polling place went unused. Moreover, the publicity given to the long waits seemed to spur people to vote early for fear of an impending election day disaster.

Election reform in Florida, including early voting reform, has not stopped. Problems bedeviled the state's subsequent elections. A highly controversial episode in Sarasota County in 2006, where there were large numbers of undervotes and lost votes, led the state to change to paper-based balloting (or DREs with voter verifiable paper trails) for 2008. Many localities switched to optical scan balloting that required the use of "ballot on demand" printing for early in-person voting. Ballot on demand brought new problems, not the least of which being that it took much longer to process each voter (McCormack, 2008). The result in 2008, when combined with a dramatic increase in early in-person voting (particularly among African Americans enthusiastic about the candidacy of Barack Obama), created long lines in many locations, with voters waiting up to four or more hours to cast their ballot. Early voting lines became such an issue that Governor Charlie Crist issued an executive order to extend early voting from eight to twelve hours. The legislature has not rested on its laurels: in the 2013 session alone, thirteen bills were proposed that change the location, length of time, and technology used for early in-person and no-excuse absentee voting.

In summary, Florida encountered many difficulties in implementing early voting reforms in 2004 and again in 2008. Some of the problems, such as long early voting lines, were also evident in other states (e.g., Georgia). Florida election officials, along with many across the nation, anticipated neither the level of interest in voting early nor the mobilization efforts targeted at this mode of balloting. Finally, elections officials took great care to avoid the problems associated with the 2000 contest, but in their efforts to make sure all ballots were counted accurately, they may have ironically dissuaded many from voting altogether.

It seems clear to us that Florida's system of election administration changed as a direct result of *Bush v. Gore* and the criticism the state received. However, the path of reform has been uneven. The state did provide new avenues for voters to cast a ballot – removing the requirement for an excuse when voting absentee and allowing early in-person voting. The result was a dramatic uptick in the proportion of Florida ballots that were cast prior to election day.

THE INDIVIDUAL VOTER: DID *BUSH V. GORE* CHANGE THE COMPOSITION OF THE EARLY ELECTORATE?

Finally, we sharpen our focus to a final level: the individual voter. In the past, scholars have shown that early voters tend to be those voters who are unaffected by the political campaign – committed partisans and experienced voters (Berinsky, 2005; Gronke and Toffey, 2008; Stein, 1998), although there are recent indications that, as the early voting electorate grows, it naturally begins to look more like the overall electorate (Stein and Vonnahme, 2010). This is especially evident after the 2008 election, where early voting spiked among many segments of the population who had previously resisted these modes of balloting. It is no surprise that committed voters would choose to cast their votes early. At the same time, voters are embedded in a legal and administrative framework, and these institutional channels will obviously encourage certain voting behaviors and discourage others. We want to capture enduring individual characteristics that are associated with early voting and to understand the impact of institutional features, but also see if there are changes in what kinds of citizens have selected the early vote option over the past decade and a half.

The 2008 election, which we have explored in detail elsewhere (Gronke and Hicks, 2009), serves as both an illustration and a caution. After 2000, a number of Southern states relaxed their early voting requirements. Therefore, *ceteris paribus*, we would expect the number of early voters in the South to

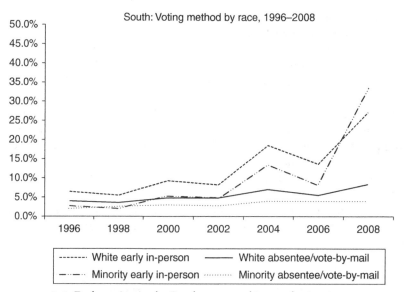

FIGURE 6.6. Early voting in the South among whites and minority voters.

increase, and this is what happened (see Figure 6.6). However, 2008 broke the mold. Once early balloting began in a number of Southern states in 2008, the historic nature of the contest manifested itself at the early voting polling place. An enduring image of the 2008 election will be long lines of African American voters waiting in Miami, Atlanta, Charlotte, and throughout the South to cast a vote for Barack Obama. With hindsight, this should have been obvious: there was virtually nothing that John McCain's campaign could have done to convince African Americans in the South, if not throughout the nation, to cast a different vote.[13] Yet, as we show in this chapter, we can find nothing *distinctive* about 2008 that does not fit the trends of the past decade and a half; African American early voting behavior fits the patterns observed in the past. As we titled our previous piece, 2008 was historic, but may be an anomaly. Only future studies will show whether the changes observed in 2008 will persist.

We next consider two sets of models that provide a more systematic evaluation of the relative impact of individual and institutional variables. The first set uses the Census Bureau's Current Population Survey (CPS), from 1996 to 2008; the second uses the 2008 and 2010 Cooperative Congressional Election Studies (CCES). The CPS provides us with a longitudinal view covering the periods both before and after *Bush v. Gore*, and therefore can be used to gauge whether any seismic shifts are evident at the level of the individual voter. The CCES is missing this depth of time, but does allow us to probe responses (such as ideology and presidential approval) that have been postulated as causes of early voting in the past. In addition, we have structured the models to be closely parallel, so we can replicate the CPS results with the CCES data.

In general, our prior expectations are that race (coded as black/nonblack, based on self-identification in the surveys) will be negatively related to the probability of casting both an absentee and early in-person ballot (except in 2008). Research on the interaction of early voting and voter uncertainty (Alvarez, 1998; Gronke, 2008) also leads us to predict that those with higher incomes and higher levels of education will be more likely to cast early ballots. We are agnostic about any gender effect. Because the legal environment is a crucial feature of a "choice" to cast an early vote, we also include a set of variables that captures the different legal regimes. States can be coded as having: no-excuse absentee balloting; *permanent* no-excuse absentee balloting; early in-person voting; or none of the above. Though we have not attempted explicitly to capture additional variation in administrative procedures, we did include regional dummy variables in an effort to control for unobserved regional heterogeneity.

With a richer set of indicators for the CCES, we added measures of presidential approval, ideological extremism, and interest in the news. In each case, our underlying assumption is that those voters who are more ideologically committed to a position, or who are highly informed, would be more likely to cast an early vote.[14] To simplify the presentation, we have included only one table of results, for the 2008 and 2010 CCES. All the results from the CPS are included in the appendix, but we have provided graphical displays throughout the body text that provide a more easily digested summary of the results. All analyses were produced via multinomial logit.[15]

The CPS is a very large survey – more than 30,000 respondents say they voted in each year – and therefore virtually every indicator is a statistically significant indicator of the mode of voting. We won't concentrate on statistical significance, therefore, but the interested reader may wish to peruse the results in the appendix (Tables A1 and A2). Instead, we want to highlight a number of important patterns that we believe help us understand the changing world of early voting, and, by implication, campaigns and elections in the United States.

In some respects, the CPS results confirm our expectations: the legal regime makes a tremendous difference in helping to predict whether a respondent cast an early in-person, no-excuse absentee, or election day ballot. This is not a "finding" as much it is a legal truism: you can't vote early if it's illegal! What we find intriguing, however, is that *independent* of the legal regime, regional differences in the use of voting by mail and early in-person balloting are robust. The top panel of Figure 6.7 plots the predicted probability of voting early in person and by mail for "average" respondents, since 1992, varying only the regions, West and South, where there has been the most dynamism in the past quarter century.[16] The graph shows that the average respondent who lives in the West has a 30 percent probability of voting by mail from 2002 onward – this compares to approximately 5 percent in the Northeast – all other things held equal *including* the early voting laws. The figure also highlights the very rapid growth of early in-person voting in the South that accompanied yet was in addition to changes in the laws. The spike in early in-person turnout in 2008 is apparent, as is the decline in 2010. Finally, we note the dramatic jump in the probability that a Westerner will vote early in person in 2008 and 2010. This is an intriguing result, one that is replicated in the 2010 CCES, and is unexpected. Up to now, Westerners have been overwhelmingly "vote by mail" voters.

What do these results imply? Obviously, election laws matter, but they seem to do more than just provide for new legal channels. These data indicate that the laws may cause a cultural shift in the way citizens in particular regions think about voting, choosing new modes at a rate above and beyond what we'd predict based on the laws alone. Alternatively, it may be that laws don't alter voting behavior as much as they alter campaign behavior, and the "above and beyond" effect evidenced here is a function of campaign mobilization.

The lower panel of Figure 6.7 reports a parallel analysis for African Americans. The data here is less surprising and replicates what we saw in Figure 6.6. Other than the unusual spike in the probability of EIP voting in 2002, the Obama effect on the probability that an African American would opt for an early ballot is obvious. What is less clear is whether 2010 shows a regression to the mean, or if African Americans are settling down to a new, higher equilibrium level of early in-person and by-mail balloting.

The results of the first CPS model are reported in the left-hand columns of Tables 6.1 and 6.2, and support most of our expectations. As predicted, better-educated voters are more likely to cast an early ballot by either mode. We also found that higher-income voters are more likely to report casting an early in-person ballot – though not an absentee ballot, contrary to previous work. Our model predicts that blacks are indeed less likely to cast an absentee ballot, but there is an insignificant relationship with early in-person voting, a relationship we examine more closely in the second model. Finally, and unsurprisingly, the legal context is tremendously influential in explaining the probability that an early in-person, absentee, or precinct ballot will be cast. Voters can't vote early if they aren't allowed to do so.

What of the effect of education? Scholars have long noticed that the early electorate is a more partisan, ideological, older, and educated electorate. Our results support some, but not all, of these observations. Older voters remain more likely to cast an early ballot (by either mode), but the relationship with income appears uneven across the years, and seems to be weakening since 2004 (compare Table A1 before and after 2004). What we find distinctive, however, is that we consistently find stronger and more statistically significant relationships between education and early in-person voting than we do for voting by mail. This result is replicated in the CCES studies. Figure 6.8 plots the logit coefficients and their 95 percent confidence intervals from 1996 to 2010 for VBM (top panel) and EIP (bottom panel). The relationship between education and VBM is always weaker, and in two cases (1998 and 2002) is

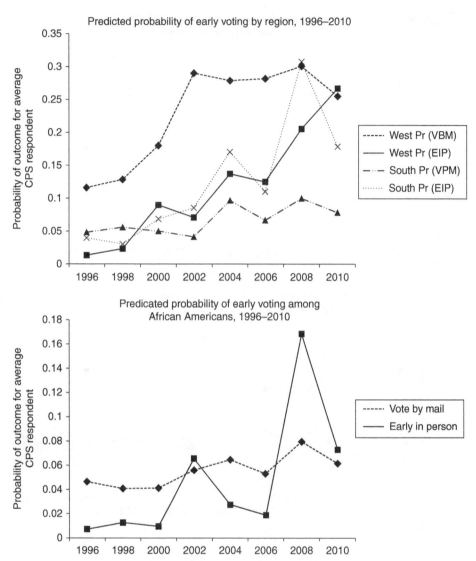

FIGURE 6.7. Region, race, and early voting, 1996–2010.

not statistically significant, indicated by the confidence interval crossing zero. The coefficients for EIP, however, are larger, significant (except for 1998), and are more precise (the 95% ranges are smaller). They are also oddly consistent, something for which we don't have a good explanation at this time, but is notable.

We remark on this pattern because it is largely replicated in the CCES, albeit with a much richer set of attitudinal and demographic indicators. Table 6.1

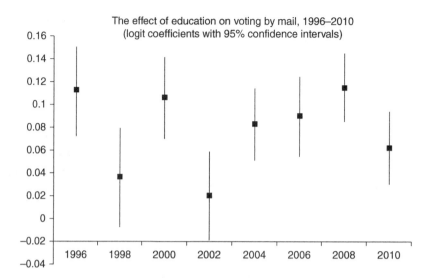

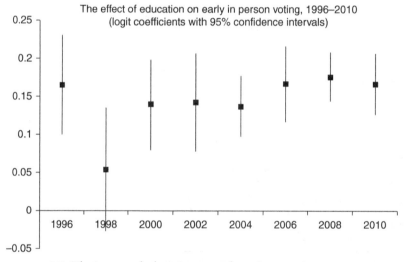

FIGURE 6.8. The impact of education on early voting, 1996–2010.

reports the results of a multinomial logit analysis of early voting (precinct voting is the baseline group) for 2008 and 2010. We will not comment in depth on the legal effects – they remain, as expected, substantial. We also find that respondents who strongly approved of President Bush's performance were less likely to vote early (by either mode) in 2008, while those who approved of Obama were more likely to vote early in the 2010 midterm elections. There are campaign-specific impacts on the patterns of early and by-mail voting that cry out for future exploration.

TABLE 6.1. *Predicting the Choice to Vote Early, 2008 and 2010*

	2008 CCES		2010 CCES	
Early in Person				
Male	−0.039	0.047	0.016	0.044
Black	**0.636**	0.123	**0.354**	0.116
Black * South	−0.081	0.131	−0.218	0.142
Hispanic	0.095	0.054	−0.023	0.079
Education	**0.142**	0.018	**0.113**	0.015
Age	**0.013**	0.002	**0.017**	0.002
Extremism	0.051	0.064	**0.184**	0.056
Presidential Approval	**−0.475**	0.075	**0.191**	0.035
Interest in the News	**0.208**	0.038	**0.307**	0.035
Early in Person	**2.831**	0.076	**2.727**	0.092
No Excuse	**−0.354**	0.048	**−0.666**	0.058
Permanent	**−1.841**	0.174	**−2.460**	0.131
West	**1.603**	0.174	**2.691**	0.158
Midwest	**0.595**	0.137	**0.547**	0.135
South	**1.822**	0.138	**1.783**	0.129
Constant	**−6.080**	0.224	**−7.178**	0.203
Vote by Mail				
Male	**−0.157**	0.077	**−0.116**	0.043
Black	−0.030	0.121	−0.037	0.075
Black * South	−0.040	0.155	**−0.643**	0.154
Hispanic	−0.092	0.096	0.087	0.081
Education	**0.046**	0.021	0.020	0.014
Age	**0.026**	0.004	**0.027**	0.002
Extremism	0.074	0.062	0.002	0.050
Presidential Approval	**−0.231**	0.057	**0.076**	0.033
Interest in the News	0.060	0.034	−0.031	0.029
Early in Person	**−1.060**	0.089	**−1.188**	0.078
No Excuse	**1.744**	0.108	**1.589**	0.088
Permanent	**0.163**	0.079	**0.433**	0.086
West	**2.658**	0.120	**2.826**	0.094
Midwest	**1.636**	0.123	**1.498**	0.093
South	**1.564**	0.123	**1.498**	0.090
Constant	**−4.885**	0.297	**−4.720**	0.169
N of Cases	22667		36905	

Notes: Data are from the 2008 and 2010 CCES. Estimates are multinomial logit coefficients. Boldface entries are statistically significant (p<.05).

What we find particularly compelling, however, is that the pattern of results mirrors the CPS in terms of education and political interest and the explicability of EIP versus VBM. Keeping in mind that the independent variables are on the same range in the top and bottom panels, the coefficient

TABLE 6.2. *Education and Early Voting in 2008 and 2010*

	2008 CCES		2010 CCES	
	EIP	VBM	EIP	VBM
Education				
No HS	0.215	0.171	0.181	0.154
HS Grad	0.238	0.172	0.198	0.154
Some College	0.263	0.172	0.216	0.153
2-Year	0.289	0.172	0.235	0.151
4-Year	0.317	0.171	0.255	0.150
Post Grad	0.346	0.170	0.276	0.148

Notes: Cell entries are predicted probabilities associated with a change in the listed variable, holding all variables at their mean or appropriate values for dummy variables. Values calculated with the SPOST procedure in Stata.

on education is three and five times as large in the EIP models as it is in the VBM models. The size of these differences is substantial – in Table 6.2 we report the predicted probabilities of EIP and VBM voting across different educational levels. The message of the table is clear: more education leads to more early in-person voting, while it makes no difference for voting by mail. Interest in the news and politics similarly provide substantial explanatory leverage for whether you cast an early in-person ballot, but not whether you cast one by mail.

What does this mean for candidates who want to harvest early votes or for election administrators who want to encourage early voting? For voting by mail, it is a case of building it, and they will come, but little else seems to encourage the VBM voter. Early in-person voting, in contrast, is not just responsive to laws, but also to politics. Sparks in political motivation, interest, and political approval translate into much higher probabilities of early in-person voting.

CONCLUSION

Scholars of American political history will remain interested in the 2000 contest, and we believe the first decade of the new millennium will be known as a decade of election reform. Early voting reform, however, was already more than a decade old in 2000. There are, on the face of it, compelling reasons to think that *Bush v. Gore* would have had altered the trajectory of early voting. The political turmoil prompted many states and local jurisdictions to reexamine their election procedures, both on their own and in response to the landmark passage of the Help American Vote Act in 2002. Was early voting swept up in a tidal wave of reform?

HAVA made few explicit references to absentee ballots and no references to early in-person voting. Most provisions dealt with standardization of the treatment of UOCAVA ballots but the act did require that states regularize their procedures for handling absentee ballots and centralize how they disseminate information about absentee ballots. It also mandated two studies that implicated vote by mail, one of vote fraud and a second of no-cost postage for absentee ballots. In short, the direct impact of HAVA on early and absentee voting was minimal.

However, the world is seldom so simple. We would argue that HAVA's impact was more substantial, although indirect. HAVA planted seeds in a soil made fertile for reform and provided funding for states to adopt new voting machines. Many turned to direct recording electronic machines (DRE) as a way to resolve past problems with elections. The new technology created opportunities for those who wanted extend early in-person voting, because delivering the many ballot styles required in an early voting location (or vote center) is far easier and cheaper using DREs. DREs made early voting with satellite locations technically and fiscally feasible, which we know leads to a higher take up among voters (Stein and Garcia-Monet, 1997). HAVA funding was key in widespread deployment of DREs, and even though HAVA did not mandate more early in-person voting, the opportunities became available as a direct result of HAVA.

However, to some extent the low-hanging fruit had already been picked: reform-minded jurisdictions (like the populist, politically active Western states) had already implemented their changes. The new entrants to the early voting states after 2002 jumped on the train that had already left the station. And voters followed suit, casting early in-person and absentee ballots in increasing numbers throughout the decade, to a point where, by 2008, more than one-third of the electorate cast a ballot at a time and place other than on election day at their local precinct. There is no indication that these trends will slow. Early voting is here to stay.

Any map of early voting has to start with the legal regime. This chapter has shown that there are many dynamic elements to early in-person voting, but voting by mail, while substantial in level, is resistant to forces beyond the specific legal regime for permissible modes voting that is in place. Laws simply set the stage. Campaigns, candidates, and vote mobilization organizations write the early voting script and play the primary role in stimulating not just turnout, but mode of turnout.

Notes

1   Chapter 7 in the case book gives extended treatment to the Court's decision.
2   See, for example, volume 29 (2001–02) of the *Florida State University Law Review* dedicated to *Bush v. Gore*, also Ackerman (2002) and Hasen (2007).

3   There is some disagreement over nomenclature in the field. For the purposes of this
     chapter, we will use the generic term *early voting* to refer to any mode by which
     voters cast a ballot prior to election day. We will use *early in-person* to designate
     early voting at an elections office or satellite location, *voting by mail* and *no-excuse
     absentee voting* interchangeably to designate ballots that are most often sent and
     returned by mail, and *precinct* and *election day voting* to describe the traditional
     practice of voting in the local precinct on election day. This usage reflects the ter-
     minology of election officials and that adopted by the Federal Election Assistance
     Commission in the Election Administration and Voting Survey, as well as that used
     in the American National Election Study (although Gronke wrote both sets of
     questions). We will attempt to avoid imprecise terms such as *convenience voting*,
     which could encompass reforms such as *voting centers*, and *advance voting*.

4   There is no agreement about terminology regarding early voting, either among
     academics or election administrators. We rely on the most common usage among
     election officials, which is also reflected in the terms and categories used in the
     Federal Election Assistance Commission's Election Administration and Voting
     Survey (http://www.eac.gov/research/election_administration_and_voting_survey.
     aspx). Gronke worked as a subcontractor on the 2008 report and helped write
     the early and absentee voting items.In this chapter, we use *early voting* as a generic
     term to describe voting prior to election day, even though the reality is that some
     jurisdictions allow voters to return absentee ballots by hand on election day (most
     notably California). We use the more specific terms *early in person* to refer to vot-
     ing early (in person) on an election machine and *no-excuse absentee* to refer to
     voting on a paper absentee ballot that is most often returned through the post. We
     will reserve *vote by mail* for those two fully vote-by-mail systems in Oregon and
     Washington.

5   See Gronke and Galanes-Rosenbaum (2008) and Fortier (2006) for an extended
     review of the history of absentee balloting.

6   Figures taken from the National Conference on State Legislatures, http://www.
     ncsl.org/LegislaturesElections/ElectionsCampaigns/AbsenteeandEarlyVoting/
     tabid/16604/Default.aspx.

7   The Military and Overseas Voter Empowerment Act (MOVE) was enacted in 2009
     as a way to provide greater protections and expand ballot access to members of the
     military and overseas citizens, often referred to by the acronym UOCAVA (coined
     from the original Uniformed and Overseas Citizens Absentee Voting Act of 1986).

8   Prior to 2000, the AP did not collect election returns broken down by mode.

9   We have chosen not to report the absentee figures prior to 1996 because only the
     tabular responses are provided by the census, and the data cannot be weighted to
     provide accurate national and regional estimates. The total number of absentee
     ballots (unweighted) prior to 1996 were very low: 2.5 percent in 1974 and 4 per-
     cent in 1980. Academic and other commercial surveys did not ask about early in-
     person and absentee voting until 2004 or later.

10   A legislative proposal database assembled by the National Conference of State
     Legislatures (http://www.ncsl.org) allows tracking of proposed (and passed) legis-
     lation on a variety of topics. These data have only been collected since 2000. We
     have not evaluated these proposals in terms of how many were eventually passed.

11   The Associated Press Elections Unit provided these data. "Advance" voting is
     reported rather than early in-person and absentee voting because, prior to 2004,

few states reported turnout via the various modes. Even in 2010, many states continued to report "advance" voting and did not separate early in-person and absentee ballots in their official return. The box plot includes the lowest and highest observations (the "whiskers"), the median (the horizontal line in each box), and the lower and upper quartiles of the distribution (the box).

12 Florida Revised Statutes 101.657 pertains to early in-person voting, and 101.6101–65 pertains to absentee ballots.

13 It is of course well known that African Americans affiliate overwhelmingly with the Democratic Party and vote at a 90 percent rate for Democratic presidential candidates, but 2008 was notable even compared to that baseline. The 2008 National Election Study found three (unweighted) African American respondents who did not say they had voted for Obama.

14 We chose not to include any measures of partisan sentiments because past work by Stein (1998) and Berinsky (2005) has shown no partisan advantage to early in-person or no-excuse absentee voting.

15 The dependent variable for all of our models is a three-outcome measure: voting on election day (always the base category), voting early in person, or voting by mail or absentee. The main difference between multinomial logit (MNL) and multinomial probit (MNP) is that MNL is more restrictive in that it assumes independence of irrelevant alternatives (IIA). This has led some to suggest the use of MNP in electoral contexts, especially multiparty races (Alvarez and Nagler, 1998). It is not clear whether the multicandidate provides guidance in other contexts. Dow and Endersby (2004) argue that the IIA assumption is not that restrictive in many instances. In one respect, we feel confident that modes of voting are not in competition the same way that candidates or parties are. On the other hand, there is the devilishly complex problem that some voters have no "choice" because early in-person or no-excuse absentee voting is not available. It should come as no surprise in the models that follow that the legal framework is overwhelmingly influential in determining whether many early votes were cast. We have deferred these complicated issues for further research. To assure the reader, we have conducted parallel analyses using MNL and MNP for all years, and have reported one such analysis in the appendix. The results are virtually identical. Ultimately, we relied on MNL for a very practical reason: there are many more post-estimation tools available for MNL to help convey results to the reader.

16 Practically speaking, this means we set all variables to their mean and set dummy variables to reasonable values (male and nonblack). We set the legal regime so that both early in-person and no-excuse absentee voting were allowed, but we did not allow for permanent no-excuse absentee voting for this comparison.

APPENDIX TABLE A1. *Multinomial Logit Results: 1996–2010 Current Population Study*

Vote by Mail	1996		1998		2000		2002		2006		2008		2010	
	Coeff	Std Err	Coeff	Std Err	Coeff	Std Err	Coeff	Std Err	Coeff	Std Err	Coeff	Std Err	Coeff	Std Err
Education	0.112	0.020	0.036	0.022	0.106	0.018	0.021	0.020	0.090	0.018	0.083	0.016	0.090	0.018
Black	-0.245	0.118	-0.278	0.131	-0.655	0.115	-0.361	0.117	-0.620	0.128	-0.607	0.105	-0.620	0.128
South x Black	-0.284	0.211	0.050	0.222	0.135	0.189	0.146	0.199	0.171	0.196	-0.058	0.160	0.171	0.196
Male	-0.113	0.042	-0.142	0.048	-0.133	0.039	-0.083	0.041	-0.190	0.037	-0.047	0.033	-0.190	0.037
Income	0.005	0.007	-0.009	0.008	-0.015	0.007	-0.017	0.007	-0.032	0.006	-0.017	0.005	-0.032	0.006
Age	0.023	0.001	0.025	0.002	0.022	0.001	0.027	0.002	0.024	0.001	0.023	0.001	0.024	0.001
No Excuse	0.683	0.063	0.909	0.067	0.548	0.058	1.010	0.070	1.667	0.085	1.659	0.067	1.667	0.085
Early In Person	-0.427	0.066	-0.304	0.065	-0.419	0.055	-0.731	0.071	-1.455	0.071	-1.090	0.062	-1.455	0.071
Permanent	0.813	0.092	0.945	0.101	1.000	0.093	-0.804	0.072	-1.007	0.071	-0.842	0.063	-1.007	0.071
West	1.282	0.083	1.805	0.104	1.698	0.079	2.698	0.089	2.979	0.089	1.818	0.068	2.979	0.089
Midwest	0.609	0.073	0.848	0.098	0.596	0.071	0.991	0.087	1.523	0.097	0.568	0.067	1.523	0.097
South	0.205	0.080	0.532	0.107	0.230	0.077	0.391	0.097	1.192	0.099	0.545	0.069	1.192	0.099
Constant	-4.749	0.142	-5.025	0.175	-4.334	0.135	-4.868	0.157	-4.894	0.152	-4.262	0.114	-4.894	0.152
Early in Person														
Education	0.166	0.033	0.055	0.041	0.140	0.030	0.143	0.033	0.167	0.025	0.137	0.020	0.167	0.025
Black	-0.079	0.288	0.896	0.260	-0.300	0.285	0.150	0.223	-0.283	0.239	0.054	0.182	-0.283	0.239
South xBlack	-0.357	0.332	-1.479	0.338	0.110	0.310	-0.308	0.260	0.015	0.265	-0.100	0.198	0.015	0.265
Male	-0.070	0.072	-0.045	0.086	-0.078	0.062	0.013	0.070	0.028	0.052	-0.042	0.042	0.028	0.052
Income	0.037	0.012	0.022	0.014	0.038	0.011	-0.001	0.011	0.003	0.009	0.023	0.007	0.003	0.009
Age	0.023	0.002	0.022	0.003	0.020	0.002	0.018	0.002	0.024	0.002	0.015	0.001	0.024	0.002
No Excuse	-1.858	0.161	-1.901	0.143	-1.640	0.096	-0.991	0.100	-0.996	0.064	-0.946	0.050	-0.996	0.064
Early In Person	3.291	0.106	3.158	0.128	3.142	0.089	2.407	0.096	2.845	0.105	3.096	0.076	2.845	0.105
Permanent	-20.842	0.137	1.355	0.478	0.702	0.594	-0.240	0.266	-0.368	0.180	0.799	0.159	-0.368	0.180
West	1.752	0.256	2.204	0.245	2.157	0.211	2.124	0.225	2.173	0.203	1.793	0.142	2.173	0.203
Midwest	1.586	0.215	0.632	0.247	1.026	0.210	0.341	0.238	-0.032	0.210	0.244	0.151	-0.032	0.210
South	1.349	0.214	1.076	0.244	1.689	0.197	1.984	0.218	1.714	0.192	1.785	0.134	1.714	0.192
Constant	-7.810	0.287	-7.142	0.351	-7.436	0.258	-7.088	0.312	-7.383	0.251	-6.736	0.168	-7.383	0.251
N of Obs	45202		35288		42887		40799		39831		53645		39831	

Note: Election day voting is the base outcome. Analyses conducted with Stata 12 using the survey module. Results for 2004 are contained in Table A2.

APPENDIX TABLE A2. *Comparing Probit and Logit Estimates for 2004*

VBM	Multinomial Probit			Multinomial Logit		
	Coeff	Std Error	T–Stat	Coeff	Std Error	T–Stat
Education	0.062	0.012	5.11	0.083	0.016	5.13
Black	−0.461	0.074	−6.2	−0.607	0.105	−5.79
South x Black	0.022	0.107	0.21	−0.058	0.160	−0.36
Male	−0.031	0.025	−1.26	−0.047	0.033	−1.44
Income	−0.013	0.004	−3.41	−0.017	0.005	−3.41
Age	0.017	0.001	20.05	0.023	0.001	20.66
No Excuse	0.918	0.051	17.94	1.659	0.067	24.82
Early In Person	−0.456	0.048	−9.44	−1.090	0.062	−17.66
Permanent	−0.351	0.053	−6.59	−0.842	0.063	−13.3
West	1.403	0.050	28.33	1.818	0.068	26.88
Midwest	0.358	0.046	7.84	0.568	0.067	8.47
South	0.410	0.047	8.71	0.545	0.069	7.91
Constant	−3.208	0.081	−39.5	−4.262	0.114	−37.51
Early In Person						
Education	0.101	0.014	7	0.137	0.020	6.74
Black	−0.047	0.115	−0.41	0.054	0.182	0.3
South x Black	−0.049	0.129	−0.38	−0.100	0.198	−0.51
Male	−0.025	0.030	−0.83	−0.042	0.042	−1
Income	0.011	0.005	2.45	0.023	0.007	3.46
Age	0.011	0.001	12.35	0.015	0.001	11.5
No Excuse	−0.623	0.038	−16.22	−0.946	0.050	−19.03
Early In Person	1.953	0.045	43.2	3.096	0.076	40.72
Permanent	0.567	0.086	6.6	0.799	0.159	5.04
West	1.150	0.073	15.68	1.793	0.142	12.61
Midwest	0.086	0.077	1.11	0.244	0.151	1.62
South	1.042	0.065	15.93	1.785	0.134	13.31
Constant	−4.499	0.102	−44.27	−6.736	0.168	−39.99
F Statistic		321.12			303.78	
N of Observations		42887			42887	

Note: Election day voting is the base outcome. Analyses conducted with Stata 12 using the survey module. Results for 2004 are contained in Table A2.

7

Absentee Ballot Regimes: Easing Costs or Adding a Step?

Jan E. Leighley and Jonathan Nagler

INTRODUCTION

There has been a revolution in voting in the United States in the past forty years. In 1972, voters in only two states had the option to request an absentee ballot without showing cause. In 2008, twenty-seven states allowed voters this opportunity. In 1972, voters in forty-five out of fifty states who were voting at a polling place did so on election day. In 2008, voters in thirty-one states could cast in-person votes on multiple days (notwithstanding the statute that designates the Tuesday after the first Monday in November as election day).[1]

There are obvious political questions about the impact of these changes. Any time an electoral institution is changed we want to know if this will advantage one particular party or another, generally by making it harder or easier for partisans of that party to vote or by changing the incentives of parties to mobilize particular voters. In the case of these laws, the most obvious question to ask is whether they have affected turnout. If we make "election day" span two weeks rather than one day, we have significantly increased the opportunities people have to vote. Will otherwise nonvoters take advantage of those opportunities, or were they nonvoters by choice: they simply do not want to vote? Much of the existing research suggests that offering additional ways of voting has not raised turnout, but simply shifted the mechanism by which people vote (Stein, 1998; Stein and Garcia-Monet, 1997).

We know that the turnout of registered voters is much higher than the turnout of nonregistered voters. So, if we make it easier for people to register, and increase the pool of registered voters, will we increase turnout? And if so, the turnout of whom? Young? Old? Rich? Poor? Democrats? Republicans?

In this chapter we look at a particular set of institutions designed to make it easier for people to vote, those associated with absentee voting. In other work we have shown that absentee voting leads to higher levels of turnout (Leighley and Nagler, 2009). But as with most changes in electoral laws, the devil can be in the details. While twenty-seven states allow for no-fault absentee voting, they differ in what persons must do to request an absentee ballot. Do these differences matter? Changes in implementation of laws have had effects on turnout for a long time. The Fourteenth Amendment gave blacks the right to vote. But poll taxes and literacy tests were quite effective at keeping black turnout low. Allowing voters to cast an absentee ballot might have minimal impact on turnout if voters cannot easily get an absentee ballot. The potential upside of absentee balloting is that it removes the cost of showing up to a specific site on election day and potentially waiting in a line for as long as three hours (or more).[2]

However, the additional hurdle imposed by absentee balloting is that the voter must *acquire the ballot*. If this process is sufficiently costly or complex, it might outweigh the convenience of avoiding the in-person balloting experience. States vary systematically in how they allow persons to request and acquire an absentee ballot. Some states allow voters to request absentee ballots by mail. And some states allow voters to request ballots electronically: either via e-mail or via the Web. In addition, in some states voters can remove this cost of requesting the ballot "in perpetuity" (or at least as long as they maintain their present address) by requesting permanent absentee ballot status (as opposed to having to request a ballot for each election).

There is good reason to believe that all of these administrative changes could affect the use of absentee balloting to vote. For thirty years political scientists have been preaching that lowering the costs of voting could increase turnout, and that a particularly nefarious cost of the American electoral system is that people go through a two-step process to vote: first register, then vote. The need to request an absentee ballot effectively makes voting a two-step process, even *after* a voter is registered. And it shares the characteristic of registration that has proven so crucial: it must happen before the election. If voters can remove this step by acquiring permanent absentee status, it should significantly enhance the impact of absentee voting.

Similarly, being able to request a ballot by mail is a much smaller cost than having to request a ballot in person. But being able to request a ballot by e-mail is a smaller cost still. We have started to gather evidence that doing tasks by e-mail can impose much less of a burden than requesting things by mail.

In this chapter we examine specifically the impact of allowing permanent absentee voter status for states that allow no-fault absentee voting. While much has been made in the press about absentee voting, there is a tension in that it eases the cost of casting a ballot, but increases the procedural burden on the voter by forcing the voter to separate the acts of requesting and returning the ballot. And there is an obvious policy question that we are addressing here: Would states that have no-fault absentee voting see larger increases in turnout if they allowed voters to request permanent absentee status? We test the impact of availability of permanent absentee status using data on turnout in presidential elections from 1972 to 2008. We describe the data and methods later on.

CHANGES IN LAWS

In *Who Votes?* Wolfinger and Rosenstone described several key provisions that function as procedural barriers to voting. The key hurdle they identified was the need to be registered *prior to election day*. And they focused on how far in advance registration was required. They also looked at other aspects of registration. But there simply was not that much variation. Thus they examined the availability of evening hours to register and the availability of places to register other than the county seat. But their key finding, repeated many times, is that the most effective reform available to increase voter turnout would be to move the closing of the registration period closer to election day. The obvious implication of this is that nothing could be more effective than moving the registration period all the way to election day and simply letting people register at the polls. This belief in the efficacy of easier registration has led many states to adopt some form of election day registration (EDR). In 2008 nine states either had some form of EDR or simply had no registration (North Dakota).[3]

However, the number of voters currently affected by EDR provisions is dwarfed by the number of voters currently affected by early voting and absentee voting. Early voting does not alleviate the burden of registration. But it does give people more opportunities to vote. Logically, it follows that this could boost turnout. Similarly, absentee voting was intended as a reform to make voting easier. In Table 7.1 we give the number of states that offered each of these voting or registration options from 1972 to 2008. The numbers are self-explanatory: the voting landscape has changed drastically over time. In 1972, voters in only two states had the option of no-fault absentee voting, whereas in 2008 no-fault absentee voting was an option in twenty-seven states. Similarly, whereas in 1972 voters in only five states had the option of in-person early voting, during the 2008 election voters in thirty-one states had this option.

These changes are so dramatic that the United States no longer has a single election *day*, but rather an election *period* that can last as long as twenty-one days preceding the Tuesday following the first Monday in November. Some estimate that approximately 33 percent of ballots in the 2008 election were cast either as absentee ballots or via some form of early voting (Early Voter Information Center, http://www.earlyvoting.net/faq). There has also been a large proportionate increase in the states offering election day registration, which was not available in any state in 1972, but was available to voters in nine states in 2008.[4] However, in absolute terms, election day registration is still available to relatively few voters in the United States.

As is often the case, the devil may be in the details. Absentee voting on its face seems to make voting easier: no waiting in line! However, to vote absentee, one needs a ballot. And the states vary considerably in the hurdles a voter must cross to receive a ballot. What should maximize the use of absentee voting would be for the state to remove the requirement of requesting the ballot by simply mailing it to the potential voter, requiring no action on the voter's part. This is in effect what eleven of the twenty-seven no-fault absentee voting states

TABLE 7.1. *Adoption of Voting Reforms*

Number of States with:

	No-Fault Absentee Voting	In-Person Early Voting	Election Day Registration
1972	2	5	0
1976	3	6	3
1980	6	7	3
1984	6	7	3
1988	6	9	3
1992	12	11	3
1996	16	14	6
2000	11	22	6
2004	14	27	6
2008	27	31	9

TABLE 7.2. *Absentee Voting Regimes*

	No-Fault Absentee Voting	Permanent Absentee Status[a]	Online Ballot Request	Mail Ballot Request	No Fault No Help[b]
1972	2	0	0	1	1
1976	3	0	0	2	1
1980	6	0	0	3	3
1984	6	1	0	3	2
1988	6	2	0	3	2
1992	12	3	0	8	3
1996	16	4	0	11	4
2000	22	7	0	13	6
2004	24	7	3	15	6
2008	27	11	6	16	7

[a] Cell entries in columns 2 through 4 are the number of states *with no-fault absentee voting* that have the indicated absentee ballot provision available.

[b] Cell entries in the last column give the number of states that offer no-fault absentee voting, but offer *none of*: permanent absentee status, online ballot requests, or mail ballot requests.

do by offering voters the option to register for permanent absentee voter status. While the other sixteen no-fault states allow for absentee voting without cause, they still require the voter to actively request the ballot for each election in which they want to cast an absentee ballot. (Though we note that none of these states goes as far as Oregon, which conducts vote-by-mail elections and mails all registered voters ballots whether they ask for them or not.)

Table 7.2 gives the distribution of how different states allow for requests of absentee ballots. In 2008, six states allowed for some form of online (Web or e-mail) request for an absentee ballot, and sixteen allowed for a mail-in ballot request. However, we note that of the twenty-seven states offering no-fault absentee voting in 2008, seven of them offered no help in obtaining the ballot. In these states voters could not sign up for permanent absentee ballot status, nor could they request an absentee ballot online or by mail.[5] And, even in the twenty-two states that allowed for either online or mail ballot requests, the burden still rests on the potential absentee voter to request the ballot prior to election day.[6]

Table 7.3 lists the states with different configurations of no-fault absentee voting rules in 2008 (states not listed do not allow for no-fault absentee voting). There does not appear to be anything systematic about which states have which sets of rules, though one might note that the West Coast states with no-fault absentee voting are more likely to allow for permanent absentee status than are non-Western states with no-fault absentee voting.

EFFECT OF REFORMS ON TURNOUT

The adoption of different forms of absentee voting by different states at different times over the period from 1972 to 2008 gives us an excellent opportunity to learn the effects of the provisions on turnout. Early work on the effects of different regulations on turnout was cross-sectional. Wolfinger and Rosenstone (1980) examined the behavior of individuals in different states with different voting rules, and when the behavior was observed to vary systematically with the rules they inferred that the rules were the cause of the observed variation. There are several caveats with this sort of inference. First, it may simply be the luck of the draw – there may be omitted variables that happen to be correlated with the presence of the measured reforms that affect turnout. Second, this may not be the luck of the draw, but rather may be the systematic tendency of states that would have high turnout regardless of the enactment of certain reforms to choose to enact said reforms. In other words, the same factors that make some states high-turnout states might also make them low-institutional-barriers-to-turnout states. If this is the case, then drawing the inference that it is the institutional factor, rather than the unobserved characteristic that led to adoption of the institutional factor, that led to increased turnout would be mistaken.

The adoption of reforms by different states over time offers a way around this inferential problem. If a given state adopts an institutional factor at time t, and turnout goes up following the adoption of the reform relative to any increase in turnout in other states, then we can have substantial confidence that the institutional factor directly caused the increase in turnout.[7] Thus we can use turnout in each state for each presidential election from 1972 to 2008, combined with the adoption of reforms in each state, to estimate a cross-sectional time series model of turnout and determine the impact of institutional changes on turnout.

We use a model here very similar to the cross-sectional time series model we used in earlier work (Leighley and Nagler, 2009). Along with the institutional

TABLE 7.3. *State Absentee Voting Regimes, 2008*

Set of Rules	States
No-Fault Absentee Voting and Permanent Absentee Status	Arkansas, Arizona, California, Colorado, Hawaii Kansas, Montana, Oregon, Utah, Washington, Wisconsin
No-Fault Absentee Voting and either *mail requests or online requests* for ballots	Florida, Georgia, Indiana, Maine, Nevada, New Jersey, Oklahoma, Vermont, Wyoming
No-Fault Absentee Voting without permanent absentee status, online ballot requests, or mail ballot requests	Maryland, Nebraska, New Mexico, North Carolina, North Dakota, South Dakota, Ohio

factors we are interested in examining, we include in the model demographic and electoral factors known to be related to turnout. As people with higher levels of income vote more than people with lower levels of income, we include state per capita income. And as older people vote more than younger people, we include a series of variables measuring the proportion of voting-aged citizens between the ages of 25–30, 31–45, 46–60, 61–76, and 76–84, with the 18–24-year-old age group the omitted category. Education is the other key demographic variable known to be related to turnout, and we include the proportion of citizens in the state who: are high school graduates; have some college; and who have college or beyond, with those who have not graduated high school the omitted group.

To account for the impact of the political (as opposed to legal) environment on voter turnout, we included dummy variables for the presence of a gubernatorial or senate election, and we included measures of the competitiveness of the presidential race in the state, and the senate and gubernatorial races. Finally, we include fixed effects for the individual states, and we include election (year) specific fixed effects. This means that any effect we observe of the institutional factors on turnout can only come from changes in those institutional factors over time. This is exactly what we would like to estimate to draw a strong causal inference.

In previous work we have examined the effects of different registration and voting reforms on the level of turnout (Leighley and Nagler, 2014). Simply comparing turnout pre adoption of EDR to post adoption of EDR, using a straightforward difference-in-differences approach, we found that the Wave I EDR states experienced a net increase of 4.5 percentage points in turnout since adopting EDR. And using more thorough cross-sectional time series analysis, we found that adopting EDR increased a state's turnout by approximately 2.8 percentage points (assuming a fifteen-day closing period for registration). We also found that absentee voting increased turnout, though we did not examine the types of ballot-request rules used.

However, here we specify the form of availability of no-fault absentee voting more thoroughly. Rather than simply coding for the existence of no-fault absentee voting, we code for the availability of no-fault absentee voting and the availability of permanent absentee status. Our hypothesis, as explained earlier, is that no-fault absentee voting should have a substantially larger effect on turnout when permanent absentee status is available.

We estimate a model of the following form, where s, t, and d index state and time respectively (we also estimate the model by demographic groups; here we suppress the d subscript):

$$T_{s,t} = \beta_0 + \beta_1 T_{s,t-1}$$
$$+ \beta_2 \, DaysToClosing_{s,t} + \beta_3 \, EDR_{s,t}$$
$$+ \beta_{23} \, (EDR_{s,t} * DaysToClosing_{s,t})$$
$$+ \beta_4 \, NoFaultAbsentee_{s,t} + \beta_{4.1} \, PermNoFaultAbsentee_{s,t}$$

TABLE 7.4. *Multivariate Model of Turnout by State – 1972–2008*

	Coefficient	t–statistic
Log–Odds Turnout (t–1)	0.532***	(6.88)
Days to Closing	−0.00152*	(−1.58)
No–Fault Early Voting	−0.081***	(−2.83)
Early Voting Period	0.00298**	(2.30)
No–Fault Absentee Voting	0.051***	(3.14)
Permanent Absentee Status	−.0037*	(−0.13)
EDR	0.01086	(0.16)
EDR * Days–to–Closing	0.0037**	(1.16)
DMV Registration	0.0049	(0.25)
State Per–Capita Income	−7.09e–06	(−1.01)
Prop Citizens Age 25–30	0.071	(0.11)
Prop Citizens Age 31–45	0.783	(1.60)
Prop Citizens Age 46–60	0.530	(1.01)
Prop Citizens Age 61–75	0.657	(1.28)
Prop Citizens Age 76–84	0.547	(0.77)
Prop Citizens High School Grad	0.59**	(2.46)
Prop Citizens Some College	0.109	(0.34)
Prop Citizens College Plus	0.861***	(2.61)
Closeness of Pres Election	0.0024	(0.51)
Closeness of Gov Election	0.0034	(0.52)
Closeness of Sen Election	−0.00012	(−0.19)
Gov Election (0/1)	0.061	(1.95)
Senate Election (0/1)	0.0145**	(2.24)
Observations	450	
R^2	0.933	

Cross – Sectional Time Series estimates, with panel corrected standard errors.
Dependent Variable: Log – Odds of Turnout for Highest Office (VAP).
Cross – Sectional Time Series estimates, with panel – corrected standard errors.
Dependent Variable: Log – Odds of Turnout for Highest Office (VAP).
*** $p < 0.01$, ** $p < 0.05$, * $p < 0.1$.

$$+ \beta_5 \text{ EarlyVoting}_{s,t} + \beta_6 \text{ EVPeriod}_{s,t}$$
$$+ \beta_7 \text{ EducDUMMIES}_{s,t} + \beta_8 \text{ AgeDUMMIES}_{s,t}$$
$$+ \beta_9 \text{ MeanIncome}_{s,t} + \beta_{10} \text{ PresMargin}_{s,t}$$
$$+ \beta_{11} \text{ SenMargin}_{s,t} + \beta_{12} \text{ GovMargin}_{s,t}$$
$$+ \Gamma \text{ (State–Dummies}_s)$$
$$+ \Psi \text{ (Year–Dummies}_t)$$
$$+ \varepsilon_{s,t}$$

The results are not as we expected. As we had previously shown, the availability of absentee voting does matter for turnout. However, we found no evidence that making permanent absentee status available to no-fault absentee voters increased turnout. The coefficients are reported in Table 7.4. The coefficient for no-fault absentee voting represents the effect of no-fault absentee voting *without* the availability of permanent absentee status. And the coefficient for permanent absentee status represents the *additional impact* on turnout that permanent absentee status yields beyond the effect just of no-fault absentee voting.

The coefficient on no-fault absentee voting is positive and statistically significant at traditional levels as expected. And it suggests that adoption of no-fault absentee voting would lead to approximately a three percentage point increase in steady state turnout. However, the coefficient of permanent absentee status is negative, though it is so small as to be estimated to be basically zero.

Because this was a surprising result, we conjectured that perhaps permanent absentee status is only useful to some voters. We reestimated the same model disaggregated by age groups. We computed state-level turnout for seven different age groups using the Current Population Survey: ages 18–24, 25–30, 31–45, 46–60, 61–74, and 76–84. When we estimated the same model to determine the impact of permanent absentee status on turnout, we found identical results. The coefficients for five of the age groups were negative. The only groups with positive coefficients for permanent absentee status were voters aged 18–24 and voters aged 76–84, but the t-statistics were 0.14 and 0.43 respectively. Thus we have to conclude that we simply can find no evidence that permanent absentee status has an effect.

There are several possible reasons for this. First, because no-fault absentee voting is a relatively recent phenomenon (see Table 7.2), it may be that not a large enough proportion of absentee voters are affected by the permanent status provision to have made a difference so far. Alternatively, it may be an implementation issue, and voters may simply not be aware of the option in some states that offer it. There might also be unanticipated consequences of permanent absentee status. It might not be as permanent as some voters think. Some voters might believe they have permanent absentee status, but moving within the state could break this status – or simply mean they never receive their ballot.

We note that while there are tremendous advantages to the cross-sectional time series approach we use here, we are also perhaps missing the trees for the forest. In analyzing the impact of the institutional reform at the state level we have not utilized any information about how many people are actually requesting permanent absentee status, much less what proportion of them *are actually voting*. We are also making finding an effect of reforms difficult: our model is saturated with fixed effects, and we are conducting a very conservative test of the impact of the reforms. However, even if we wanted to examine the data at a finer grain level, most states simply do not make available the raw data on how many voters are selecting permanent absentee status nor on how many votes such people are casting.

We examined the publicly available data on voting for all thirteen states that allow voters to request permanent absentee status. Only two states, California and Colorado, provide any data at all. And they each provide limited, though informative, data. In 2008, California issued 7,303,263 absentee ballots. Of those, 5,560,112, or 76.1 percent, were issued to voters with permanent absentee status. Thus there is apparently widespread knowledge of, and use of, the permanent absentee feature. And it *may* be responsible for the widespread use of absentee voting in California, where 43.1 percent of votes were cast absentee in 2008. However, while we know what proportion of ballots were *issued* to voters with permanent absentee status, we do not know what proportion of ballots were *returned* by voters with permanent absentee status. In Colorado, 61.9 percent of active voters had permanent absentee status in 2010. And for larger counties, this number was as high as 74.7 percent. However, we have no information about the absentee status of persons who cast votes in Colorado.

Thus looking at the trees rather than the forest, we can see that many voters take advantage of permanent absentee status to request ballots. However, we do not know if the persons who take advantage of this as a means to receive their ballots are any more likely to submit ballots than persons who do not.

We believe that understanding the effect of absentee voting requires understanding implementation of it. And we think that the effect of any electoral reform is likely to depend on how much it really changes the costs of voting for people. We see it as something of a paradox that we cannot determine that such an obvious step in making voter easier has in fact led to increased turnout. However, we also point out the obvious caveats. Our failure to find an effect of the availability of permanent absentee status does *not* imply that there is no effect. We may simply lack the statistical power necessary to observe it. We are looking to distinguish between the effect of absentee voting *without* permanent absentee status and the effect of absentee voting *with* permanent absentee status on turnout – without ever observing in the data how many people are voting via absentee balloting.

Beyond the statistical caveats we have to offer, though, there is an important substantive caveat. This chapter presents an analysis of the impact of absentee voter rules on voter turnout *in presidential elections*. Even if such rules had no impact on turnout, the most visible and salient and highest turnout elections in the United States, it would *not* imply that such rules had no impact on turnout in other elections. Whereas the burden to request an absentee ballot may not be a large hurdle in a presidential election when all voters know the election is approaching – and thus know that requesting the ballot is necessary – it might be a substantial hurdle in less prominent elections during which it is easier to forget or be unaware that an election is approaching.

Notes

1 See Cemenska and colleagues (2009) for a summary of changes in non-precinct place voting laws since 1972.
2 Of course the availability of early voting means that it is not election day, but perhaps election weeks, suggesting that the impact of absentee voting might be less in states that allow for generous early voting periods.

3   We note, however, that the Montana legislature has recently passed a bill to repeal EDR.

4   This count does not include North Dakota, which simply does not have voter registration.

5   Further, none of the states that offered mail ballot requests allowed phone requests.

6   The length of advance notice required varies by state.

7   We are still hostage to the possibility that other factors caused the state to adopt the institutional reform and to experience greater turnout. But such factors would have to be changes in the state over time, which seem much less likely than simply cross-sectional variation in states.

PART III

REMAINING CHALLENGES

8

The Evolution (or Not) of Ballot Design Ten Years after *Bush v. Gore*

Martha Kropf

INTRODUCTION

Few stories in the election world are as unfortunate as that of Theresa LePore, the former supervisor of elections for Palm Beach County, Florida and designer of the now infamous butterfly ballot with the multiple-column presidential contest that confused so many voters during the 2000 election. In defending the butterfly ballot, LePore noted, "Palm Beach County has a lot of elderly voters. I was trying to make the ballot so that it would be easier for the voters to read, which is why we went to the two-page, now known as the butterfly ballot."[1]

Yet, four years after that fateful decision, on August 24, 2004, National Public Radio's Melissa Block noted that Palm Beach had a new balloting system for absentee ballots: connect-the-arrow optical scan ballots. Block interviewed LePore, who noted that the arrow design had been around the United States for almost twenty years and was used in thirty-three states and DC. The interview continued with LePore saying that the connect-the-arrow ballot is easy to vote.

LEPORE: "[W]e decided to use the arrow because it was easier for voters to draw a line than to fill in the bubble as per a lot of studies that are out there."
BLOCK: "Easier to draw because you basically take one end of the arrow, there's a gap in the middle and you connect it to the opposite end."
LEPORE: "Correct, it's basically connecting the head and tail of the arrow by just drawing a line – a simple straight line."
BLOCK: "And the arrow is pointing to the candidate of your choice?"
LEPORE: "Correct."[2]

The author would like to thank David C. Kimball for his intellectual contribution. All errors contained herein are the author's.

Interestingly, what LePore declared with such faith – that several studies had indicated that connect-the-arrow ballots were usable – was not completely correct. Not only were there not several studies, but maybe two, both negative. One was a pilot study (using theory drawn from those who study item non-response in surveys) examining paper ballot design in five states that revealed that the connect-the-arrow format was associated with a 413 percent increase in the expected number of over-votes (Kimball and Kropf, 2005, 525–26; see also Bullock and Hood, 2002).

By all accounts, LePore just wanted to make it easier for the elderly people in her jurisdiction to vote. She was not aware of graphic design principles about which scholars now know. She was not alone in poor ballot design. Another often-cited example of poor ballot design is that of Sarasota County, Florida, one of the counties in the Thirteenth Congressional District, in 2006. Two different contests appeared on one DRE screen – making it difficult for voters to tell the difference between the contests. Evidence indicates that many voters failed to cast a vote for the second race – the Thirteenth District congressional race (Frisina et al., 2008) – because of the design (see also Kropf and Kimball, 2012). These are just two examples, but scholarship (Frisina et al., 2008; Herrnson et al., 2008; Herrnson, Hanmer, and Niemi, 2012; Kimball and Kropf, 2005, 2008; Kropf and Kimball, 2012; Neeley and Cook, 2008; Norden et al., 2008; Wand et al., 2001) has shown that the ballot design of optical scan and the user interface (ballot) on electronic voting machines has the potential to and has changed political outcomes. While scores of jurisdictions nationwide have made important changes in voting equipment and implemented other election reforms in the past decade and a half, a key question to consider is how much attention has been paid to ballot design and how much progress has been made.

The research presented herein indicates that the federal government has done little to effect change in ballot design. I also show that state legislatures introduced a flurry of legislative changes to ballot design, but early changes in response to the 2000 election focused most on modernizing voting technology. Finally, using a framework of ballot design suggestions developed by Kimball and Kropf (2005) and Kropf and Kimball (2012), I show that ballot design has not improved substantially since *Bush v. Gore*. While the framework is specifically applied to paper ballots (optical scan ballots), the Sarasota County, Florida example indicates that ballot design on DREs is also important.

To analyze ballot design, I operationalize "good ballot design" as having a few relatively simple design features that are suggested by usability research and studied extensively by those designing self-administered public opinion surveys to minimize item nonresponse (Kimball and Kropf, 2005, 2008; Kropf and Kimball, 2012; Lausen, 2007). This research analyzes ballot design in three states that were originally part of the Kimball and Kropf (2005) ballot study published in 2005: Iowa, Florida, and Kansas. These states are chosen because of the lack of centralization in election policy among counties in these states before the 2000 election landmark. Also, the three were part of a content analysis of ballots conducted in 2002, allowing for comparison of ballots.

FEDERAL REACTION TO BALLOTS

The fateful 2000 election was ultimately decided by the Supreme Court of the United States when it made its decision to stop the Florida ballot recounts. The Court noted that counting standards varied among the counties, and even among counting teams within counties. In other words, the decision was made on the equal protection of the right to vote. According to the *per curiam* opinion:

> The question before the Court is not whether local entities, in the exercise of their expertise, may develop different systems for implementing elections. Instead, we are presented with a situation where a state court with the power to assure uniformity has ordered a statewide recount with minimal procedural safeguards. When a court orders a statewide remedy, there must be at least some assurance that the rudimentary requirements of equal treatment and fundamental fairness are satisfied.

Yet the Court attempted to limit the precedential value of the decision to the specific situation by noting, "[t]he recount process, in its features here described, is inconsistent with the minimum procedures necessary to protect the fundamental right of each voter in the special instance of a statewide recount under the authority of a single state judicial officer. Our consideration is limited to the present circumstances."

Thus, the limitation of *Bush v. Gore* and ultimately HAVA were partially about state autonomy. Saphire and Moke note, "[b]y endorsing a highly deferential model of federalism that encourages state autonomy at the cost of uniform federal rights, HAVA is fundamentally at odds with the framework for voting reforms that has evolved over the last four decades since the adoption of the Voting Rights Act" (2006, 245). Yet, even though there is the idea of state autonomy, the equal protection of voters within states seems important; improving ballot design could help effect that goal. Reducing variation in residual votes among voters within states that may occur because of voting equipment is important, but what of the voter interaction with the equipment via the ballot? What did federal legislation say?

The 2002 Help America Vote Act (HAVA) focused mainly on providing incentives for election jurisdictions (states, counties, cities, townships) to replace old-fashioned voting equipment, for example, lever machines and punch card equipment of all types. The federal legislation also created an administrative body – the Election Assistance Commission (EAC) – with no rule-making authority. The EAC would serve as a clearinghouse of election research in addition to providing best practices for issues such as ballot design and design of election administration (Montjoy, 2005). Specifically in HAVA, there was little concern for ballot design itself; the emphasis was more on the usability of technology. According to HAVA:

Not later than 1 year after the date of the enactment of this Act, the Commission, in consultation with the Director of the National Institute of Standards and Technology, shall submit a report to Congress which assesses the areas of human factor research, including usability engineering and human-computer and human-machine interaction, which feasibly could be applied to voting products and systems design to ensure the usability and accuracy of voting products and systems.

Finally, in 2007, voluntary standards for ballot design were issued by the Election Assistance Commission. The guidelines concerned ballot design and election administration design more generally (e.g., voter materials such as signs posted at the precinct as well as various ballot designs and DRE screen design and usability suggestions).[3] The EAC report stemmed from the initiatives of the AIGA's Design for Democracy initiatives (see Lausen, 2007). However, a report from the Brennan Center for Justice notes that Voluntary Voting System Guidelines have not "required vendors to fully support the ballot design recommendations made in *Effective Designs for the Administration of Federal Elections*."[4] Interesting, empirical study has not yet revealed whether states and/or election jurisdictions have adopted these guidelines – or any changes in ballot design for that matter. Improvement in ballot design will be addressed in the third part of this chapter; given the Court's attention to state autonomy, it is important to examine state efforts as well as federal.

CHANGING BALLOT DESIGN: WHAT HAVE STATES DONE?

In 2002 President George W. Bush signed HAVA into law. HAVA represented some of the first federal legislation passed that would provide incentives in the form of funding for states to replace so-called outdated or old-fashioned voting equipment. HAVA was largely state focused in that it required states to take action; the legislation ordered that states establish a chief election officer, mandated states to create state plans, and noted that states could receive funding for new equipment and other reforms. By not mandating uniformity in equipment, administration, and designs but asking the states to centralize election administration more, the federal legislation would work to provide equal protection within states, rather than among states.[5] How much have state legislatures acted to change ballot design?

Clearly, how much a state has acted to change ballot design would require an in-depth study into whether the state uses administrative rules or statutes to govern issues such as ballot design. (Not that a state that wanted to give local administrators less discretion could not change the policy process utilized, but that it may be more of a regular practice for the state actors to effect change via one process or another.) For example, in examining law pertaining to ballot design in Kansas, one finds that state statutes are rather detailed about what should be included on the ballot, but not the design per se. As an example: "[t]he secretary of state shall prescribe the ballot format but the state offices part of the official general ballot for national and state offices shall follow the national offices part substantially as is shown in this section."[6] The statutes do not necessarily reflect the reality of ballot design and administration in the state. In terms of ballot design, Bryan Caskey, who assists in handling elections in the secretary of state's office, states that the office does not have "statutory authority to tell them [counties] how to design ballot[s],"[7] other than a few things in statute. He noted that ballot design is recommended, but not mandated. This stems from the election philosophy of Ron Thornburgh, who served as secretary of state for sixteen years, according to Caskey. Thornburgh believed that because all but four county clerks were elected by their county, they would be more responsive to voters than a centralized state officer could be. At the time of this interview, Caskey reported that he and the newly elected secretary of state, Republican Kris Kobach, had not had a conversation about whether election administration should be more centralized.

Within the past two or three years, Kansas contracted with a design firm in Kansas City, Missouri called Willoughby Designs. In May 2010, the secretary of state's office rolled out the new suggested designs at the May annual meeting of the County Clerks Association (see Figure 8.1). Interesting, the designs are very similar to those the Election Assistance Commission provided in its 2007 report (see Figure 8.2). Caskey noted that his office has only recommended ballot design changes, but the secretary of state's office had not mandated any of them.

An important question to address is the source of state regulations concerning ballot design. Does the state legislature enact legislation concerning the design, or is ballot design promulgated as administrative rules or guidance by the state's chief election officer? In examining the policy process on the state level, scholars will often examine the legislative process, yet comparatively less attention is focused on the administrative process at the state level. In examining Kansas ballot regulations, most of them are statute and Constitution based. Only the color of the ballot is regulated by administrative rule, but other states may be very different.

That said, assuming state legislatures have taken action, one might see such actions by tracking state legislation since *Bush v. Gore*. In this part of the analysis, I examine the amount of legislation proposed in the fifty states during the ten years of 2001–10. In order to do so, I queried the National Conference of State Legislatures database on election reform legislation. In particular, I searched for legislation concerning "ballot format & design." Predictably, immediately following the 2000 election, much more legislation was proposed in statehouses around the country (see Figure 8.3), and much more passed. Note that some of the 2001 legislation included making butterfly ballots a thing of the past, except when specifically approved by the state's chief election officer (e.g., as happened in Missouri; see Kropf, 2005).

However, even as late as 2011 – more than ten years after *Bush v. Gore* – states such as Florida were making changes to ballot design and making them via statute. Florida's state legislature recently passed an omnibus election bill

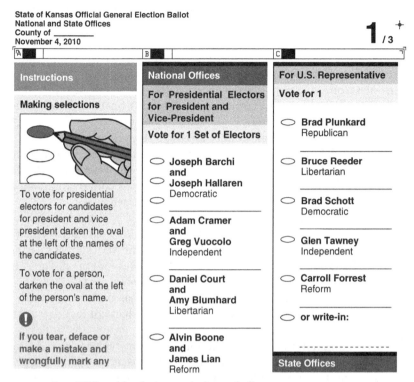

FIGURE 8.1. Willoughby design optical scan ballot.

that included a number of controversial factors such as third-party voter registration, polling place procedures, and maintaining a statewide registration database (required by HAVA). Buried within the bill was a section about ballots: "[t]he bill revises the appearance of the ballot to clarify the order of the offices on the ballots and eliminate header requirements that currently precede office titles."[8] One election official with whom I communicated speculated the change was the result of the EAC report:

I can only speculate that the bill sponsor (House Bill 1355) wanted to adopt a portion of the "best practice" examples provided within the "Effective Designs for the Administration of Federal Elections" report that was released by the U.S. Election Assistance Commission in June of 2007. The "best practice" examples within that report do not include "office headings."

Section 6.14 of the aforementioned document refers to the "office headings" as "subheads." Item four of that page refers to the subheads as "inconsistent" and "redundant."[9]

Examining newspaper coverage of the bill reveals that much of it – especially the third-party registration guidelines – was controversial. But there is almost

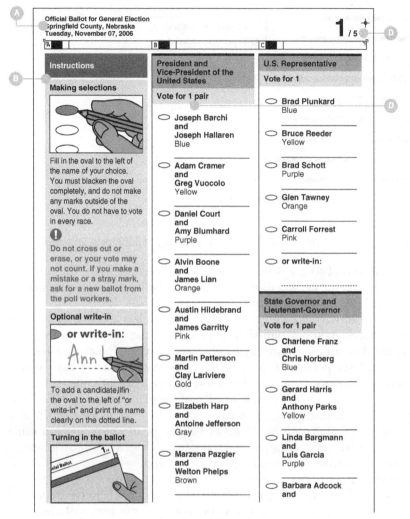

FIGURE 8.2. Ballot portion taken from EAC report.

no information about the ballot design changes. I argue that this is emblematic of the attention that most states have paid to good ballot design – minimal at best. One may expect to see the minimal attention reflected in actual ballots.

HAS BALLOT DESIGN IMPROVED? COMPARING ACTUAL BALLOTS

So, while many voters within the same state may use the same type of equipment, the question remains whether those voters are seeing an improved, more

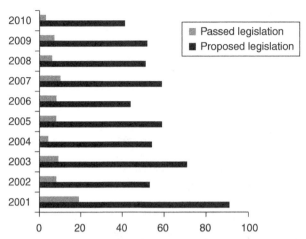

FIGURE 8.3. Proposed and passed legislation concerning ballot layout and design.

usable ballot (and of course, whether the federal standards were "helpful"). By the 2004 election, the answer to the question of whether ballots were "better" was "not yet" (see Kropf and Kimball, 2012, chapter 5).

On the state level, ballot design has received much less attention than other election issues, even though one of the core issues of the 2000 election was the unfortunate design of the butterfly ballot (see Wand et al., 2001). However, scholars also have pointed to a number of features that make both voting equipment and ballots more usable and less likely to foment under-votes and over-votes (Herrnson et al., 2007; Kimball and Kropf, 2005, 2008; Niemi and Herrnson, 2003; Lausen, 2007; Norden et al., 2008).[10] In particular, Kimball and Kropf (2005) analyzed the design of ballots for the 2002 election using graphic design techniques suggested by the research of Dr. Don Dillman, a survey methodologist who has extensively analyzed what features of self-administered surveys lead to item and survey nonresponse.[11] In the 2002 research, Kimball and Kropf (2005) identified seven ballot features associated with residual votes, over-votes, and under-votes in gubernatorial elections. Further, the research indicates that well-designed ballots minimize the impact of race on residual votes (Kimball and Kropf, 2005). Some ballot features are specific to the instructions, such as their location and readability. Other features are specific to the layout of the candidates, such as where the voter marks the ballot, shading and bolding of candidate names and office titles, and clutter around candidates (see Table 8.1). Jenkins and Dillman (1997) distinguish these features as symbolic and verbal language. Included in the various empirical examinations of survey design are not just whether pictures matter, but where text is placed and its size and whether it is bolded, are considered part of the visual features of the survey (e.g., Tourangeau, Couper, and Conrad, 2004).

TABLE 8.1. *Features of Ballots Analyzed*

Features Coded From the 2002 Study	Features Coded From 2010 Comparison
• Instructions in the Top Left Corner	• Instructions in the Top Left Corner
• Grade Level of Instructions	• Grade Level of Instructions
• Warning about Consequences of a Spoiled Ballot	• Warning about Consequences of a Spoiled Ballot
• Bolded Text to Differentiate Offices and Candidates	• Bolded Text to Differentiate Offices and Candidates
• Lack of Clarity about Where to Mark the Vote (proximity of vote mark area to candidate name is important, but this was less objective in 2002)	• Lack of Clarity about Where to Mark the Vote (Adjusted: is the "response box/oval" right next to the candidate names)
• Clutter around the Candidates	• Clutter around the Candidates
• Is it a connect – the – arrow ballot?	• Is it a connect – the – arrow ballot?
	Additional Features Coded:
	• Are pictures included to guide the voter?
	• Is there a line or a space between the candidates for the office of interest?
	• Does the ballot include the instruction to turn over the ballot?
	• Font:
	i) Size of instructions, candidates, offices
	ii) Capital letters used?

Table 8.1 notes the various features coded in the research, including the present study. In terms of ballot instructions, the first concern is *location* of the instructions. Survey methodology research indicates that they should appear right before the first response task to which the instructions apply. Thus, typically, the instructions should appear in the upper left hand corner of the ballot. The next concern is with *readability* of ballot instructions – they should be easy to read and written in active and affirmative style. To analyze readability, following Kimball and Kropf (2005) and Kropf and Kimball (2012), I typed instructions into Microsoft Word and computed Flesch-Kincaid Grade Level scores.[12] Higher scores indicate documents that are harder to read. Also following the earlier Kropf/Kimball work, in terms of instructions, I analyze whether the ballot directs voters as to what constitutes a spoiled ballot and what do about it if they spoil it. Americans try to correct mistakes when they make one, often creating a residual vote (a good ballot warns the voter not to do this, but to trade in the ballot for another), but also HAVA requires jurisdictions with paper ballots to include instructions on the effect of multiple votes

for a single office and how to correct a spoiled ballot (HAVA 2002, Title III, section 301.a.1.B).

There are a few features analyzed here that are not included in the 2002 study, but are in the more recent work (see Kropf and Kimball, 2012, chapter 5). Larger fonts are easier to read than smaller fonts (Roth, 1998). I assess whether capital letters are used for instructions, candidate names, and offices. Capital letters are more difficult to read, possibly making voting more difficult (Lausen, 2007; Long et al., 1996, 91). Thus, I record both the font size and whether various text on the ballot is all caps or not. A further analysis is whether, consistent with the EAC recommendations, ballots include an illustration of what to do to completely fill in the oval (see also Lausen, 2007; Norden et al., 2008).

Finally, I also analyze whether there is a direction to turn over a ballot when the first side or page is completed; in keeping with the law of proximity, directions to turn the ballot over should appear right after the last response task or office on a page for which one must make a selection.

Kimball and Kropf (2005) also analyzed how the layout of the offices and candidate names affected the level of residual votes. In the present study, I code the ballots for the presence of *shading and bolding* that may help guide the voter through the ballot. Another large concern is whether there is ambiguity in the box, circle, or arrow to mark for the voter's candidate of choice. This issue has several dimensions. Ballot designers often divide a page into two or three columns of offices and candidate names, so confusion may arise if spots for marking a vote appear on both sides of a candidate's name. In the Kimball/Kropf study, we coded ballots for whether there were response options on both sides of the candidate's name, as well as for whether there was potential confusion about which box, circle, oval, or arrow to mark for one's candidate of choice. Thus, I do so here as well.

However, in analyzing ballots, as noted, Kimball and Kropf (2005) found that in counties with so-called connect-the-arrow ballots, there was a large increase in over-votes over counties with ballots with ovals, circles, or squares (see also Bullock and Hood, 2002). I code for this feature partially because voters are generally less familiar with the arrow format than the oval format (which is common on standardized tests and many government forms). Furthermore, the crux of the problem may also be that there are often arrows on both sides of candidate names on connect-the-arrow ballots. In this study, I simply code whether the ballot uses the arrow format.

Finally, the Kimball/Kropf study analyzed whether there was clutter around candidates' names, which could confuse people about their response options. Election officials or state legislatures sometimes require that ballots include extra detail (such as a candidate's occupation or hometown). Survey researchers advise against putting any extraneous text near the response options on a questionnaire (Dillman, 2000). Niemi and Herrnson (2003) apply that criterion to ballots, arguing that ballots include too much information beyond a candidate's name and party affiliation. In a presidential race, some states require that the names of the electors appear on the ballot. Another possible cause of clutter is translating a ballot; thus, I also code whether the ballot is bilingual, following the lead of the Kropf/Kimball study.

The Kropf and Kimball (2012) study also considers additional factors, for which I code here. First, ballots may seem less cluttered if there are *lines or spaces between the candidate names*. Second, if there are *spaces between* the office name and the first response choice, it may make the ballot more navigable. Finally, Dillman (2000) notes that the effects of clutter on surveys may be mitigated if one demotes some of the less important information.

Additionally, I code for whether a straight party feature is included. Herrnson, Hanmer, and Niemi (2012) find that the straight party option is a source of confusion and increased voting errors. However, because straight party ballots are used statewide in whatever state they are used, I do not consider this feature in the current chapter. Of the states analyzed in the 2010 election in the present chapter, only Iowa has a straight party feature.

Finally, because one of the overriding interests of this chapter is whether the EAC recommendations for good ballots diffused to the states, I also code for whether the ballot the county/city used resembled the ones the EAC recommended in its 2007 report (see Figure 8.1).

METHODOLOGY

Five states are considered in the larger analysis of which this chapter is a part: Florida, Kansas, Iowa, Illinois, and Missouri. In each of these states, elections are administered at the county level (or at the city level in the case of eight Illinois cities and two Missouri cities). In this particular chapter, I consider three of the five states for which I have obtained ballots (N = 271). For each county, I either located a paper-based ballot online from the largest precinct or requested one from the largest precinct in the county from the relevant county official. Even counties with DREs as the principal equipment in this sample use an optical scan/paper ballot for absentee voting by mail (for example, Johnson County, KS). I was able to obtain and code 115 ballots (approximately 40 percent of the possible ballots). These ballots are compared to the ballots used in the 2002 election. I focus on these three states because of the relatively decentralized nature of their election administration.

Note that in creating the coding scheme, every effort was made to utilize measures that either existed on the ballot or did not. In other words, coding the ballot did not require much subjectivity, except in the case of "clutter around the candidates" (see Appendix A for the coding sheet). Also, note that for some ballots, I was unable to accurately code certain features because I had a faxed ballot, certain electronic files that do not accurately represent the true font size, or a sample ballot from a newspaper; this problem affected my ability to code things such as font size, but also sometimes factors such as whether the "turnover instruction" was right after the last task on the front of the ballot.

RESULTS

Again, because an overriding interest of the study is whether the EAC recommendations diffused to the states, I first analyzed whether the ballots had the "look" of the EAC/Design for Democracy Ballots (the county had adopted all or most of the recommendations). Interesting, of the ballots assessed in this analysis, only eight – less than 10 percent – resembled the EAC recommendations. As noted earlier, the Kansas secretary of state's office contracted out ballot design to a graphic design firm and presented them to the clerks in May 2010. Ironically (?), the firm designed a ballot that appeared much more like the EAC recommendations than most of the ballots in Kansas. (Kansas elections are fairly decentralized.) However, almost all of the ballots that resembled the EAC design were in Kansas; one Kansas ballot appeared to adopt some of the EAC recommendations, but rejected others.

Table 8.2 indicates the results of 2010 ballot coding and includes a rough comparison to the 2002 sample. Because the ballots do not come from exactly the same counties, the comparison is only approximate, but I would argue it gives the reader a good sense of the changes in ballot design. A couple of things are worth noting. No counties in this sample used connect-the-arrow ballots, which is a good thing from the perspective of usability. However, note the small average font sizes of instructions, candidates, and the political party of the candidates. Such small font could affect the ability of the older voters in particular to cast a vote as intended.

Something worth noting that the table cannot tell the reader is how the ballot instructions vary in terms of telling the voter not to spoil the ballot. In 2010, many Florida counties were very direct:

If you make a mistake, don't hesitate to ask for a new ballot.

If you erase or make other marks, your vote may not count.

In contrast, most Iowa counties were much less direct:

4. Do not cross out. If you change your mind, exchange your ballot for a new one.

This is actually a difficult coding decision, as the voter may not realize that crossing out a vote because of changing his mind may void his vote. Nevertheless, for illustrative purposes, the Iowa language was counted here as telling the voter not to spoil his ballot and what to do if he did. So, while counties are more likely to warn of a spoiled vote if the voter makes a mistake, there are differences in the language used, some of which could be confusing.

TABLE 8.2. *Ballot Features for 2010 Compared to 2002 Findings*

Ballot Feature	Florida 2010	Florida 2002	Iowa 2010	Iowa 2002	Kansas 2010	Kansas 2002
Instructions in the Top Left Corner	35%	33%	33%	77%	83%	57%
Grade Level of Instructions	6.05 (0.72)	6.7 (0.6)	6.81 (0.74)	6.9 (1.2)	9.49 (1.36)	10.2 (1.1)
Warning of Consequences of Spoiled Ballot	100%	98%	8%	0%	100%	30%
Warning about Correcting Spoiled Ballot	100%	100%	93%	72%	100%	80%
Bolded Text (Candidate Different from Office)	91%	87%	36%	14%	22%	31%
Shading for Different Offices	5%	44%	0%	71%	31%	2%
Possible Confusion in Marking Governor Vote		23%		8%		34%
Is There a Space Between Candidates for Governor?	95%		90%		80%	
Is the Oval Right Next to the Candidate?	59%		67%		28%	
Clutter around the Candidates (for Governor)	18%	12%	24%	72%	83%	100%
Pictures to Guide Voter	0%		14%		22%	
Turnover right after last response task?	5%		17%		19%	
Font Size of Instructions	10.01 (0.91)		10.54 (0.95)		9.78 (1.13)	
Font Size of Candidates	10.08 (0.95)		10.58 (1.03)		9.5 (1.02)	
Font Size of Party	9.47 (1.12)		9.32 (1.78)		8.5 (0.86)	
Number of Ballots Coded	22	52	42	78	36	95

Note: 2002 data taken from Kimball and Kropf, 2005, 519.

Another observation from Table 8.2: while scholars have prominent examples of where shading and bolding can help guide the voter (the situation in Sarasota County might have been helped by it), Table 8.2 provides evidence that counties are not using shading and bolding more.

What is striking about this table is that it is NOT striking that ballots in the United States have made improvements in many basic design features. Some states indicate improvements in some areas, but have gotten worse in others.

CONCLUSION

The federal efforts to spirit election authorities into buying new equipment has resulted in approximately 75 percent of local jurisdictions using different voting equipment than they did in the 2000 election (Kropf and Kimball, 2012, chapter 2). By the 2010 election, almost 60 percent of counties used optical scan balloting (either precinct or central count); another one-third of voters used DREs in the 2010 midterm. Only about 2 percent used hand counted paper ballots (Kropf and Kimball, 2012). However, in examining the ballots herein, there have *not* been many dramatic changes, nor much political attention to ballots.

However, empirical research indicates that ballot design matters. In analyzing ballot design, Kropf and Kimball conclude:

> The accuracy problem of elections in 2000 was not just a voting equipment problem. All in all, the evidence indicates that ballot design matters in terms of helping to increase the accuracy of election results. Building on the idea that voting a ballot is much like completing a public opinion survey a person receives in the mail, we are able to advance a series of suggestions for creating better ballots. Our research on actual ballots indicates these suggestions can improve the accuracy of voting.... If elections are supposed to reflect the voice of the people, then well-designed voting systems are a must. (Kropf and Kimball, 2012: 94–95)

Furthermore, as policy makers reform elections in ways that include more challenging voting tasks such as instant run-off voting, cumulative voting, and complicated direct democracy ballot measures, more attention to ballot design is vital (see Kimball and Kropf, 2011; Neeley and Cook, 2008).[13] In the next decade – and perhaps longer – I argue that usability research should continue.

However, before this chapter closes, it is important to emphasize one more thing: the issue of usability is not just about paper ballots, despite the bulk of empirical work presented herein. The combination of the federal legislation and concerns about computer security with direct recording electronic voting machines has certainly meant that paper optical scan ballots are now the most popular way of registering citizen electoral preferences. Thus, ballot design – and at this point in time, especially that of paper ballots – is more important than ever, especially because scholarly research has indicated that ballot design does affect the ability of the voter to express his or her preferences in voting.

All in all however, using computerized interfaces to register citizen preferences will continue to grow. And policy makers designing computerized user interfaces (including overseas/absentee voting on the Internet) should take a lesson from survey design and the ballot design literature more generally. Survey methodology scholars who examine Web-based data will likely give us even more lessons for the future (Couper, 2008). This research should be taken seriously going forward.

APPENDIX A: CODING FOR 2004 AND 2010 BALLOT STUDY

County and state:_____
Coder:_____

2010 Only:
EACLook: Does the ballot look like the EAC ballot (images, font, bolding/shading/color?)
1=yes
0=no

2004/2010

2004 and 2010:

INSTRUCT: Are the instructions in the top left of the first column?

1—top left of first column (if there are more than one set of instructions, but they start with the basics in the top left of the first column, code it "1".)
2—spread across top
3—instructions on a separate page
4—instructions come after response task
5—Doesn't tell you what to do to vote (may include, for example, straight ticket instructions, but nothing else
____—Not available (instructions missing)

SHADE: Location of shading
0—no shading on ballot
1—shading for groups of offices
2—shading for each office (includes reverse shading)

BOLD: Boldness of candidates v. office they are running for
1—is the same
2—office is bolder than candidates
3—candidates is bolder than office

LINEBT: Horizontal lines between candidates for office
0—no
1—yes

SPACE: Is there space between the candidate lines (between candidates for the same office)?

0—no, squished
1—yes, not squished

TYPEBAL: *Ballot type*

0—oval (or circle)
1—arrow
2—square

CAPINS: *Are the instructions in all capital letters?*

1—yes
0—no

CAPCAN: *Are the candidate names in all caps? (both presidency and state level: we do not expect them to be different, but we need to be cognizant it is possible)*

1—yes
0—no

GRADEINS: *Grade level of instructions*_____
         • Type the ballot instructions in the "ballot instruction file" and then analyze grade level using MS Word. (see word count function)

READABLE: *Readability score of instructions*_____
         • Type the ballot instructions in the "ballot instruction file" and then analyze readability using MS Word (see word count function)

SPOIL: Instructions of what to do in the case of a spoiled ballot (HAVA!)

0—nothing
1—Warning not to spoil ballot
2—What to do if you spoil your ballot
3—Both 1 and 2
_____—No instructions at all available

INSTFONT: *Instruction font size*

CANFONT: *Candidate font size*

OFFFONT: *Office font size*

JUST: Justification of candidate names and circles/arrows/squares for vote

1—circle/arrow/square and candidate names left justified and next to each other
2—circle/arrow/square and candidate names left justified but **not** next to each other

3—circle/arrow/square and candidate names right justified and next to each other

4—circle/arrow/square and candidate names right justified but **not** next to each other

TURNOVER: Does the ballot tell the voter to turn over the ballot (or look at a second page)?

1—yes, right after the last contest on the page
2—yes, printed across bottom of ballot
3—yes, somewhere else on page
0—no

[leave blank if there is only one page to the ballot]

CLUTPRES: *Clutter for president (more than candidate and party listed) (Party column ballots usually are cluttered by our judgment; listing hometowns is usually cluttered.)*

1—yes
.5—yes, but demoted (i.e., smaller or different font clutter where candidate stands out)
0—no

CLUTGOV: *Clutter for president (more than candidate and party listed)(Party column ballots usually are cluttered by our judgment; listing hometowns is usually cluttered.)*

1—yes
.5—yes, but demoted (i.e., smaller or different font clutter where candidate stands out)
0—no

CLUTS: *Clutter for STATE RACE (more than candidate and party listed)) (Party column ballots usually are cluttered by our judgment; giving hometowns is usually cluttered.)*

1—yes
.5—yes, but demoted (i.e., smaller or different font clutter where candidate stands out)
0—no

Notes

1   ABC News. 2000. "Butterfly Ballot Designer Speaks Out: Election Official LePore Talks about the Controversial Butterfly Ballot." http://abcnews.go.com/Politics/story?id=122175&page=1.

2   Block, Melissa. 2004. "New Ballot Design in Florida County." All Things Considered, August 26, 2004, available at http://www.npr.org/templates/story/story.php?storyid=3873016.

3   See U.S. Election Assistance Commission. Effective Designs for the Administration of Federal Elections, June 2007, available at http://www.eac.gov/assets/1/Page/EAC_effective_election_Design.pdf.

4   Brennan Center for Justice citing *Voluntary Voting System Guidelines Recommendations to the Election Assistance Commission* (prepared at the direction of the Technical Guidelines Development Committee) (Aug. 31, 2007), available at http://www.eac.gov/files/vvsg/Final-TGDC-VVSG-08312007.pdf.

5   Montjoy, Robert. 2005. "HAVA and the States." In Daniel J. Palazzolo and James W. Ceaser, eds., *Election Reform: Politics and Policy.* Lanham, MD: Lexington Books.

6   Kansas State Statutes, Article 6, "Official Ballots," §25–616, available at http://www.kslegislature.org/li/statute/025_000_0000_chapter/025_006_0000_article/025_006_0016_section/025_006_0016_k/.

7   Caskey, Bryan. Election Representative, Secretary of State's Office. Personal Interview, April 8, 2011, Topeka, Kansas.

8   Florida House of Representatives Staff Analysis. 2011. Bill#CS/HB 1355, Elections. http://www.flsenate.gov/Session/Bill/2011/1355.

9   E-mail communication with a Florida election official (name withheld). May 25, 2011.

10 *Under-votes* refers to the concept of the voter failing to vote in a certain contest – it may be intentional, but it may be unintentional. *Over-votes* refers to the situation when an individual casts more than the allowed number of votes for a particular contest, thus voiding the vote altogether. Over-votes are not usually intentional. Together, these concepts pair to create residual votes, usually operationalized by examining voter turnout in a given jurisdiction and subtracting the number of votes cast in a particular contest.

11 Kropf and Kimball discuss Dr. Dillman's significant role in redesigning census report forms to make them more usable (2012, chapter 5). The federal government spent considerable resources making these self-administered surveys more user friendly.

12 The Flesch-Kincaid scores indicate the grade level needed to understand the text. The Flesch-Kincaid Grade Level scores are based on the length of words and sentences. The formula for computing the score is (.39 x ASL) + (11.8 x ASW) − 15.59, where ASL is the average number of words per sentence and ASW is the average number of syllables per word. In Microsoft Word, the "Spelling and Grammar" feature in the "Tools" menu computes Flesch-Kincaid scores for a document. The use and validity of Flesch-Kincaid scores are supported by other studies (Heilke, Joslyn, and Aguado, 2003; Sanders and McCormick, 1993; Tefki, 1987).

13 For more information about alternative voting mechanisms, see http://www.fairvote.org.

9

Poll Workers and Polling Places

Thad E. Hall and Kathleen Moore

INTRODUCTION

In the year after the 2000 presidential election debacle in Florida, there was a sharp focus by many organizations, commissions, and interest groups to determine how to address the problems associated with ensuring that the events of November 2000 did not occur again (e.g., Caltech/MIT Voting Technology Project, 2001; Carter and Ford, 2002). In general, these organizations considered issues related to voting technologies and voter registration. The Florida recount illustrated that it can be difficult, if not impossible, to determine how to count certain ballots, especially when the intent of the voter is not discernable from the marks on the ballot. Therefore, there was great interest after this experience in determining how to design a voting system that was easy to use and that accurately captured voter intent. It was also clear, based on the events in Florida and in other states, that many voters had never been able to get to the point of being able to mark – or mismark! – a ballot because problems with the voter registration system had not allowed them to be authenticated as valid voters.

Not surprising, election reforms passed in 2001 and 2002 tended to focus on solving these two technology problems. The Help America Vote Act (HAVA) focused most of its funding and reforms on modernizing voter registration systems by creating statewide implementations and procedures for addressing problems with voter registration through provisional voting requirements and on modernizing voting systems by banning punch card voting in federal elections and requiring the adoption of new voting systems that were auditable and that provided users with feedback regarding any errors they might have made in voting.

This chapter was written when Moore was a master's student at the University of Utah.

However, as several authors have noted, voting and other operations management are about the intersection between people, processes, and technology (e.g., Alvarez and Hall, 2008). HAVA focused almost exclusively on the last two factors: processes and technology. But, strong evidence has emerged over the past decade and a half that the human component of elections – especially the poll workers who actually run the elections – is of critical importance to making elections functional events in which the public has confidence.

Consider, for a moment, the role of poll workers in an election. At the start of election day, they set up the polling place, including putting up all signage, setting up the voting machines, and preparing the voter rolls. Mistakes at this point can result in a polling place not being accessible to people with disabilities or the voter rolls and ballots not being appropriately audited. Once voters start to vote, it is the poll worker who enforces all election laws – from voter identification requirements to voter privacy requirements to explaining to voters how to use the voting technology. These same poll workers also have to implement the "fail safe" procedures such as provisional voting that are used if there are problems with a person's voter registration. At the end of the night, it is the poll worker who ensures that the votes are initially tabulated correctly, and that the ballots and election materials are appropriately secured and are not susceptible to fraud.

Unfortunately, for much of the past decade and a half, there has been little research regarding poll workers in the United States (cf. Hall, Monson, and Patterson, 2007, 2008, 2009; Magleby, Monson, and Patterson, 2008). Instead, the media continuously repeats urban myths about poll workers – such as that the average age of poll workers is seventy years old, that most poll workers have been doing their job for dozens of years, or that most poll workers lack any technological savvy and find new voting equipment too hard to use. A quick search of the Internet or *LexisNexis* produces numerous examples of how these myths have existed since the 2000 election and continue today. Even more troubling, there have been only a few efforts to link poll worker characteristics and training to the effective implementation of voting technologies or election procedures.

As we discuss in this chapter, poll workers play a critical role in elections and we have only recently developed a full understanding of that role. These workers are more diverse than the media suggests; they are not all old ladies. Moreover, the linkages between poll worker training and the subsequent quality of elections, such as problems at the polls with voting equipment or implementing election laws regarding voter identification or provisional voting, illustrate that funding training for them is as important as funding technology. We also show that the quality of the poll worker-voter interaction affects the way poll workers are evaluated and how elections overall are evaluated. However, many research questions about poll workers still need greater study.

VOTING AS A PROCESS

Across the United States, poll workers are the face of the electoral process, yet they receive limited training from local election offices (LEO) and, on election day, they do their jobs with little direct supervision by staff from the LEO. This delegation means that poll workers are the ones who are responsible for setting up and implementing the voting system used in each polling location and interpreting the election laws and procedures in that jurisdiction. For the voter, this means that their ability to exercise the franchise is mediated by workers who represent the state but are not permanent or professional government employees.

This delegation of election activities from the LEO to the poll worker creates a principal-agent problem for the election officials (Alvarez and Hall, 2006). The election officials have to delegate responsibility for polling place operations to the poll workers, but the mechanisms for overcoming principal-agent problems – staff selection, monitoring, training, clear standard operating procedures – are attenuated by the single-day nature of elections.[1] Poll workers in a problematic precinct can be better trained for the next election but the voter may not get much solace from this if they were not able to vote in *this* election.

The consequences of the principal-agent problem have been highlighted in numerous newspaper articles.[2] For example, there are many documented cases of poll workers failing to properly fill out outer provisional balloting envelopes, which invalidates the provisional vote, disenfranchising the voter. There are also cases where voters in consolidated precincts (where two or more precincts are consolidated into a single polling location) have been given the wrong ballots, and such actions have potentially affected the outcome of a local election. In both cases, the election officials are generally not in a position to fix the problems after the fact. Such problems can reduce voter confidence in the election process.

Poll workers also interpret state election laws and determine how such laws will be implemented. In several reports and studies, Atkeson, Alvarez, and Hall (2007, 2010) have found that poll workers often implemented voter identification laws incorrectly. In addition, there was bias in the implementation; poll workers of all races and political persuasions asked Hispanics – especially Hispanic men – to show identification more than other subpopulations. Poll workers in New Mexico have discretion over how to implement the state's voter identification law, which allows for multiple means of authenticating a voter's identity. Such discretion can lead to diversity in the implementation of a given law.

In the largest study of the voting experience ever conducted, the Caltech/MIT Voting Technology Project (VTP) found that a sizable population of voters are not asked for identification consistent with state law (Alvarez et al., 2009). This is true both in states with strict voter identification laws and in those with minimal voter identification laws. In states with strict voter identification laws, approximately 25 percent of voters showed photo identification only because it was convenient, not because they were asked. By contrast, approximately one quarter of all voters in states with liberal voter identification laws responded that they would not have been allowed to vote had they not produced a photo ID.[3] The VTP analysis also found that, as was the case in the study by Atkeson and colleagues (2010), that minority voters were asked to show photo identification more than were white voters.[4]

THE AMERICAN POLL WORKER

So who are these poll workers who implement laws and implement elections? When poll workers are discussed in the popular media, one phrase is often used, without any citation or substantiation: the average age of poll workers is seventy years old. The most interesting aspect of this statement is that it is made authoritatively, even though there have been only a few poll worker surveys conducted since 2000, and none of them were national surveys of poll workers. Most poll worker surveys have been conducted at the county level, and none of them suggest that poll workers are as old as the urban myth states.[5] Taken together, these surveys give shape to the attributes of the post-HAVA poll worker. We consider the various demographic factors of the American poll worker and then consider the implications of these findings in the section on voter confidence.

THE SEVENTY-YEAR-OLD FEMALE POLL WORKER

Are American poll workers really seventy years old and female? In a May 2006 Cuyahoga County survey, this seemed true; the average poll worker was sixty-nine years old (Monson, Patterson, and Warren, 2006, 31). However, in the 2006 Ohio general election, workers' median ages were lower (from 55 to 67) when analyzed across three counties (Magleby et al., 2008, 21). In 2006 in New Mexico, 33 percent of poll workers were 55–64 years old and 24 percent were 45–54 years old. In 2008, New Mexico and Ohio workers had an average age of fifty-eight years (Atkeson et al., 2009, xii; Mockabee et al., 2008, 21). In Los Angeles, poll workers were mostly middle aged; the average worker in the 2010 primary election was fifty-two years old and was forty-eight years old in the 2010 general election (Alvarez et al., 2010, 8; Alvarez et al., 2011). Although poll workers do tend to be older than the average person in their community, they are not as old as is typically represented in the media.

However, the gender aspect of the urban myth is true. In all surveys analyzed (Alvarez et al., 2007; Alvarez et al., 2010; Alvarez et al., 2011; Atkeson et al., 2009; Magleby et al., 2008; Mockabee et al., 2009; Monson et al., 2006), the majority of poll workers were female. Typically, two-thirds of poll workers are female, although this was slightly lower in Los Angeles County in the 2010 primary election.

TRAINING AND PROBLEMS AT THE POLLS

Poll workers are not the elderly people the media suggest. However, the question remains, regardless of how old the poll workers are, whether they are prepared well for their job on election day. The primary mechanism that LEOs have to mitigate against problems at the polls is poll worker training. However, as Hall, Monson, and Patterson (2008) note, very little of the standard practice of training front line workers in either the public or private sectors can be applied to poll workers. For example, the "tell-show-do" method – where supervisors explain a process and demonstrate it and the trainees practice it – can be done in preelection training but not in on-the-job training for poll workers; there just are not enough supervisors to engage in such training on election day.[6] In addition, unless the LEO conducts debriefings after the election, they are unlikely to develop a learning culture and then use that culture to improve the training.

Using a pooled set of poll worker surveys, we examined the factors that affected the poll workers' confidence that votes were counted accurately, focusing specifically on factors related to training. Many things could affect workers' perceptions of the integrity of the vote count: problems with polling place setup and closing, inability to operate voting machinery, not garnering enough information and guidance from training opportunities, difficulty authenticating voters, and worker uncertainty in administering provisional voting procedures. When asked about problems, we found the following:

1) More than 70 percent of poll workers disagreed or strongly disagreed with the statement that "there were problems setting up the polling place."

2) More than 80 percent of poll workers disagreed or strongly disagreed with the statement that "there were problems closing down the polling place."

Problems at the polls are directly linked with poll workers being confident that the votes in the election were counted accurately. Poll workers who are confident in the vote counts are also likely to have not experienced problems at their polling place. In addition, we compared the relationship between the vote count confidence question and the question "the training was easy to understand." We found that more than 85 percent of workers either strongly agreed or agreed that the training was easy to understand. Looking at the association between this training variable and the vote count confidence variable, we see that higher levels of confidence occur with a belief that the training was understandable.

POLL WORKERS AND VOTER CONFIDENCE

Obviously, understanding the issues poll workers face in elections is important, especially from a public administration and a management perspective. However, what is also important is the way the voter-poll worker interaction affects voter confidence in the election process and voters' attitudes about elections in the United States. For voters, their poll workers are the face of elections, the individuals who make the election work. In the 2000 election, little consideration had been given to this issue, but recent research has found several important linkages that help to explain the importance of the poll worker-voter interactions. These linkages have important implications for managing elections and for ensuring that voters have confidence in the election results.

Theoretically, poll worker-voter interaction is important because this interaction is the sole one a voter has with the election process and is one where the LEO is dependent on the poll worker to ensure that the voter has a high-quality experience (Alvarez and Hall, 2006). This interaction is affected by the discretion that poll workers have to make decisions about how to implement election law (Hall et al., 2009). Poll workers use their discretion in ways that can affect voter confidence in the electoral process both positively and negatively. For example, a poll worker may decide to ask for photo identification, even though it is not required under state law, simply to make it easier to look up a voter's name on the registration rolls. Likewise, an experienced poll worker may know how to assist voters in casting their ballot in a way that maximizes voter privacy and the secrecy of their ballot. Claassen and colleagues (2008) also note that voting is a government service activity where voters respond to the voting experience like they do to any other service experience. Given that the poll workers are responsible for the setup of polling places and the operations of the location, they are critical for providing a quality experience to the voter who comes out to vote, especially on election day.

A recent study of the voting experience was conducted by the Caltech/ MIT Voting Technology Project (Alvarez et al., 2009). The 2008 Survey of the Performance of American Elections (SPAE) was a fifty-state survey with 10,000 respondents (200 in each state) that examined the voting experience during the 2008 presidential election.[7] Hall and Stewart (2011) used data from this study to evaluate voter interactions with poll workers (Oregon and Washington State were excluded because neither state has significant in-person voting) and to evaluate early voting, something previous studies have not done. In addition, the SPAE asked voters a set of questions regarding the race and age of the poll workers in the polling place. This allowed them to evaluate the effects of the race and age of poll workers on the evaluation of poll worker performance. Given that, as was shown previously, poll workers tend to not be highly representative of their communities – especially along the racial dimension, where they tend to be whiter than average – the question arises as to whether this lack of representativeness affects voter evaluations of poll workers.

The SPAE report and the analysis by Hall and Stewart had several key findings. First, race is an important factor in how voters evaluate their poll workers. Specifically, voters who have a same-race experience are more likely to rate their poll worker as excellent compared to voters who have a cross-race experience. This was true, however, only in election day voting, not in early voting. Part of the reason for the difference may be that, when voters vote on election day, the precinct is normally in their neighborhood. Given the segregation that is common in American housing, a different race poll worker is viewed as an "other" or "intruder" who does not belong. By contrast, in early voting, voters go to a government building or similar locale where they expect to encounter a government employee; there is no expectation these individuals will look like the voter. The congruence of voter–poll worker race increased satisfaction in the poll worker encounter for both white voter–white poll worker encounters and for black voter–black poll worker encounters.

Second, voters who know their poll worker rate them much higher than poll workers who are not known to the voter. Interestingly, though, this is not very common. The SPAE study found that only one in five election day voters and one in ten early voters stated that they knew their poll worker. However, when it does occur, there is a sizable percentage point increase in voters' satisfaction with their poll worker. This may be a function of voters not wanting to attribute bad outcomes to people they know (Hall and Stewart, 2011).

Third, age effects were also important in poll worker evaluations. Voters do not tend to rate very old or very young poll workers highly. They instead rate poll workers of middle age – between 30 and 70 – highly. This was not affected by the age of the voter; neither very old nor very young voters rated their counterparts highly. In early voting, younger poll workers were not rated as low as they were in election day voting, but very old poll workers were rated low in early voting. Magleby, Monson, and Patterson (2008) also suggest that the age of the poll worker may affect the way voters evaluate poll workers.

Problems at the polls greatly affect the evaluation that voters give about their poll workers. Voters are very sensitive to problems that occur during voting and they hold their poll workers responsible for such problems. Problems at the polls result in voters: (1) evaluating their poll workers much lower and (2) being much less confident that their vote was counted accurately.

Finally, we know that voter confidence is predicted by the quality of the voting experience, including voters' interaction with their poll worker. Hall, Monson, and Patterson (2009) found that voter confidence on election day in Utah and Ohio in 2006 was most affected by partisanship (Republicans were more confident than were Democrats) and the quality of the voter-poll worker interactions. Voters who were very satisfied with their poll worker were also much more likely to think that their votes would be counted accurately and also to have stronger views on the fairness of the outcome of the election. As

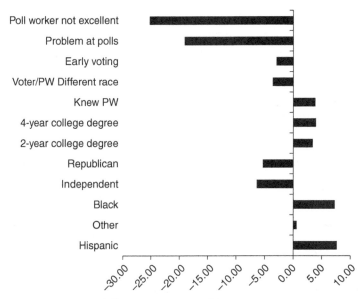

FIGURE 9.1. First differences, voter confidence.

we see in Figure 9.1, moving to having an "excellent" evaluation of the poll worker leads a hypothetical respondent to have a sizable improvement in confidence – between a ten and thirty-six percentage point improvement. If a voter has a good experience voting, and they know that the poll worker is the person who will be getting the ballots ready for counting, they will be more confident that the votes will in fact be counted correctly. If there are problems with a poll worker doing simple tasks or they otherwise question the quality of the poll worker, they may question too whether the poll worker will make an error that affects confidence.

Using the national data from the 2008 *Survey of the Performance of American Elections*, we see that poll workers are important to voter confidence. In Table 9.1, we present the results of a logistic regression, where the dependent variable is whether the voter is very confident that their vote is counted accurately. We include in the model demographic variables, political variables, and experiential variables regarding the voting experience.[8] The easiest way to interpret these variables is by looking at the first differences, presented in Figure 9.1. Here, we see that having a bad experience with a poll worker can be extremely detrimental to voter confidence. Voters who have a low rating of their poll worker were twenty-five percentage points less likely to be very confident in the votes in the election being counted accurately compared to other voters. This holds true even controlling for other problems, such as encountering a problem in the precinct, waiting in line, having a different race poll worker, and the like.[9]

TABLE 9.1. *Factors Affecting Voter Confidence in Vote Counts*

	Coefficient	Standard Error	Confidence
Poll Worker Not Excellent	−1.050	0.060	0.00
Knew Poll Worker	0.120	0.063	0.06
Race Congruence	−0.383	0.066	0.00
Problem Voting	−0.186	0.069	0.01
Early Voter	0.639	0.085	0.00
Obama Voter	−0.179	0.079	0.02
Democrat	−0.176	0.081	0.03
Republican	−0.029	0.114	0.80
High School or Less Education	0.017	0.109	0.88
Some College Education	0.044	0.082	0.60
Two–Year Degree	0.279	0.078	0.00
Graduate Degree	0.331	0.119	0.01
African American	0.229	0.083	0.01
Voter's Age	0.012	0.002	0.00
Constant	0.582	0.146	0.00
N	7298		
Log Likelihood	−3795.10		

CONCLUSIONS AND IMPLICATIONS

The work on poll workers has only occurred in small increments in a small number of jurisdictions nationally. With the exception of the poll worker questions that were included on the 2008 *Survey of the Performance of American Elections*, there have been no national efforts to understand the role of poll workers in American elections. However, from these various studies, certain policy lessons can be drawn but many research questions also remain. As Hall and Stewart (2011) note, the 2008 survey does suggest clear policy lessons can be learned from asking voters about their experience with poll workers. First and foremost, voting is an interpersonal activity and election officials need to be sensitive to this fact as they select polling places and poll workers. Voters are sensitive, especially in the election day context, to the race of their poll workers and their ages. It also suggests that efforts to recruit teachers, principals, and other "middle manager" types into the voting process would be good; voters like people in that middle age group – 30 to 50 – as poll workers.

Second, several of these studies suggest the importance of poll worker training. Given the sensitivity of voters to problems at the polls and the fact that training is closely linked to poll worker confidence as well as to the incidence of problems opening and closing the polls, training remains an important part of the election process. There are some indications that certain types of training may work better than others – small group, hands on training may be better than large group lecture – but there is a need to study if different types of training make for a better experience for either voters or poll workers.

Third, there is some indication in the 2008 survey results that the voting experience is different for early voting compared to election day voting. Early voting has grown dramatically since 2000, but our understanding of the implications of this change, from a management and experiential perspective, has been limited. Given that voters view the interpersonal aspects of early voting different in some respects compared to election day voting, it would be helpful to study this component of the voting process more effectively and extensively.

Fourth, Alvarez and Hall (2006) wrote that standard operating procedures are a critical component of the voting process. More recently, work on election audits also suggests that evaluating the processes that occur in election management – including activities that occur in polling places and the manuals and checklists that contain the election management protocols – should be a critical part of any postelection evaluation of the voting process. However, little work has been done on what kind of protocols, manuals, or checklists make the election go more smoothly for either the voter or the poll worker. Given that, nearly a decade and a half after Florida, we still have a highly decentralized voting system with great variation in administration across counties within states, determining how to best manage elections, the types of materials that ensure that election results are accurate, and ways to ensure that steps in the process are not missed would all be valuable improvement to the research on elections.

Finally, it would be helpful if policy makers recognized that, when they change election laws, voting technologies, and voting procedures, they have to invest in the human side of the equation as well. Investing in training may not be sexy and considering the effect that the implementation of new voting laws and procedures has on poll workers may be secondary, but when policy makers implement change without considering the human part of the voting process, they are remiss.

Notes

1   Obviously, in early voting, which can last many weeks, election officials can address many principal-agent problems because the fewer number of early voting sites means that local election officials can engage in better oversight with permanent LEO staff who are at early voting sites. In addition, jurisdictions like Washington, DC often rotate precinct captains – the lead poll worker in a precinct – through early voting sites before they work on election day to observe their performance.

2   See Hall et al., 2007, 2009 and http://electionupdates.caltech.edu for summaries of these problems.

3   This analysis controlled for the fact that first time voters are required under HAVA to show identification in most circumstances.

4   Specifically, 70 percent of African Americans, 65 percent of Hispanics, and 51 percent of whites were asked to show photo identification.

5   Because of the local variation inherent in election administration, poll worker studies are typically confined to smaller geographies. Studies were conducted in Cuyahoga County, Ohio after the 2006 primary election and later that year, surveys were conducted with workers from primary and general elections in several counties from Ohio and Utah (Magleby et al., 2008) and general elections in New Mexico (Alvarez et al., 2007). A large study on the New Mexico 2008 election included a survey of poll workers from several counties (Atkeson et al., 2009). Also in 2008, Ohio poll workers were surveyed (Mockabee et al., 2009). L.A. County workers were surveyed around their participation in online training (Alvarez et al., 2010) and after the 2010 general election (Alvarez et al., 2011).

6   One way that LEOs can get around this problem is to train workers during early voting, which is sometimes used to evaluate or train precinct managers and limited numbers of election day poll workers.

7   The 2008 *Survey of the Performance of American Elections* was funded by The Pew Charitable Trusts/JEHT Foundation *Make Voting Work* Initiative. The views expressed in the work of Hall and Stewart are those of the authors and do not necessarily reflect the views of The Pew Center on the States or The Pew Charitable Trusts.

8   These variables are all coded the same as in Hall and Stewart (2011).

9   We can do the same analysis in a two-stage model, where we first predict the probability that someone would rate their poll worker's performance as high as a function of voter attributes, the poll worker's attributes, poll worker-voter comparisons, and voting experience variables, as was done in Hall and Stewart (2011). We can then compute a second model, where we predict the probability that someone would have high confidence in vote counts as a function of voter attributes, if the voter voted on election day, and the predicted probability that the voter would rate a poll worker's performance as excellent. In this analysis, we again see that poll workers are important to voter confidence.

10

Resolving Voter Registration Problems: Making Registration Easier, Less Costly, and More Accurate

R. Michael Alvarez and Thad E. Hall

INTRODUCTION

The practice of voter registration has a long history in the United States. In 1800, Massachusetts was the first state to impose a voter registration requirement. By Reconstruction, a handful of states used voter registration, typically in urban areas, as a tool to prevent multiple voting. By early in the twentieth century, most states required voter registration.[1]

In recent decades, there have been many initiatives to make voter registration easier and more convenient for voters. At the federal level, the National Voter Registration Act (NVRA, 1993) and the Help America Vote Act (HAVA, 2002) both sought to ease the registration process for eligible voters. For example, NVRA made the registration process available in government agencies and by mail and HAVA required that most states develop statewide computerized voter lists, among other reforms. At the same time, many states shortened preelection registration deadlines, allowed for election day voter registration, and worked in other ways to make the registration process easier.[2]

Voter registration regulations in the United States currently look like a patchwork quilt: states have different deadlines for registration before an election, they use different registration forms, and some states even allow some eligible citizens to register online.[3] Despite these varying practices, there are some important commonalities in how voter registration is practiced in every state. In the United States, voter registration is voluntary (eligible citizens do not have to register) and is passive (eligible citizens have the responsibility for registering with the appropriate government authority in their state).[4] From an international perspective, the voluntary and passive nature of voter registration in the United States is not unique, but many other nations have voter registration systems that are compulsory and/or active (appropriate governmental authorities are required to find and register eligible citizens).[5]

In this chapter, we argue that, despite federal and state efforts to make voter registration easier and more convenient for voters, the existing patchwork quilt of registration practices and regulations remains a barrier to some eligible citizens. This patchwork quilt has produced a voter registration system that is likely more costly and less accurate than other types of voter registration systems. Thus, the United States should consider a process for implementing an active, rather than passive, voter registration process. Implementation of an active voter registration process should make registration issues less of a burden for many eligible citizens, lower the costs of election administration, and produce a voter registry that is both more accurate and more comprehensive.

DEFINING THE PROBLEMS WITH THE CURRENT VOTER REGISTRATION PROCESS

In the wake of the 2000 presidential election, there was a great deal of attention paid to voting technology and election administration issues. In 2001, the Caltech/MIT Voting Technology Project (VTP) issued a study that estimated that between 4 million and 6 million votes were lost in the 2000 presidential election. Surprisingly, most of these lost votes (up to 3 million) stemmed from voter registration problems (Caltech/MIT VTP, 2001). This report, and other studies of voter registration problems in the 2000 presidential election, led to significant efforts at both the federal and state levels to reform the process of voter registration in HAVA and other state legislation.[6] Despite these efforts, the VTP estimated that roughly 2.2 million votes were lost during the 2008 presidential election because of registration problems, an estimate nearly identical to that for the 2000 presidential election.[7]

Interestingly, in research dating back nearly three decades, political scientists have studied how changing regulations associated with voter registration affect voter participation. Wolfinger and Rosenstone (1980) were the first to document how moving the registration closing date closer to election day, and using other registration mechanisms like election day registration, could lead to increased voter participation. Subsequent research has continued to examine how changing the regulations associated with preelection deadlines can increase voter turnout (e.g., Knack, 1995; Leighley and Nagler, 1992; Nagler, 1991; Rhine, 1995).

However, despite the efforts of reformers – especially recent reforms intended to make the registration and voting process easier and more convenient – there is a debate in the research literature about whether these reforms have actually sparked additional voter participation, or have simply made it easier for already high-propensity voters to participate (Berinsky, Burns, and Traugott, 2001). Others have noted that the effects of these reforms might have been counterbalanced by other changes, most notably the precipitous decline in unionization in the United States (Leighley and Nagler, 2007).

Considerable data indicates that more work is needed to improve the process of voter registration. For example, in the U.S. Census Bureau's recent Current Population Survey (CPS) Voter Supplement, registered nonvoters have been asked why they did not vote; registration problems were one of the explanations for nonvoting. It was this data that the VTP used to produce its estimate of lost votes due to voter registration problems – the 2000 CPS reported that 6.9 percent of registered nonvoters said that they did not vote in that election because of registration problems (CPS, 2002). The same CPS study estimated that there were approximately 18,723,000 registered nonvoters in 2000; simple math indicates that an estimated 1,291,887 registered nonvoters did not participate because of a reported registration problem.

The same calculation can be done using the 2008 CPS (CPS, 2010). In 2008, 6.0 percent of the registered nonvoters said that registration problems kept them from voting. The CPS estimated that there were 15,167,000 registered nonvoters in that election; by the same type of calculation we find that an estimated 910,020 registered nonvoters did not participate because of registration problems. It is important to note the similarity in these estimates between 2000 and 2008; despite federal reform efforts like HAVA, and efforts in many states to improve the registration process, the CPS estimates of registration problems have only fallen slightly in percentage and numerical terms.

In 2008, a nationwide survey was conducted in all fifty states to assess the performance of the electoral process (Alvarez et al., 2009a). Unlike the CPS, this survey probed in detail the registration process, including problems that registered nonvoters experienced with the registration process. This survey found that 22.4 percent of registered nonvoters said that registration problems were either a major or a minor factor deterring them from participating in the 2008 general election (Alvarez et al., 2009a, 64). Significantly, this survey found that registration problems were more likely to be reported by registered but nonvoting racial and ethnic minorities. Specifically, 16.5 percent of registered nonvoting whites reported not voting because of a registration problem, but 37.0 percent of registered nonvoting blacks, 31.9 percent of registered nonvoting Hispanics, and 78.2 percent of registered nonvoting Asians reported not voting because of a registration problem (Alvarez et al., 2009a, 81). Registration problems were also more likely to be reported by younger voters (Alvarez et al., 2009a, 88). These data indicate that many registered nonvoters perceived that the registration process is keeping them from voting and that this perception is not uniformly distributed across the potential electorate.

The exact nature of these problems needs further study. For example, the 2008 survey just discussed provides some indications that this might be the case, as in a number of states where there are relatively easier registration procedures (for example, many of the election day voter registration states) the percentages of registered nonvoters reporting registration problems are lower (Alvarez et al., 2009a, 67–68).[8]

TABLE 10.1. *Reasons for Not Registering, 2008 CPS*

Reasons for not registering	Percentage
Not interested in the election/not involved in politics	46.0
Did not meet registration deadlines	14.7
Not eligible to vote	8.6
Other	6.1
Permanent illness or disability	6.0
Don't know or refused	5.7
Did not know where or how to register	4.2
My vote would not make a difference	4.0
Did not meet residency requirements	3.5
Difficulty with English	1.4

The 2008 CPS asked those who were not registered to vote in that election why they were not registered, and we report those results in Table 10.1 (CPS, 2010). Of the reasons for not being registered, a variety are issues that further reforms to the registration process are unlikely to resolve – for example, making registration easier or more convenient would not likely make Americans more interested, more involved, or more likely to believe that their vote would matter (reasons that total 50 percent of the reasons provided). But note that nearly 15 percent of the nonregistered said they did not meet registration deadlines, 6 percent had an illness or disability that kept them from registration, 4 percent did not know how or where to register, and more than 1 percent had difficulty with English. These reasons make up more than 25 percent of the reasons provided for not being registered, and they are the sorts of problems that could be resolved by reforming or rethinking the registration process in the United States. With approximately 60 million citizens older than age eighteen who are not registered to vote, this means that roughly 15 million Americans would benefit from such reforms.

Recent research has assessed the accuracy of statewide voter registration lists, which might be another problem confronting otherwise eligible voters when they try to participate. For example, McDonald (2007) compared 2004 state voter registration files with data from the CPS and the media consortium exit polls; he found the three generally agreed on gender, but not on age or race.[9] Another indication of the inaccuracies in voter registration lists comes from New York City. Levitt, Weiser, and Munoz noted that "an audit conducted after attempting to match 15,000 records in the voter registration database against those in the state motor vehicle database revealed that almost 20% of those records did not match because of typos by election officials" (2006, 4–5). Gronke (2005) studied undeliverable ballot rates in 2004 in Oregon, which uses all vote by mail, from a selected set of Oregon counties. The study identified undeliverable ballot rates of between 3 percent and 7 percent; this is the accuracy of voter registration data in a state where election officials are in frequent mail contact with registered voters. Although some of these undeliverable mail rates might be due to mistakes or errors, some of these problems no doubt arise because of the highly mobile nature of American society.[10]

Although we have not undertaken a comprehensive study of the accuracy of any state's voter registration database, we undertook a preliminary examination of voter registration data from Ohio. Using Ohio's public release file (dated February 8, 2009), with 8,316,482 records of registered voters, we found a variety of typographical errors. Simply looking at the last name field of this database, we found obvious errors such as instances where the voter's county identification number was incorrectly copied into the voter's last name field, a case where the voter's last name was given as "%", and a voter whose last name was listed as ".Allen" (with the leading period) Other potential errors or issues appear in the database: for many registered voters, their date of registration is given as 1/1/1900, 85,416 records have year of birth entries of "1800", nearly 200 record birth years between 1825 and 1899, and 14,204 list the year of birth as "1900".[11] Although more research on the accuracy of voter registration databases is needed, indications are that voter registration data have many errors, either due to data entry problems, missing information, or because of a highly mobile society.

Other recent research has dug more deeply into these problems. A recent study by Ansolabehere and Hersh (2010) found that of the 185,445,103 listed registration records in the United States, 16,130,325 of those were estimated to be invalid (which is nearly 9 percent of registration records). Furthermore, in a typical state, 1 in 65 registration records are duplicates; 1 in 25 records have a mailing address that is undeliverable; and 1 in 100 listed registrants are likely to be deceased. These errors and problems in voter registration databases seem profound, again despite all of the reforms that have been implemented in recent decades in federal and state efforts like HAVA and NVRA to clean up these lists.

A further issue with the passive American voter registration system is that tertiary organizations – political parties, interest groups, and other advocacy organizations – currently spend considerable resources to register voters. These third-party registrations are important because they seek to register potentially difficult to reach populations, but they are also controversial because there have been concerns of voter registration fraud involving such groups.[12] In talking to election officials, there is evidence that the third-party process also introduces duplication (individuals who already have a valid registration register again) and errors (forms are difficult to read) into the system. Research that we conducted in 2010 showed that in Franklin County, Ohio, the bulk of registration applications in 2008 came from third-party groups or other political organizations – perhaps 70,000 applications in the 2008 election cycle came from such organizations in just Franklin County, Ohio.[13] These groups exist, however, because the government does not engage in active registration.

Claims and concerns about fraud can arise because of these duplications and errors in registration.

MOVING TOWARD ACTIVE REGISTRATION

There are three clear rationales for implementing an active voter registration process: ease, cost, and accuracy. First, as we noted before, the cost for the voter of navigating through the current voter registration process can be difficult. As Alvarez, Hall, and Llewellyn (2007) found, the individuals who have the most difficulty navigating the process are minority and socioeconomically disadvantaged individuals. These "less resourced" individuals are more likely to encounter difficulties registering. Moreover, even when registered, these individuals seem to have more problems keeping their registrations current and problem free (Alvarez et al., 2009a).

Because of these difficulties, many eligible American citizens are not registered to vote. In the most recent census data, nearly 136 million Americans were registered to vote for the 2006 federal elections, of the 210 million citizens, voting-aged eligible Americans. That means there are 74 million American citizens older than eighteen who are not registered to vote. The failure to register is important for two reasons. First, once someone is registered, they are very likely to participate; the Census Bureau reported that in 2006 71 percent of registered voters reported voting in that midterm election. Second, with 74 million eligible American citizens who cannot participate because they are not registered, their preferences are not being reflected in the political process. As registered voters are more likely to be older, married, better educated, more wealthy, and white, it is probable that the political preferences of the unregistered nonparticipants differ from those who are registered to vote.[14]

Second, the current localized system is costly to administer. In a local election office, the process of passive registration can lead to inefficient processing of registration forms in local election offices. In Figure 10.1, we provide an example of this, using data on voter registration flows from Franklin County (Columbus), Ohio for 2007 and 2008. The gray line represents voter registrations received from the Ohio State Bureau of Motor Vehicles (BMV) from individuals who registered to vote when they received or renewed their driver's license. Note that this line is relatively smooth with similar number of registrations coming in each of the twenty-four months from January 2007 through December 2008.

This smooth line can be compared to the total number of registrations processed by the Franklin County Board of Elections. From January to August 2007, the total number of registrations track relatively closely to the number of registrations received from the BMV; roughly two-thirds of all registrations during this period are coming from the BMV (4,818 registrations per month). In the months leading to the November 2007 statewide general election and the March 4, 2008 primary elections (September to February), the number

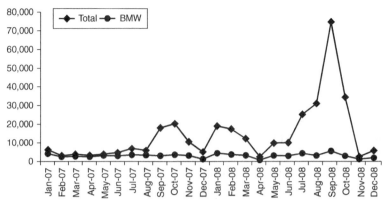

FIGURE 10.1. Voter Registration Form Flows, Franklin County, Ohio.
Source: Franklin County Board of Elections, 2009.

of total registrations increases to approximately 15,118 per month. There is a lull in registrations from March to June 2008 and a slight bump in registrations in July 2008. However, in the three months before the presidential election, 46,742 voters were registering every month, with 74,680 registering in September 2008 alone! More people registered to vote in this three-month period – August to October 2008 – than registered from January 2007 through March 2008.

Handling this large volume of registrations – many of which are duplicates – requires the local election office to hire numerous temporary workers to process the registrations. According to a recent study by the U.S. PIRG Education Fund, maintaining the current voter registration rolls, fixing voter registration problems, and addressing the errors involved in this process is quite costly.[15] In addition, they note that the costs associated with voter registration have to also include the costs of provisional balloting, mailing last minute voting roster changes, and similar activities, all of which raise the costs of voter registration.

Third, the current passive voter registration process lacks accuracy. The processing of so many registration applications – which are typically reentered by hand – increases errors in the file and introduces the likelihood of duplicate registrations. The system also is inefficient in noting movements of people; in a given election, the number of actual registrants in a given precinct may be overestimated or underestimated because of errors in the file. The problems of the inaccuracy in voter registration data can be very costly: poll worker allocations, precinct locations, and other services are based on the voter registration files. Voters can face problems of long lines or understaffing when they go to vote on election day because of these inaccuracies.

HOW WOULD ACTIVE VOTER REGISTRATION WORK IN THE UNITED STATES?

An active voter registration system would remove the burden of voter registration from the shoulders of the voter and place that burden on government agencies. It should be more accurate, as it would largely eliminate the use of registration forms, and would minimize the potential for typographic errors. It should also be more cost-efficient and streamline the election administration process. There are many models for how active voter registration works in other nations. Here, we outline the basic structure for how an active voter registration system might be established in the United States.

The goal would be to develop an active voter registration system that meets international standards, such as the IDEA standard: "The international standard for voter registration is that the register must be comprehensive, inclusive, accurate, and up to date, and the process must be fully transparent. The process should facilitate the registration of a qualified voter but, at the same time, safeguard against the registration of ineligible persons" (IDEA, 2002, 45). Although research needs to be done regarding the quality and coverage of other local, state, and federal databases, we here will focus on a hypothetical example of a statewide demographic database that has very accurate and up to date information on all residents of a state, a database that includes the resident's name, residential address, date of birth, and citizenship.[16] In our example, the state also maintains a fully functional computerized statewide voter registration database, with the full name of each currently registered voter, their residential address, date of birth, mailing address, and voting history information. We assume as well that the demographic and voter registration databases have been constructed using a single database standard to ensure that all of the information in both databases is easily comparable.[17]

Periodically, the demographic file would be matched to the voter registry and a list of voting-eligible individuals who are on the demographic file would be added to the voter registration database in such a way that these records would be marked as new additions to the file of unregistered but otherwise eligible individuals. These unregistered but voting-eligible individuals would then be notified before the election about their registration status – where they were being officially registered, the precinct in which they were to vote, and any change in their status that had occurred since the last time they voted. These individuals would then be given an opportunity to alter their information or to opt off the registration list if they desired or if their name was placed on the registration list in error.[18] Any newly registered voters would have to follow all state and federal laws regarding the provision of appropriate identification when they tried to vote for the first time, either in person or by mail. Upon the verification of their eligibility the first time they voted, they would then be made an active registered voter in the state database. For those voting-eligible individuals whose information does not appear in the state demographic database, or whose information in that database was not updated in sufficient time for them to be included in the list of potential voters, some sort of election day voter registration would be in place so that, once their voting eligibility has been verified, they can cast a ballot and have their identity added to the voter registry.

It is quite easy to argue that the Help America Vote Act of 2002 was intended to create statewide databases that are fully integrated into a state's other data networks. The reports of the National Commission on Federal Election Reform (Carter and Ford, 2002) and the Caltech/MIT Voting Technology Project (VTP, 2001) both recommended the creation of such integrated statewide voter registration systems. Moreover, the language in Section 303 of HAVA is rather specific regarding what a voter registration database should look like. It states:

SEC. 303(a)(B) each State, acting through the chief State election official, shall implement, in a uniform and nondiscriminatory manner, a single, uniform, official, centralized, interactive computerized statewide voter registration list defined, maintained, and administered at the State level that contains the name and registration information of every legally registered voter in the State and assigns a unique identifier to each legally registered voter in the State (in this subsection referred to as the "computerized list"), and includes the following.... (iv) The computerized list shall be coordinated with other agency databases within the State.

As this section of HAVA suggests, Congress proposed a rather specific voter registration system – a state-administered, single, uniform, official, centralized, interactive computerized one that can interact with other state databases. However, Congress also left the statute open to interpretation by the states, which led to wide variation in how states administered this aspect of HAVA in practice, based on guidance from the United States Election Assistance Commission (EAC).[19]

The EAC's 2010 Election Administration & Voting Survey Statutory Overview asked states about the type of registration database that they have and the linkages that the database has with other governmental databases. There are thirty-five states with top-down databases and several of these states have very robust linkages with other databases. These linkages can suggest how, if used correctly, states already have access to an array of information that could be used to populate a voter registry. If we use Georgia as an example, we see that a voter registration system *links to the* following databases for the following purposes (see Figure 10.2):

- Department of Driver Services, which provides a driver's license number, Name, Date of Birth, street address, and information on U.S. Citizenship;
- Social Security Administration, for death records;
- Department of Community Health, for death records;
- Department of Revenue, which can provide Name, Date of Birth, Gender, and a social security identifier;

FIGURE 10.2. Links between voter registration system and other government databases.

- Administrative Office of the Courts and the Department of Corrections, for information on felon records.

Other states also link to the Postal Services National Change of Address system and its national street address record systems. Together, these linkages can be used to create a database of potential voters, as well as people who should be removed from such a list – such as people who may violate a state's felon voting provisions and people who are deceased. These databases are also dynamic – each entity updates its data on some regularized schedule, based on the organization's own standard operating procedures. A state can tap into these systems as necessary for its efforts to build a voter registry.

These statewide registries could, in turn, be interconnected to create a national voter registry that still maintained the state control that would be politically required under our federal system of government. The interconnectivity of such databases is not difficult, once there are protocols for voter registries (Alvarez and Hall, 2008). One reason such systems seem so foreign today is that only fourteen states have top-down voter registries that are also well connected to other state databases.

CONCLUSION

We have presented a broad-brush portrait of a hypothetical active voter registration system. In this system, the primary effort for registering to vote is moved from the voter to the government. Voters are placed on (and removed from) the voting rolls by the government, using data sources that are managed by the government, such as motor vehicle registries, state assistance records, death records, tax records, and related databases. This voter registry would be the primary registration method, with election day voter registration providing a failsafe system.

More research is necessary before this type of system can be fully implemented. First, there is a technological issue: What are the appropriate demographic databases for such a process and are these databases sufficiently interoperable, with data that can be easily compared and linked with a state's existing voter registration database? Managing data interoperability can be difficult because these databases will reside in various agencies that have their own uses for the data. Making this type of voter registration system effective will also require thinking about how these data will be pushed to the local level, and then to the precinct level, for elections.

Second, potential legal barriers may hamper the creation of active registration systems. Many states have laws that govern voter registration and that govern data use that may pose a barrier to voter registration reform. If a state will not allow for certain data to be used for voter registration because of privacy, for example, or limit the way voter registration databases are created, that could stymie reform. Third, there is need to carefully delineate the procedures associated with the development of the list of potential voters, and how their eligibility and identity will be verified the first time they vote. In addition, states will have to determine how a potential election day voter registration system would be implemented as part of this active registration system.

However, the need for study should not stand in the way of pilot projects, in a state or set of states, in the near future aimed at developing and implementing such an active voter registration system. Such pilot projects would allow for policy learning and for the various issues related to the implementation of an active voter registration system to be identified and addressed before large-scale implementation. We have recently been seeing steps that are slowly but steadily moving some states toward the direction of an active registration system. For example, Oregon and Washington have worked on interstate database matching, and have also worked to ascertain how tertiary data matching might improve the accuracy of their voter registration systems.[20] In 2008 and 2010, we have seen states implement different approaches to election day or other same-day voter registration procedures. And we have also seen states like Arizona and Washington integrate their DMV and voter registration processes in ways that allow those with existing DMV records to electronically update or change their voter registration information (Barreto et al., 2010). All of these innovations are steps toward the development of more active voter registration procedures in the United States, and we recommend that these efforts continue.

Notes

1 For details of the evolution of voter registration practices in the United States, see Bensel (2004, 139); Harris (1929, 65–89); Keyssar (2000, 65–66, 151–59).

2 According to information from the U.S. Election Assistance Commission, in the 2008 general election, eight states had election day voter registration (Idaho, Iowa, Maine, Minnesota, Montana, New Hampshire, Wisconsin, and Wyoming), one state had registration and voting at absentee/early voting sites (North Carolina), and one state has a centralized voter file that is updated on election day by voters (North Dakota). Of the remaining states, their preelection voter registration deadlines generally were between two and four weeks prior to the election.

3 Currently Arizona and Washington allow online voter registration for eligible citizens who already have a driver's license; California is soon to implement such a system as well.

4 One exception is North Dakota, which does not require that eligible citizens register to vote, though North Dakota does maintain a central list of voters called the "Central Voter File" (Chapter 16.1–02, North Dakota Election Laws, 2008).

5 See Rosenberg and Chen (2009).

6 See, for example, U.S. Commission on Civil Rights. Voting Irregularities in Florida during the 2000 Presidential Election. Washington, DC: GPO, June 2001 and "Revitalizing Democracy in Florida," a report by the Florida Governor's Select Task Force on Elections Procedures, Standards and Technology.

7 VTP (2009, 59).

8 For example, 9.4 percent of registered nonvoters in Wisconsin (an election day voter registration state) reported registration problems as keeping them from voting, and 6.7 percent in New Hampshire. No registered nonvoters in the sample from Minnesota reported that registration problems kept them from voting.

9 McDonald found that the media consortium exit polls showed a younger electorate than either the voter registration files or the CPS, and that the media exit polls in 2004 showed fewer white voters than the CPS or the voter registration files.

10 The U.S. Census Bureau estimated that 40.1 million American residents moved between 2002 and 2003, with 59 percent of these being moves within the same county, 19 percent to a different county in the same state, 19 percent to a different state, and 3 percent from abroad (Schachter, 2004).

11 While some of these entries might be correct, they appear to occur with too great a frequency, or have other problems that seem illogical. Consider, for example, the voter whose date of registration is given as 1/1/1900, and whose birth year is given as 1952! Our inference is that birth year entries like "1800" or date of registration entries like "1/1/1900" are being used as missing data indicators, or in some cases might be typographical errors.

12 For competing views on this, see "The New Crackdown on Voter Registration Drives," http://brennan.3cdn.net/d3f8df8f1a5316dba6_ncm6bxts8.pdf and "Stolen Identities, Stolen Votes: A Case Study in Voter Impersonation," https://www.policyarchive.org/bitstream/handle/10207/13529/lm_22.pdf.

13 See figure 9.3, "Franklin County Total Registration Applications by Source, 2008"; Alvarez, Hall, and Llewellyn (2010).

14 For example, in the 2006 Census CPS Voting Supplement data (File [2008], the most recent CPS report currently available), table 2 provides detailed data on the national population of registered voters. In 2006, 69.5 percent of citizen voting-aged whites were registered to vote, compared to 60.9 percent of blacks and 53.7 percent of Hispanics. Forty-six percent of the 18–24-year-old citizens were registered to vote, compared to 77.1 percent of those citizens aged fifty-five and older. In terms of education, 47.5 percent of voting-aged citizens who had less than a high school degree were registered, compared to 77.9 percent of voting-aged citizens with a college degree.

15 See http://www.uspirg.org/uploads/d_/yo/d_yoJms3xiodWDrSojL_Eg/USP-Saving-Dollars-Saving-Democracy.pdf.

16 There have been a number of proposals recently for similar voter registration processes; see for example Weiser, Waldman, and Paradis (2009). See also McDonald (2008) for discussion of the reasons for making voter registration more portable. A database like this would need to be constructed from a variety of other government databases, for example the state's database of those with driver's licenses and government-issued identification cards, data from educational institutions, and other information from government agencies. Clearly there are many issues that need to be resolved: technically, these databases all need to be integrated so that matching and merging are efficient; legally, state regulations associated with the use of many of these forms of data may likely need to be revised; procedurally, the privacy and security of these databases if used for voter registration need analysis. This is an area that needs to be studied.

17 For a discussion of such database standards and their importance in applications like these, see Alvarez and Hall (2005).

18 Legislation would be necessary to ensure that any individual whose name was incorrectly placed on the registration list solely by the action of the government would not be subjected to any criminal penalties.

19 The Section 305 of HAVA notes, "The specific choices on the methods of complying with the requirements of this title shall be left to the discretion of the State." This language allowed states to decide what was or was not a statewide database. The EAC guidance for statewide voter registration systems can be found at http://www.eac.gov/assets/1/workflow_staging/Page/330.PDF (last accessed September 27, 2012).

20 For a report of the Oregon-Washington interstate database matching effort, see Alvarez and colleagues (2009b).

11

Felon Disenfranchisement after *Bush v. Gore*: Changes and Trends

Khalilah L. Brown-Dean

On November 7, 2000, Marie Jackson attempted to cast a ballot in what would become one of the most contested elections of our time. She gave her name and identification to a poll worker but was told that she wasn't on the list of registered voters. Despite her pleas, Jackson was not allowed to vote. She later learned from a neighbor working the polls that her name appeared on a list of more than 80,000 Florida residents who were barred from voting because of a prior felony conviction. The list also contained the names of thousands of state residents who were "suspected felons" and matched by simple characteristics such as name or date of birth. Individuals with common names ran a high risk of being mistakenly included on the list. Another 8,000 Florida residents who were convicted of misdemeanor offenses were erroneously included in the felon purge list while nearly 5,000 citizens whose voting rights had been restored were still banned from voting. In all, nearly 1 million Florida residents were barred from voting in the 2000 presidential election. The brunt of that exclusion was particularly harsh for African Americans, who comprised about 32 percent of Florida's disenfranchised population (Brown-Dean, forthcoming). One in every three black male residents of Florida was barred from voting.

Two years prior, the state of Florida had signed a $4 million contract with a company called Data Base Technologies to cleanse the voting rolls of felons and create a central voter file. The push to cleanse the voting rolls resulted from allegations that the former mayor of Miami, Republican Xavier Suarez, received votes from felons, noncitizens, and the deceased during his 1997 bid for office (Navarro, 1998). The investigation into fraudulent voter rolls resulted in the arrest of the city commissioner and his staff and Suarez's removal from office. In theory, the creation of a central voter file seemed like an appropriate way of protecting the integrity of the electoral process. In practice, this process set in motion a protracted national conversation regarding the fairness and consequences of felon disenfranchisement.

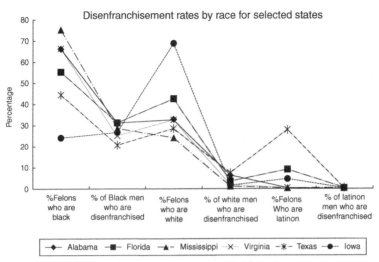

FIGURE 11.1. Disenfranchisement rates by race for selected states.

Felon disenfranchisement laws prohibit current, and in many states, former felony offenders from voting. In forty-eight states and the District of Columbia inmates are barred from voting. The overwhelming majority (approximately 80%) of America's disenfranchised population, however, is citizens who have already served their time. Currently more than 5 million Americans are *permanently* barred from voting because of a prior felony conviction. Together blacks and Latinos comprise more than 40 percent of America's disenfranchised population. As Figure 11.1 indicates, the impact is particularly pronounced in states like Virginia with sizeable minority populations. However, even in states like Utah with relatively small minority populations, disenfranchisement restrictions sharply constrain access to the ballot. In Iowa, for example, 27 percent of African American men are barred from voting compared to 4.5 percent of Hispanic men and 1.5 percent of white men. The overrepresentation of communities of color within America's criminal justice system coupled with state-level autonomy diminishes access to the simplest tool of democracy: the vote.

The massive national and international attention devoted to irregularities surrounding Florida's role in the 2000 presidential election coupled with the racially disparate impact of disenfranchisement provisions prompted a number of states to revisit their disenfranchisement provisions. Since 2000, forty-two state legislatures have introduced legislation concerning the existence and administration of disenfranchisement provisions. This reexamination is part of a national restoration trend that has brought hundreds of thousands of American voters back into the electorate (King, 2006). These changes have occurred in a variety of contexts such as Democratic and Republican-controlled legislatures, Southern and non-Southern states, and states with varying levels of crime problems.

This chapter is a review of the major legislative and judicial developments that have occurred since 2000. Though a number of states have made significant progressive reforms to their statutes, some have also adopted more punitive reforms aimed at solidifying the presence and impact of disenfranchisement. These revisions have addressed four major areas of concern:

1) Should felons be permanently disenfranchised? On what should states base their decisions regarding the terms and length of disenfranchisement?
2) How do we gauge the discriminatory motivations and/or consequences of felon disenfranchisement?
3) What civil penalties (e.g., monetary fines, restrictions on access to housing, education, etc.) should be attached to sentencing?
4) How should inmates be counted within apportionment plans?

JUDICIAL DEVELOPMENTS

A total of seven major cases challenging the merits of felon disenfranchisement have emerged since 2000: *Farrakhan v. Washington* (9th Circuit, 2003), *Johnson v. Bush* (11th Circuit, 2005), *Hayden v. Pataki* (2nd Circuit, 2006), *Danielson v. Dennis* (CO Supreme Court, 2006), *Madison v. Washington* (WA Supreme Court, 2007), *Simmons v. Galvin* (1st Circuit, 2009), and *Farrakhan v. Gregoire* (9th Circuit, 2010 (2)). While the jurisprudence of state and circuit courts does not technically hold beyond their jurisdiction, the rationale presented often informs similar cases that arise across the country. This is particularly important given that the Supreme Court has continuously refused to issue a writ of certiorari to review any of these cases.

Farrakhan v. Washington seemed to open the door to increased judicial intervention in the realm of felon disenfranchisement.[1] The majority opinion of the Ninth Circuit Court stated that "felon disenfranchisement is a voting qualification, and Section 2 is clear that *any* voting qualification that denies citizens the right to vote in a discriminatory manner violates the VRA [Voting Rights Act]."[2] Under the guidelines set forth by the court's decision in the monumental *Hunter v. Underwood* case, previous plaintiffs focused on the "intent requirement" to show a discriminatory denial of the franchise. However, *Farrakhan* eased this burden by requiring that future plaintiffs "show, based on the *totality of the circumstances*, that the challenged voting practice results in discrimination on account of race," including evidence of discrimination in the justice system.[3] However, this ruling would not be echoed in similar cases across the country.

Johnson v. Bush was the name given to a class action suit against the state of Florida on behalf of "all Florida citizens convicted of felonies who have completed their sentences but nonetheless remain ineligible to vote."[4] The highly controversial 537-vote margin that separated George W. Bush and Al Gore focused intense attention on Florida and allegations of improper conduct. In

December 2000 Governor Jeb Bush created the bipartisan Select Task Force on Election Procedures, Standards, and Technology to study and make written policy recommendations and/or propose legislation to improve election procedures, standards, and technology employed in each of Florida's sixty-seven counties.[5] Although the task force made a number of important recommendations concerning ballot design, upgrading equipment, and standardizing procedures for counting ballots, it did little to address the high rates of disenfranchisement in the Sunshine State.[6]

The Florida Election Reform Act of 2001 was passed by state legislators in direct response to the task force's recommendations. However, the final legislation was sharply criticized by advocacy groups such as the ACLU and the state NAACP for failing to adequately address the disproportionate number of Florida residents who were barred from voting because of a prior conviction. In 2001 the ACLU assisted in filing a class action lawsuit alleging that the state's Department of Corrections failed to comply with state law concerning the clemency process to have one's civil rights restored. The case, *Florida Conference of Black State Legislators et al. v. Moore*, successfully forced the Florida Parole Commission and the Office of Executive Clemency to revamp their arduous clemency process. The two offices streamlined the application process and created new procedures for assisting offenders *before* they are released from supervision. However, these procedural changes still did not result in comprehensive re-enfranchisement.

Florida legislators revisited the issue with a 2006 law that requires correctional institutions to distribute the restoration of civil rights application to inmates at least two weeks before they are released from custody. Shortly after his election in 2007, Republican governor Charlie Crist amended the state's clemency process for restoring the rights of former felons convicted of non-violent crimes. Under the prior rules for executive clemency Florida residents could not have their rights reinstated unless the state clemency board approved them on an individual basis. Florida residents who have paid all fines and restitution and have no new criminal charges may now pursue automatic reinstatement. Critics such as the Brennan Center for Justice (2007) argue that these streamlined procedures are still problematic because they impose a financial burden on former offenders seeking to have their rights restored.[7] Further, they allege that the restoration procedures remain unnecessarily cumbersome. In 2008, notifications were sent to the more than 115,000 former felons who qualified for this restoration. A report issued by the Florida Parole Commission shows that more than 55,000 cases await review.

The Eleventh Circuit Court rejected the federal constitutional claims raised in *Johnson v. Bush* by noting a provision in the Fourteenth Amendment allowing for the exclusion of felons from the vote, and similarly rejected appeals to the Voting Rights Act of 1965. The court noted that "the case for rejecting the plaintiffs' reading of the statute is particularly strong here, where Congress has expressed its intent to *exclude* felon disenfranchisement provisions from Voting

Rights Act scrutiny."[8] While the court reaffirmed that disenfranchisement laws may not be used to intentionally discriminate on the basis of race, the justices claimed no clear evidence on the question of intent and stated clearly that "federal courts cannot question the wisdom" of any given state policy outside of its constitutionality.[9]

Hayden v. Pataki, a 2005 New York case submitted on behalf of currently incarcerated felons and parolees, was decided in favor of maintaining the ban on a similar interpretation of the Voting Rights Act found in *Johnson v. Bush*. However, the court's opinion was careful to note that "this case poses a complex and difficult question that, absent Congressional clarification, will only be definitively resolved by the Supreme Court."[10] One issue raised by outside organizations in *Hayden v. Pataki* was the question of congressional apportionment. The National Voting Rights Institute and the Prison Policy Initiative filed an amicus brief challenging the current law that apportions felons as residents of the district their prison is located in despite the fact that they cannot vote in that district.[11] The Census Bureau has used the Usual Residence Rule since its inception in 1790 to identify "the place where a person lives and sleeps most of the time."[12] It's important to note, however, that usual residence is not synonymous with legal residence. In most states legal residence is defined as the place where "you have your permanent home or principal establishment and to where, whenever you are absent, you intend to return."[13] The usual residence standard is also used to count groups such as college students and military personnel. However, the enumeration of prisoners differs from the counting of these other groups. Inmates in the United States are counted as residents of the town they are incarcerated in as opposed to their place of legal residence. In turn, areas with larger prison populations receive the direct economic benefit of prison hosting as well as a disproportionate share of valuable political resources such as legislative districts and funds for the delivery of social service programs.

In *Danielson v. Dennis*, the Colorado Supreme Court heard a case submitted on behalf of more than 6,000 parolees seeking to have their right to vote restored. The case was based on a clause in the Colorado Constitution that states "that persons who were qualified electors prior to their imprisonment and who have served their full term of imprisonment shall have their rights of citizenship restored to them."[14] However, the Court found that those "serving a sentence of parole" could be said to have "not served his or her full term of imprisonment," and thus no constitutional violation occurred.[15]

Madison v. Washington, the second of three Washington state cases cited here, was also challenged on both federal constitutional grounds and the privileges and immunities clause of the Washington Constitution. The plaintiffs challenged the denial of "the right to vote to convicted felons who have not completed all of the terms of their sentences, including full payment of their legal financial obligations (LFOs)," claiming it discriminated improperly based on wealth.[16] (The clause reads: "[n]o law shall be passed granting to any citizen, class of citizens, or corporation other than municipal, privileges or immunities which upon the same terms shall not equally belong to all citizens, or corporations.")[17] Finding that voting rights were a privilege extended as part of state citizenship that could be rightly stripped from felons in part, the court chose to rule solely on whether the felon disenfranchisement passed a rational basis test, determining state interests were connected plausibly enough to justify the prohibition.[18]

Like many of the prior cases, *Simmons v. Galvin* challenged the disenfranchisement of Massachusetts felons based on the Voting Rights Act, but the plaintiffs also cited the *ex post facto* clause on behalf of inmates who were incarcerated prior to the tightening of laws in 2000. The court first rejected the VRA claim, appealing to the standard of discriminatory intent.[19] It then rejected the *ex post facto* claim, holding that disenfranchisement was a regulatory, not punitive measure, thus exempting it from the clause.[20] Justice Juan Torruella's dissent echoed Justice Sotomayor's in *Hayden v. Pataki*, protesting that the Voting Rights Act was being reinterpreted based on dubious intent grounds despite clarity of wording.[21]

Farrakhan v. Gregoire, a challenge to Washington state law following directly from the 2003 *Farrakhan case*, is emblematic of the direction in which judicial decisions have progressed. After an initial decision by the traditionally liberal Ninth Circuit Court that "discrimination in the criminal justice system on account of race" existed within Washington State and could be a contributing factor to validating a claim of racial disparity, the case was reheard and reversed as a matter of law. Citing *Johnson*, *Hayden*, and *Simmons*, the court "conlude[d] that the rule announced in Farrakhan I sweeps too broadly," returning the standard to that of intentional discrimination.[22]

LEGISLATIVE DEVELOPMENTS

In response to the national impact of Florida's disenfranchisement provision and subsequent purging errors, a number of congressmen sought a federal solution to the problem during the subsequent 2001–03 legislative session. Rep. John Conyers (D-MI) introduced a bill at the beginning of the congressional session, reproduced in the Senate, that would have permitted all ex-felons to vote in federal elections.[23] The legislation met with sharp opposition from conservative legislators such as Senate Minority Leader Mitch McConnell (R-KY), who stated, "those who break our laws should not dilute the vote of law-abiding citizens," while others like Senator Jeff Sessions advocated continuing to defer to the "different standards" of the individual states "based on their moral evaluation, their legal evaluation, their public interest."[24] In the end, the legislation failed to pass in either chamber while raising significant questions regarding the constitutionality of a federal right to vote and its relationship to states' rights.

In many ways the failure to enact reform at the federal level stimulated a great deal of activity at the state level. While legislative change on the subject of felon and ex-felon voting was not unique to the period after *Bush v. Gore* – George W. Bush had signed a law as governor of Texas in 1997 eliminating a two-year waiting period for former felons to regain voting rights – the volume of change rose significantly from the decade prior. Looking back from 2010, the *New York Times* pinpointed the 2000 presidential election as the tipping point politically for bringing many of these bills to the dockets of state legislatures.[25] According to the *New York Times's* analysis of the Sentencing Project's report on the subject, 800,000 citizens had their voting rights restored over the course of the decade following the 2000 presidential election because of the rolling back of laws against felon and ex-felon voting.[26] However, not all trends have been in favor of greater openness of the franchise. The following is a state-by-state breakdown of major changes made by state legislatures and governors since 2000:[27]

GREATER RESTRICTION

*In 2002, the Kansas legislature passed a law to include probationers in the "excluded felon" category.

MIXED RESULT

*In 2005, Iowa Governor Tom Vilsack used an executive order to restore voting rights for all former felons; his successor, Governor Terry Branstad, repealed this order in 2011.

*In 2007, Florida's Office of Executive Clemency approved the automatic restoration of rights for many persons convicted of nonviolent offenses, but the decision was reversed in 2011, with former felons now required to wait five years after completion of sentence to seek restoration of the franchise.

LESSER RESTRICTION

*In 2001, New Mexico repealed its lifetime ban on ex-felon voting, followed by a 2005 provision requiring the Department of Corrections to directly inform the secretary of state when incarceration was completed.

*In 2001, Connecticut approved a bill extending voting rights to felons on probation – a measure led by the Connecticut Black and Puerto Rican Caucus.[28]

*In 2003, Nevada approved an automatic restoration of voting rights for first time nonviolent offenders immediately after completing their sentence.

*In 2005, Nebraska replaced its prior lifetime ban on felon voting with a two-year ban following incarceration.

*In 2007, Maryland replaced all provisions of the state's lifetime voting ban with an automatic restoration of voting rights for all former felons after completion of their sentence.

GREATER EASE OF APPLICATION

*In 2001, Kentucky approved a measure requiring eligible offenders to be informed of and assisted in efforts to restore their voting rights post imprisonment.

*In 2003, Alabama adjusted its disenfranchisement law to allow most felons to apply for a certificate of eligibility to register to vote following time served.

*Also in 2003, Wyoming adjusted its felon voting ban to allow nonviolent first time offenders to apply for restoration of the franchise five years after the completion of their sentence.

*In 2006, Tennessee simplified "the country's most complex restoration system" by allowing all former felons (with the exception of those convicted of "electoral or serious violent offenses") to apply for a "certificate of restoration" from the Board of Probation and Parole after satisfying outstanding financial obligations.

*In 2009, Washington State eliminated the requirement of full payment of fines/fees/restitution for former felons seeking the restoration of their voting rights.

Though many states have clearly trended in a direction of reducing the severity of disenfranchisement – though executive order is more prone to reversal – none completely abolished its existing restrictions on both felon and ex-felon voting after 2000. Of the fifty states, only two – Maine and Vermont – maintain no restrictions on felon voting whatsoever. This figure stands in sharp contrast to other democratically comparable countries who reserve disenfranchisement for very serious crimes of electoral fraud.

Even as laws may appear to trend in the direction of greater openness, the application process for the restoration of civil rights may be too cumbersome to render progressive reform effective. Florida again offers a particularly important angle. Governor Charlie Crist's efforts in Florida to make it easier for former offenders to restore their voting rights drew much attention. However, only a ninth of the 950,000 felons and former felons denied the franchise had their rights restored, not least because of the financial burden of paying restitution required before one could obtain restoration. It remains unclear how many of those eligible for readmittance to the ballot were even aware of how to restore their rights.[29]

What was the impact of the 2000 presidential election and *Bush v. Gore* on the area of disenfranchisement in the public arena? In the realm of jurisprudence, the impact might be considered minimal. Though a number of cases arose over the next decade, perhaps inspired by the 2000 situation, no case besides *Farrakhan v. Washington* seriously broke with Supreme Court precedent, and even that break was later reversed. *Bush v. Gore* itself was intentionally designed to narrowly address the case at hand, and even the four dissents do not address the issue directly. However, the political impact of the election brought the issue of felon disenfranchisement back into the public sphere, and likely helped the overall push toward liberalization. A study conducted in 2010 by Brown-Dean (forthcoming) found that more Americans were opposed to the idea of lifetime disenfranchisement than ever before. Similarly, respondents were more likely to question the motives behind disenfranchisement after receiving information about the racially disparate impact and political consequences.

THE IMPACT

The issue of felon disenfranchisement is inextricably tied to the racial politics of the country. Because of a variety of factors ranging from outright racism to national class dynamics, American blacks face much higher incarceration rates than the nation on the whole – 10 percent of African Americans are under some kind of "correctional supervision" versus 2 percent of the country on the whole.[30] Despite Kentucky's 2001 nominal effort to assist some former offenders in regaining their rights through petition to the governor, one in four African Americans in Kentucky remains disenfranchised.[31] Going beyond disproportionate impact, racial politics appears to inform the design of these laws as well. Though many felon disenfranchisement laws date back more than a century – some prior to federally mandated enfranchisement of blacks – it appears that "large nonwhite prison populations increase the odds of passing restrictive laws" against felon voting rights in the modern era.[32] A number of the laws in the American South can be directly traced to efforts to prevent freed slaves from being able to exercise the franchise.[33] However, emphasis on this history has proven a double-edged sword for opponents of disenfranchisement law, while knowledge of this racial history can contribute to the law's unpopularity.

There is some disagreement among social scientists as to the degree to which extensive disproportionate disenfranchisement actually impacts election outcomes. Christopher Uggen and Jeff Manza suggest in their 2002 paper "Democratic Contraction?" that felon disenfranchisement laws not only changed the outcome of the 2000 presidential election, but seven Senate races in recent history as well.[34] However, Thomas Miles has suggested projected turnout rates for former felons in many papers "may be optimistic" because of low voter registration rates prior to arrest, having claimed the overall impact on election outcomes is low.[35] Work by Traci Burch (2013) makes a similar argument that the socioeconomic profile of felons even before their time of conviction makes it highly unlikely that even with access to the franchise, they would exercise it. Other work by Brown-Dean cautions that in understanding the relationship between disenfranchisement and electoral politics, the scope must be widened to consider not just the individual convicted of a crime, but the broader community to which s/he belongs. In my forthcoming book, I examine the impact of disenfranchisement on what I term *concentrated punishment communities*: communities with disproportionate rates of crime, disenfranchisement, and punishment and disruptive rates of civic retreat.[36]

While current and former felons may be denied their right to vote, their procedural impact on congressional apportionment cannot be erased. As noted earlier in the discussion of *Hayden v. Pataki*, continuing to count felons as residents of the prison in which they are held rather than their former communities while simultaneously denying them the vote can function as a "representation drain" where high-crime communities lose legislative representation to communities hosting prisons. In New York, the subject of *Hayden v. Pataki*, the racial implications were particularly clear. As cited by the Prison Policy Initiative, "rural white counties with additional population based on the presence of disenfranchised prisoners in upstate prisons" gained representation while "diminish[ing] the voting strength of non-incarcerated persons of color in the prisoners' home communities."[37] This representation calculus is used for both state and federal apportionment, thus diminishing poor and minority communities' ability to receive adequate representation relative to their size. One cannot help but draw a parallel between this system and the amended Three-Fifths Clause of the U.S. Constitution, allowing slave societies to draw apportionment power from their slaves held in bondage while preventing them from obtaining the franchise.

WHAT CAN BE DONE?

The development of felon disenfranchisement policy since *Bush v. Gore* has been a tale of two trends: continued but increasingly defined conservatism in terms of judicial unwillingness to overturn legislative action, and a slow liberalization of legislative policies. The opportunity for the latter should be seized, particularly given the potential for reversal in executive-level decisions, as in Iowa and Florida. Unless the atmosphere of the Supreme Court changes, it may be considered ill advised for opponents of disenfranchisement to put greater pressure on the high court to take up a case to clarify the interpretation of the Voting Rights Act and Fourteenth/Fifteenth Amendments that the Court sees as appropriate at this time. Even if the Court broke with its prior conservative interpretation, any more liberal interpretation would be out of step with current jurisprudence to the extent that the clear language cited by Justice Sotomayor in the Voting Rights Act prohibiting all discriminatory voter qualification practices might be in danger of being repealed by a reactionary Congress concerned with preserving state prerogative.

Though the goal of voting rights for both current and former felons may be maintained, a focus on parolees and former felons may prove more fruitful because of higher levels of public support for effective reentry. As of 2005, only 26 percent of the 5,000,000 disenfranchised through anti-felon legislation were currently serving jail time.[38] Efforts such as the Democracy Restoration Act – an updated version of the Conyers bill cited earlier – focus primarily on permitting these ex-felons to vote in federal elections, and would entirely change the landscape of the issue if passed.[39] However, it will not be enough to merely allow for a process of restoration. While any legislative progress on the state level may be encouraging for opponents of felon disenfranchisement, this incremental development may rest as a hollow victory for those seeking to regain their voting rights. The automatic restoration of civil rights for eligible current and former felons, particularly where application for restoration is intended to be mostly perfunctory, should be sought as a crucial advancement over existing laws.

On the topic of representation and responsiveness, more complex reforms may be required. Advocates of reform may also seek to address "constituent drain" by adjusting the ways "primary residence" is determined for prisoners – as has occurred in Maryland, New York, and Delaware.[40] The enumeration of American prisoners is intimately tied to larger debates over disenfranchisement, representation, and democracy. In general, advocates for greater political inclusion must seek to improve and expand political representation for those groups most effected – not just for individual felons, but for the broader demographic communities to which they belong. Another possible pathway to reform may be shaping public opinion on and support for re-enfranchisement. To date only three states have offered referenda on the issue of felon disenfranchisement: Utah in 1998, Massachusetts in 2000, and Rhode Island in 2006. Utah and Massachusetts voters chose to "stri[p] persons incarcerated for a felony offense of their right to vote," while Rhode Island voters chose to restore voting rights to those serving probation or parole. Still, if the greater populace can be educated about the pernicious nature of current disenfranchisement policy, the most representative body may very well end up being the populace itself.

Notes

1 Section 2 is a permanent provision of the Voting Rights Act of 1965 that prohibits discrimination on the basis of race, creed, color, or membership in one of the federally identified language groups. Section 2 is designed to ensure that minority voters have equal access to the political process. In 1982 the provision was amended to address electoral rules that have a discriminatory *impact* even when intent cannot be proven.

2 *Farrakhan v. Washington*, 10139.

3 Ibid., 10142–44.

4 *Johnson v. Bush*, 214 F. Supp. 2d 1333, 1335.

5 Bush, Jeb. 2002. "Election Reform in Florida: Meeting the Challenge." *Election Law Journal* 1(3): 311–14.

6 Florida's reform bill became an important model for the federal government's Help America Vote Act (HAVA) that became law in 2002. Much like the Florida bill, HAVA mandated that punch card systems be replaced and that interested voters be provided with provisional ballots during disputes over eligibility.

7   The Brennan Center for Justice. "Progressive Changes in Laws 2006–2007." (August 21, 2007).

8   *Johnson v. Bush* (2005 – 11th circuit, *en banc*).

9   Ibid., 40.

10 *Hayden v Pataki*, 310.

11 http://www.prisonpolicy.org/news/pr06222005.html.

12 *Source:* U.S. Census Bureau (2000), "Plans and Rules for Taking the Census, Residence Rules."

13 U.S. Department of Defense, Federal Voting Assistance Program, http://www.fvap.gov/laws/legal.html.

14 *Danielson v. Dennis*, 3.

15 Ibid.

16 *Madison v. Washington*, 1.

17 Ibid., 8.

18 Ibid., 13, 15, 31.

19 *Simmons v. Galvin*, 2.

20 Ibid., 41.

21 Ibid., 47–48. Pointed out to me here: http://electionlawblog.org/archives/014188.html.

22 *Farrakhan v. Gregoire*, 2–5.

23 Behrens, Uggen, and Manza, "Ballot Manipulation and the 'Menace of Negro Domination,'" 596.

24 Ibid., 572–73.

25 http://www.nytimes.com/2010/10/20/opinion/20wed4.html?ref=felonydisenfranchisement.

26 Ibid.

27 The Sentencing Project Report, "Felony Disenfranchisement Laws in the United States," March 2011.

28 Behrens, Uggen, and Manza, "Ballot Manipulation and the 'Menace of Negro Domination,'" 596.

29 http://www.nytimes.com/2008/06/30/opinion/30mon3.html?ref=felonydisenfranchisement.

30 Behrens, Uggen, and Manza, "Ballot Manipulation and the 'Menace of Negro Domination,'" 574.

31 http://www.brennancenter.org/blog/archives/kentuckys_disturbing_disenfranchisement_numbers/.

32 Behrens, Uggen, and Manza, "Ballot Manipulation and the 'Menace of Negro Domination,'" 559.

33 http://www.nytimes.com/2010/03/22/opinion/22mon3.html?ref=felonydisenfranchisement.

34 Uggen and Manza, "Democratic Contraction?" 794.

35 Miles, "Felon Disenfranchisement and Voter Turnout," 177.

36 Khalilah L Brown-Dean, forthcoming. *Once Convicted, Forever Doomed: Punishment, Citizenship, and Civil Death*. Yale University Press.

37 http://www.prisonpolicy.org/news/pr06222005.html.

38 Uggen, Behrens, and Manza, "Criminal Disenfranchisement," 308.

39   http://www.nytimes.com/2010/03/22/opinion/22mon3.html?ref=felonydisenfranc
     hisement.
40   See *Baltimore Sun* article for coverage of one: http://articles.baltimoresun.
     com/2010–04–27/news/bs-ed-baltimore-prisons-20100427_1_prison-inmates-
     residents-legislative.

Epilogue: *Bush v. Gore* and the Constitutional Right to Vote

Samuel Issacharoff and Richard H. Pildes

The purely partisan perspective on *Bush v. Gore*[1] focuses on the ongoing, contested dimensions of a close election and the controversial role of the Supreme Court in declaring game over. On this telling, the *Bush v. Gore* decision was a denial of the right of every vote to be counted amid an institutional power grab for the Republican Party. From this point of view, the main legacy of that dramatic moment in constitutional and political history is that everything possible should be done to allow postelection validation of all votes, including the expanding role for provisional ballots. The reform upshot was the Help America Vote Act[2] (HAVA), a complicated legislative gambit that tried to rationalize state voter registration records at the state level, created a generally useless Electoral Assistance Commission, and enshrined a system of post-election challenges to provisional ballots that, while perhaps better than the other available options, is also a litigation nightmare just waiting to happen.

Perhaps the passage of time will allow an alternative story, one in which the postelection partisan scramble was even more important as a window into the much more pervasive and structural dysfunctionalities of the American electoral system. This alternative account begins at the top with a winner-take-all Electoral College system that created the cliff effect necessary for Florida 2000 – the ability of a few hundred actual votes to determine whether Florida's twenty-five Electoral College votes would be entirely captured by George Bush or Al Gore. From there, the story of electoral dysfunction would cast attention on how control of federal elections is still, more than 200 years since the Constitution's creation, overwhelmingly left in the hands of the states and, ultimately, in those of local county administrators. Voting lists are kept in local polling books; volunteers (mostly female and mostly senior, even on a more probing reexamination) staff election administration generally with inadequate training and little more than episodic engagement with complicated election rules. This account would add in the local administrators who purchase voting machines from friendly vendors and devise ballots based on whimsical expectations of voter capabilities. And the list would run to partisan control of the machinery of elections. Here we would engage the devotion of major electoral resources to combat illusory claims of in-person fraud by constricting early voting, adding identification requirements, and generally clogging the machinery in ways that invite a takeover by Starbucks or Cheesecake Factory, or any competent market-tested firm able to satisfy basic consumer needs.

Under this alternative viewpoint, the *Bush v. Gore* decision may have been partial, incomplete, hesitating, right on substance but wrong on remedy – the list is by no means exhausted. Yet it may also have been the opening wedge in defining a broader claim of citizen expectation that voting should be accessible and fair. Any legal requirement of basic fairness would place a bull's eye on the structural guarantees of dysfunctionality of the electoral system, starting with its partisan overseers and continuing right on through its localized administrators. On this more far-reaching reading, the Supreme Court's efforts to find a guiding legal principle for constitutional oversight might provide a foothold for challenging some of the more bizarre excesses of our electoral system. A single case study of Ohio provides evidence whether this attempt to rescue a broader constitutional commitment to the right to vote is simply Panglossian, or whether the moment has finally come to integrate a conception of proper democratic functioning into the Constitution.

We look to Ohio because the past three presidential elections have either turned on the outcome in Ohio or, perhaps more significant, because the past three presidential campaigns were waged on the presumption that Ohio could be the touchstone of the entire election.

I

As the chapter by Paul Gronke nicely chronicles, perhaps the most significant change in voting law and practice in the decade after *Bush v. Gore* was the sudden emergence of early voting (EV) as a central feature of American elections. Although early voting existed in some places before 2000, it has exploded since then, with thirty-two states now adopting some form of pre–election day voting. As their work documents, the proportion of ballots cast early grew by around 50 percent in each presidential election from 2000 to 2008 (with some dips in midterm elections). For the 2008 presidential election, about 34 percent of the electorate (44 million voters) voted early. Preliminary indications are that the percentage was even higher in the 2012 election, despite the fact that some large states, such as Ohio and Florida, cut back on the number of early voting days available. As Gronke argues, this dramatic flourishing of early voting since 2000 is directly attributable to the combined forces of the 2000 election, *Bush v. Gore*, and the enactment of HAVA.

Yet while early voting has been among the most significant practical changes to the election system since 2000, the courts had not been required to grapple with this new category of voting in any significant way until the 2012 election cycle. The essential legal question is how to understand early voting as a legal matter, including for purposes of constitutional law. Indeed, the most significant election litigation in 2012 was about early voting, with cases in Ohio and Florida (including cases litigated the weekend of the election) leading to more than 106,000 people in Ohio alone making use of judicial decisions to vote the weekend before the election. The judicial decisions that resulted will be important for the future of election law for two reasons: first, because they indicate how courts are going to conceive of early voting as a legal category; and second, because these decisions continue the evolution of jurisprudence concerning the right to vote and show how courts are beginning doctrinally to integrate *Bush v. Gore* into that evolving jurisprudence.

On the first issue, one way to frame the question of how to treat EV as a legal category is to reason by analogy: Should the courts treat EV more like traditional election day voting or more like absentee voting? Is EV best understood, legally, as expanding election day back in time a bit, so that the legal and constitutional framework should be thought about much like the framework that applies to election day in general? Or is EV best understood as more like traditional absentee voting, in which states have long made decisions about which groups of voters have sufficiently good "excuses" for not being able to show up on election day to justify their access to an absentee ballot? Doctrinally, any lines that a state draws on who can cast a vote at the ballot box are going to be subject to the most exacting scrutiny and upheld only for purposes of ensuring bona fide residency, eligibility, and the like. Yet for absentee balloting, the doctrine is exactly the opposite: the Supreme Court decided more than forty years ago, in a fairly obscure case called *McDonald v. Board of Election Commissioners*,[3] that the lines states drew in deciding which voters would have access to absentee ballots should be subject only to a minimal rational basis standard. Although commentators have questioned that decision, courts of appeals continue to apply it in absentee balloting cases.

This question was the fundamental one underlying the most consequential piece of election litigation in the 2012 cycle. Long lines and other problems in the 2004 election had led Ohio to create an expansive early voting system, which had helped the 2008 election process run more smoothly. Yet in the run-up to the 2012 election, the Ohio legislature cut back on the amount of early voting, including eliminating it on weekends. Through a crazy quilt pattern of bills, repealed bills and, the qualification of a voter referendum on voting issues, Ohio had ended up in a situation in which, on the weekend before election day, some voters – military and overseas voters, as defined by federal law – would have access to early voting while all other voters would not. Indeed, Ohio might have simply stumbled into the situation it created: the state actually enacted two separate statutes, one that would have treated everyone equally for early voting, and one that permitted only military voters to vote the final weekend. Election officials had resolved this conflict in favor of the latter result.

The Obama campaign then brought a constitutional challenge to this differential access to early voting. Invoking *Bush v. Gore* and many of the Court's seminal right-to-vote cases, the campaign argued that Ohio could not open its polling doors to some voters but not others without at least some credible, compelling justification supported by a factual foundation. Thus, that challenge suggested EV should be seen as much like traditional election day voting, just expanded backward in time. In turn, Ohio assumed that EV should be treated under Supreme Court precedents that apply to absentee voting, and that the state should only draw lines on access as long as any conceivable rational basis existed for those distinctions.

Every federal judge to address the merits of these issues (in the district court and a unanimous Sixth Circuit) rejected Ohio's position. The Sixth Circuit held that the Constitution and the Court's right-to-vote cases required Ohio to open its early voting doors to all voters on an equal basis; the Supreme Court denied Ohio's effort to stay that decision. As a result, more than 106,000 voters in Ohio voted early the weekend before the election.

These decisions are now the most important window into the way federal courts are beginning to understand EV as they work out its legal meaning. The Obama campaign did not challenge Ohio's decision to eliminate EV for all voters on weekends; it challenged only Ohio's decision to open those doors selectively to some voters and not others. As a matter of the actual practice on the ground, EV looks in virtually every way like election day voting: voters line up in person, sometimes for hours, at state polling locations, go in, and cast their vote. Unlike with absentee voting, no state has ever tried to carve up its electorate during early voting and insist that some voters can vote early but others cannot. Since early voting has been developed, it has always been open in all states to all voters on equal terms, just as election day voting is. Everything about the way early voting is covered in the media and treated by campaigns is the same as it is on election day. And voters use early voting in massive numbers that dwarf the traditional absentee ballot process. In terms of the experience of voters with EV, the atmospherics of EV, and the emerging norms of EV, there is little difference from election day voting. No state had previously adopted a policy of selective access to early voting like Ohio's.

In rejecting that policy on federal constitutional grounds, the federal courts cited not just *Bush v. Gore*, but many of the classic right-to-vote cases, such as *Kramer v. Union Free School District No. 15*,[4] *Dunn v. Blumstein*,[5] and *Harper v. Virginia State Board of Elections*.[6] These are the cases that not only fleshed out the constitutional right to vote, but also asserted a muscular role for courts in policing the wrongful denial of the franchise. That citation list is itself a further, powerful signal that the courts viewed EV as much like election day voting that was simply extended earlier in time. In these important first decisions, the courts rejected the position that EV should be viewed through the lens of absentee voting. That is why the courts invoked these foundational precedents that preclude states from opening their polls to some voters but not others. Thus, one of the most significant changes in election practice since 2000, the dramatic rise of EV, now has an accompanying legal response: in their initial confrontations, at least, with EV, courts are inclined to conceptualize EV as more similar to traditional election day voting than to traditional absentee voting.

Could a state ever permit some voters to vote early and not others, if the state truly had some compelling reason for picking and choosing among early voters? That is unknown at this early stage of the development of the jurisprudence of early voting. Arguably, that issue was not squarely presented in the Ohio litigation, given the convoluted path through which Ohio had ended up opening its early voting doors to some voters but not others. Given that path, the federal courts found it hard to credit any post hoc claim that powerful and convincing reasons had justified Ohio in opening its polls for EV to some voters but not others. But the very fact that the federal courts examined the Ohio scheme in a rigorous way, and were unwilling to defer to the state's post hoc efforts in court to justify that scheme, leads to the second area of legal significance that emerged from the 2012 election cycle: the continuing evolution of the right-to-vote jurisprudence and the integration of *Bush v. Gore* into that jurisprudence.

II

Ohio provides a window into a deeper and more general transformation of the election jurisprudence, the second major legal development in 2012. In *Baker v. Carr*,[7] the Court rested the justiciability of constitutional challenges to the election system on these cases being integrated into what Justice Brennan termed the "well developed and familiar" contours of equal protection law.[8] That approach recognized claims that state conduct violated a fundamental right or that it drew distinctions along classifications that were deemed suspect because they reflected the historic subordination of racial or ethnic minorities.

The Ohio litigation posed challenges along both these dimensions. The initial cases in which the Court recognized voting to be a fundamental right mostly involved direct qualifications on political participation: failure to meet those qualifications (a poll tax, a durational residency requirement) meant complete exclusion. In the current generation of cases, however, the courts typically confront regulations on the processes by which voting is done, often without complete exclusion from participation. In Ohio, even following the restrictions imposed for 2012, EV was still widely available, anyone could vote absentee for any reason, and of course, general election day voting remained open to all. Should the courts, then, nonetheless conceive Ohio's differential access to EV the weekend before the election as a severe burden on the fundamental right to vote? If the law was instead looked at primarily in terms of whether it invidiously classified voters, Ohio's attempt to distinguish overseas voters, particularly military overseas voters, from in-state voters for purposes of access to the

EV sites on the weekend before the election may have been maladroit, but did not implicate any of the traditional categories of suspect classes. The overarching issue, then, was how the modern right-to-vote jurisprudence, which now spans almost fifty years, ought to be synthesized and applied in the context of emerging new forms of voting regulation.

In *Obama for America v. Husted*,[9] the Sixth Circuit upheld a district court preliminary injunction against discriminatory restrictions on access to early voting the weekend before the election, a decision that allowed more than 100,000 Ohio voters to take advantage of enhanced opportunities to vote. As a formal matter, the Ohio law did not deny anyone the right to vote, because these other avenues remained open; hence, the Sixth Circuit concluded that the burden on the right could not be severe. But the Court also realistically noted that, for a significant number of Ohioans, weekend voting might in fact enhance their ability to vote, given job and family constraints when general election day takes place on a Tuesday.

As a result, the Court was not prepared to dismiss the burden on the right to vote as trivial or nonexistent. Instead, the Court found that constitutional doctrine permitted recognition of a category between these extremes: burdens that were "real" and meaningful, even if not severe, would trigger a kind of intermediate judicial scrutiny. Moreover, major counties in Ohio filed briefs arguing that, despite the state law (and the state's arguments), experience had shown that EV eased the burdens on election administrators and smoothed the election day path for voters. For the Court, one critical fact was that the State of Ohio previously "had granted the right to in-person early voting to all Ohio voters" and that "[i]n 2008, thousands of Ohio voters cast their votes in person in the three days prior to Election Day. Then, the State retracted that right, imposing a 6 P.M. Friday deadline."[10] Having established the significance of EV as part of the American electoral process, the Court could conclude that "thousands of voters who would have voted during those three days will not be able to exercise their right to cast a vote in person."[11]

Once the Court recognized that significant burdens on the right to vote, even if not severe, required serious judicial scrutiny, the Court turned to crafting the legal doctrine to offer relief. EV was a relatively new development and did not trigger the more classic outright denial of the franchise evident in the voting as fundamental right line of equal protection cases. Nor did the categories of privileged and nonprivileged voters easily map onto the race-based distinctions that populate the constitutional right-to-vote cases. Instead of the classic forms of equal protection, courts (and the Sixth Circuit in particular in dealing with a series of cases from Ohio) began to formalize the elements of an intuitive sense of unjustified regulations of the electoral process or, put in other terms, illegitimate political behavior. This intuition turned on three elements: the creation of a real-world obstacle to voting, including the denial to some voters but not others of a previously granted ability to vote more easily; proximity of a change in voting procedures to election day, thereby creating an aura of partisan manipulation about the change; and an inability to articulate a reasonably credible account of why the change was necessary.

Together these three elements combined to defeat the normal deference granted to state administrative decision making, even in the electoral arena. No one element seemed to stand alone. For example, no court in this line of cases ever intimated that early voting, once granted, could not be rescinded. The Obama campaign, as well, did not challenge the elimination in Ohio of EV altogether on weekends, but only the discriminatory access to it the week before the election. Thus, the courts did not subject administration of the franchise to a one-way ratchet, even with regard to EV, but if changes were to be made, they had to be evenhanded. Similarly, no court imposed an elevated burden of justification on even bureaucratic decision making unless struck by the likely impact on the realistic ability of voters to cast their ballot. At the same time, bureaucratic indifference proved insufficient to overcome a burden on the franchise. As the Sixth Circuit emphasized in *Hunter v. Hamilton County Board of Elections* in 2011, *"unanticipated* inequality is especially arbitrary."[12]

Much of the Sixth Circuit's development of the right to vote has been built on the foundation of *Bush v. Gore.* The Sixth Circuit has elaborated this new equal protection jurisprudence across cases involving the use of inferior voting machines in some parts of the state,[13] disparities in election administration across counties,[14] and the inconsistent treatment of provisional ballots.[15] In each case, the Sixth Circuit comes back to *Bush v. Gore* as standing for the proposition that the right to vote encompasses, in the language of *Bush v. Gore,* "more than the initial allocation of the franchise. *Equal protection applies as well to the manner of its exercise."*[16]

In *Hunter,* the most expansive of the Sixth Circuit cases prior to 2012, the Court's focus was on the statement in *Bush* that there is a constitutional requirement under equal protection to "the nonarbitrary treatment of voters."[17] From this, the Sixth Circuit established the new equal protection of the franchise: "We are therefore guided in our analysis by the important requirement that state actions in election processes must not result in 'arbitrary and disparate treatment' of votes."[18] As a matter of doctrine, the new equal protection of the right to vote expanded judicial scrutiny beyond the constricted categories of outright denial of the franchise and the protection of vulnerable minorities against mistreatment on account of race or some other specified characteristic. As critically applied in *Hunter,* the contested treatment of provisional ballots was "not the result of a broader policy determination by the State of Ohio that such distinctions would be justifiable. Therefore, they are especially vulnerable to equal-protection challenges."[19]

Rather than carve out new categories of specific entitlements (e.g., all voters must have a certain number of EV opportunities), the new equal protection limited the prospects for strategic manipulation of access to the franchise by state officials, most notably the partisan aspirations of legislatures or elected secretaries of state. Constrained were the aims of state regulation, an "expressive" command that governmental conduct in the domain of elections not further improper purposes, including the arbitrary or unjustifiable conduct at issue repeatedly in Ohio.[20] In practical terms, this meant that Ohio was free to alter the conduct of an election, but that the combination of a suspected constriction of voting opportunities and lack of substantial reasons would be constitutionally fatal.

In 2012, the new equal protection was tested – and strengthened – in two major cases challenging the restriction on early voting for nonmilitary voters[21] and on the disqualification of provisional ballots cast at the wrong precinct as a result of poll worker error.[22] In each case, the appellate court upheld lower court injunctions against Ohio regulatory restrictions on the ability to cast a vote. And, in each case, the court ruled unanimously, with panels of Republican and Democratic appointees on the frequently fractious Sixth Circuit.

Rejecting the formalism of some constitutional law on the right to vote, the Sixth Circuit announced candidly that it needed to calibrate the level of equal protection scrutiny to "[t]he precise character of the state's action and the nature of the burden on voters."[23] In *Obama for America*, the district court had made the critical factual findings, again relying on *Bush v. Gore* as the ultimate legal authority for a constitutionally supple standard of review:

The issue here is *not* the right to absentee voting, which, as the Supreme Court has already clarified, is not a "fundamental right." ... The issue presented is the State's redefinition of in-person early voting and the resultant restriction of the right of Ohio voters to cast their votes in person through the Monday before Election Day. This Court stresses that where the State has authorized in-person early voting through the Monday before Election Day for all voters, "the State may not, by later arbitrary and disparate treatment, value one person's vote over that of another." *Bush v. Gore* ... which is precisely what the State has done.[24]

The Sixth Circuit elaborated the new model of equal protection:

If the State merely placed "nonsevere, nondiscriminatory restrictions" on all voters, the restrictions would survive if they could be sufficiently justified.... On the other hand, if the State merely classified voters disparately but placed no restrictions on their right to vote, the classification would survive if it had a rational basis. However, the State has done both; it has classified voters disparately and has burdened their right to vote. Therefore, both justifications proffered by the State must be examined to determine whether the challenged statutory scheme violates equal protection.

Although states are permitted broad discretion in devising the election scheme that fits best with the perceived needs of the state, and there is no abstract constitutional right to vote by absentee ballot, eleventh-hour changes to remedial voting provisions that have been in effect since 2005 and have been relied on by substantial numbers of voters for the exercise of their franchise are properly considered as a burden ... To conclude otherwise is to ignore reality.[25]

This new equal protection helps insulate the right to vote from naked efforts at partisan manipulation. Though an election law is not unconstitutional merely because it might reflect partisan motivations in part, the Supreme Court in cases like *Crawford v. Marion County Election Bd.*[26] had left open the possibility, or perhaps even suggested more strongly, that a restriction on voting whose only plausible justification was pure partisanship might well not survive constitutional scrutiny. As Justice Stevens wrote for the *Crawford* Court: "If [partisan] considerations had provided the only justification for a photo identification requirement, we may also assume that [such a law] would suffer the same fate as the poll tax at issue in *Harper.*"[27] This greater judicial sensitivity in recent years to partisan manipulation of the democratic process is also beginning to be reflected at the margins of redistricting cases; even though state redistricting was traditionally subject to a 10 percent "safe harbor" for populations deviations from perfect equality, one lower federal court (in a decision the Supreme Court summarily affirmed) has now held that it is unconstitutional for state legislatures to hide behind this safe harbor for partisan purposes.[28]

Thus, recent years, culminating in the 2012 presidential election, have seen a continuing evolution in the constitutional jurisprudence of the right to vote. Just as the 2000 election made all of us, including, unfortunately, partisan legislatures, far more aware of how micro-manipulations of electoral rules might change outcomes, so too with the courts. Major Supreme Court decisions that some have seen as nothing more than retrenchments in this jurisprudence – *Crawford*, upholding photo identification laws, and *Bush v. Gore*, terminating the recounting of ballots – have also become the building blocks for an initial new stage of constitutional scrutiny of the electoral process.

In this emerging approach, voting remains constitutionally unique and its protection continues to warrant a special, if modified, judicial role. Even if burdens on the right to vote are not severe, and even if they do not involve complete exclusions from participation based on irrelevant criteria, the courts are starting to apply a kind of intermediate scrutiny that tests in a serious way a legislature's actual justifications for new regulations of the voting process. In addition, courts are showing greater sensitivity to the risk that these regulations are based on purely partisan aims; even if the courts do not directly condemn laws in these terms, they are willing to examine electoral laws in a more intensive way and, if the public-regarding and neutral justifications for those laws cannot be credibly supported, to strike down those laws – while leaving unsaid the more bald-faced statement that the law is a purely partisan act.

Ohio has remained the most important crucible for constitutional challenges to voter exclusion from 2004 to 2012. And in the major series of cases that have emerged there, the courts turned once and again to *Bush v. Gore* for an expansive view of equal protection, one that was nowhere else "well developed and familiar."

Notes

1   *Bush v. Gore*, 531 U.S. 98 (2000).
2   Pub. L. 107–252.

3 394 U.S. 802 (1969).

4 395 U.S. 621 (1969).

5 405 U.S. 330 (1972).

6 383 U.S. 663 (1966).

7 369 U.S. 186 (1962).

8 Ibid., 369 U.S. at 226.

9 697 F.3d 423 (6th Cir. 2012).

10 *Obama for America v. Husted*, No. 2:12-CV-0636, 2012 WL 3765060, at *7 (S.D. Ohio Aug. 31, 2012), *aff'd*, 697 F.3d 423 (6th Cir. 2012).

11 Ibid.

12 635 F. 3d 219, 238 n.16 (6th Cir. 2011).

13 *Stewart v. Blackwell*, 473 F.3d 692 (6th Cir. 2007).

14 *League of Women Voters v. Brunner*, 548 F.3d 463 (6th Cir. 2008).

15 *Hunter v. Hamilton County Bd. of Elections*, 635 F.3d 219 (6th Cir. 2011).

16 *Bush v. Gore*, 531 U.S. 98, 104 (2000) (emphasis added).

17 *Hunter v. Hamilton County Bd. of Elections*, 635 F.3d 236 (6th Cir. 2011) (quoting *Bush v. Gore*, 531 U.S. at 105).

18 Ibid., 635 F.3d at 234 (quoting *Bush v. Gore*, 531 U.S. at 104).

19 Ibid., 635 F.3d at 238.

20 Expressive Harms, "Bizarre Districts," and Voting Rights: Evaluating Election-District Appearances after *Shaw v. Reno*, 92 *Mich. L. Rev.* 483 (1993) (with Richard Niemi); "Expressive Theories of Law: A General Restatement," 148 *U. Pa. L. Rev.* 1503 (2000) (with Elizabeth Anderson).

21 *Obama for America v. Husted*, 697 F.3d 423 (6th Cir. 2012).

22 *Northeast Ohio Coalition for the Homeless v. Husted*, 696 F.3d 580 (6th Cir. 2012).

23 *Obama for America v. Husted*, 697 F.3d at 428.

24 *Obama for America v. Husted*, No. 2:12-CV-0636, 2012 WL 3765060, at *10 (S.D. Ohio Aug. 31, 2012), *aff'd*, 697 F.3d 423 (6th Cir. 2012).

25 *Obama for America v. Husted*, 697 F.3d at 432, 442 (citations omitted).

26 553 U.S. 181 (2008).

27 Ibid., 553 U.S. at 203.

28 *Larios v. Cox*, 300 F. Supp. 2d 1320 (N.D. Ga. 2004), *aff'd*, 542 U.S. 947.

References

Aberbach, Joel D. 1969. Alienation and Political Behavior. *American Political Science Review* 63(1): 86–99.

Ackerman, Bruce. 2002. *Bush v. Gore: The Question of Legitimacy.* New Haven, CT: Yale University Press.

Adamany, David W. and Joel B. Grossman. 1983. Support for the Supreme Court as a National Policymaker. *Law and Policy Quarterly* 5(4): 405–37.

Alvarez, Lizette. 2011. Republican Legislators Push to Tighten Voting Rules. *New York Times,* May 28. Available at: http://www.nytimes.com/2011/05/29/us/politics/29vote.html?_r=1&ref=lizettealvarez.

Alvarez, R. Michael. 1997. *Information and Elections.* Ann Arbor: University of Michigan Press.

Alvarez, R. Michael and Jonathan Nagler. 1998. When Politics and Models Collide: Estimating Models of Multiparty Elections. *American Journal of Political Science* 42(1): 55–96.

Alvarez, R. Michael, Stephen Ansolabehere, Adam Berinsky, Gabriel Lenz, Charles Stewart III, and Thad E. Hall. 2009. 2008 Survey of the Performance of American Elections. Caltech/MIT Voting Technology Project.

Alvarez, R. Michael, Stephen Ansolabehere, and Charles Stewart III. 2005. Studying Elections: Data Quality and Pitfalls in Measuring of Effects of Voting Technologies. *Policy Studies Journal* 33(1): 15–24.

Alvarez, R. Michael, Lonna Rae Atkeson, and Thad E. Hall. 2007. The New Mexico Election Administration Report: The 2006 November General Election. University of New Mexico.

Alvarez, R. Michael, Lonna Atkeson, and Thad E. Hall. 2012. *Evaluating Elections: A Handbook of Methods and Standards.* New York: Cambridge University Press.

Alvarez, R. Michael, Dustin Beckett, and Charles Stewart III. 2011. Voting Technology, Vote-by-Mail, and Residual Votes in California, 1992–2008: A Preliminary Report.

Alvarez, R. Michael and Thad E. Hall. 2004. *Point, Click and Vote: The Future of Internet Voting.* Washington, DC: Brookings Institution Press.

2005. The Next Big Election Challenge: Developing Electronic Data Transactions Standards for Election Administration. IBM Center for The Business of Government.

2006. Controlling Democracy: The Principal-agent Problems in Election Administration. *Policy Studies Journal* 34(4): 491–510.

2008. *Electronic Elections: The Perils and Promise of Digital Democracy.* Princeton, NJ: Princeton University Press.

2009. Provisional Ballots in the 2008 Ohio General Election. Pew Charitable Trusts, The Center for the States, Provisional Ballots: An Imperfect Solution. Available at: http://www.pewcenteronthestates.org/initiatives_detail.aspx?initiativeID=54789.

Alvarez, R. Michael, Thad E. Hall, Stephen Ansolabehere, Adam Berinksy, Gabriel Lenz, and Charles Stewart III. 2009. 2008 Survey of the Performance of American Elections. Caltech/MIT Voting Technology Project. Available at: http://vote.caltech.edu/drupal/node/231.

Alvarez, R. Michael, Thad E. Hall, and Susan Hyde. 2008. *Election Fraud: Detecting and Deterring Electoral Manipulation.* Washington, DC: Brookings Institution Press.

Alvarez, R. Michael, Thad E. Hall, and Morgan H. Llewellyn. 2007. How Hard Can It Be: Do Citizens Think It Is Difficult to Register to Vote? *Stanford Law & Policy Review* 18(349): 382–409.

Alvarez, R. Michael, Thad E. Hall, and Morgan Llewellyn. 2008a. Are Americans Confident Their Ballots Are Counted? *Journal of Politics* 70(3): 754–66.

2008b. Who Should Run Our Elections?: Public Opinion about Election Governance in the United States. *Policy Studies Journal* 36(3): 325–46.

2009. *The Winner's Effect: Voter Confidence Before and After the 2006 Elections.* California Institute of Technology.

Alvarez, R. Michael, Thad E. Hall, and Morgan H. Llewellyn. 2010. Making Voter Registration Easier: Evaluation of the "Welcome Kit" Voter Registration Pilot Project. Caltech/MIT Voting Technology Project.

Alvarez, R. Michael, Thad E. Hall, and M. Kathleen Moore. 2010. 2010 Poll Worker Survey of the Performance of LA County Elections: Spring 2010 Study, Initial Survey Report. Prepared for LA County Clerk's Office.

2011. 2010 Poll Worker Survey of the Performance of LA County Elections: Fall 2010 Study, Initial Survey Report. Prepared for LA County Clerk's Office.

Alvarez, R. Michael, Jeff Jonas, William E. Winkler, and Rebecca N. Wright. 2009. Interstate Voter Registration Database Matching: The Oregon-Washington 2008 Pilot Project. 2009 Electronic Voting Technology Workshop/Workshop on Trustworthy Elections, online proceedings. Available at: http://www.usenix.org/event/evtwote09/tech/full_papers/alvarez.pdf.

Alvarez, R. Michael, Lonna Rae Atkeson and Thad E. Hall. 2012. *Confirming Elections: Creating Confidence and Integrity through Election Auditing.* New York: Palgrave Macmillan.

American Association for Public Opinion Research. 2008. *Standard Definitions: Final Dispositions of Case Codes and Outcome Rates for Surveys,* 5th edition. Lenexa, KS: AAPOR.

Anderson, Christopher J. and Andrew J. LoTempio. 2002. Winning, Losing, and Political Trust in America. *British Journal of Political Science* 32(2): 335–51.

Anderson, Christopher J. and Yuliya V. Tverdova. 2003. Winners, Losers, and Attitudes about Government in Contemporary Democracies. *International Political Science Review* 22(4): 321–38.

Ansolabehere, Stephen. 2009. Effects of Identification Requirements on Voting: Evidence from the Experiences of Voters on Election Day. *PS: Political Science & Politics* 42(1): 127–30.

Ansolabehere, Stephen and Eitan Hersh. 2010. The Quality of Voter Registration Records: A State-by-State Analysis. Department of Government. Harvard University.

Ansolabehere, Stephen and Phillip Edward Jones. 2010. Constituents' Responses to Congressional Roll Call Voting. *American Journal of Political Science* 54(3): 583–97.

Ansolabehere, Stephen and Nathaniel Persily. 2010. Measuring Election System Performance. *New York University Journal of Legislation and Public Policy* 13(3).

Ansolabehere, Stephen and Charles Stewart III. 2005. Residual Votes Attributable to Technology. *Journal of Politics* 67(2):365–89.

2008. Function Follows Form: Voting Technology and the Law. In *America Votes!: A Guide to Modern Election Law and Voting Rights*, ed. B. E. Griffith. Chicago: ABA Publishing.

Atkeson, Lonna Rae, R. Michael Alvarez, Alex N. Adams, and Lisa Bryant. 2011. The 2010 New Mexico Election Administration Report. University of New Mexico. Available at: http://www.unm.edu/~atkeson/newmexico.html.

Atkeson, Lonna Rae, R. Michael Alvarez, and Thad E. Hall. 2009a. Are They the Same or Different? An Examination of Trust in Government, External Efficacy and Voter Confidence. Presented at the Midwest Political Science Association's Annual Meeting, Chicago Illinois, April 1–4.

Atkeson, Lonna Rae, R. Michael Alvarez, and Thad E. Hall. 2009b. Assessing Electoral Performance in New Mexico Using an Ecosystem Approach: Combined Report.

2009c. Provisional Voting in New Mexico. Pew Charitable Trusts. The Center for the States. Provisional Ballots: An Imperfect Solution. Available at: http://www.pewcenteronthestates.org/initiatives_detail.aspx?initiativeID=54789.

2010. The 2008 New Mexico Election Administration Report. University of New Mexico. Available at: www.unm.edu/~Atkeson.

Atkeson, Lonna Rae, R. Michael Alvarez, Thad E. Hall, Lisa A. Bryant, Yann Kereval, Morgan Llewyllen, and David Odegaard. 2008. The 2008 New Mexico Post Election Audit Report. University of New Mexico.

Atkeson, Lonna Rae, Lisa A. Bryant, Alex N. Adams, Luciana Zilberman, and Kyle L. Saunders. 2011. Considering Mixed Mode Surveys for Questions in Political Behavior: Using the Internet and Mail to Get Quality Data at Reasonable Costs. *Political Behavior* 33: 161–78.

Atkeson, Lonna Rae, Lisa A. Bryant, Thad E. Hall, Kyle L. Saunders, and R. Michael Alvarez. 2010. A New Barrier to Participation: Heterogeneous Application of Voter Identification Policies. *Electoral Studies* 29(1): 66–73.

Atkeson, Lonna Rae and Nancy Carrillo. 2007. More is Better: The Impact of Female Representation on Citizen Attitudes Toward Government Responsiveness. *Gender and Politics* 3(1): 79–101.

Atkeson, Lonna Rae and Kyle L. Saunders. 2007. Election Administration and Voter Confidence: A Local Matter? *PS: Political Science & Politics* 40: 655–60.

Atkeson, Lonna Rae and Lorraine Tafoya. 2008a. Close, but Not Close Enough: Democrats Lose Again by the Slimmest of Margins in New Mexico's First Congressional District. In *The Battle for Congress: Iraq, Scandal, and Campaign Finance in the 2006 Election*, eds. D. Magleby and K. Patterson. Boulder, CO: Paradigm Publishers.

    2008b. Surveying Political Activists: An Examination of the Effectiveness of a Mixed Mode (Internet and Mail) Survey Design. *Journal of Elections, Public Opinion and Parties* 18(4): 367–86.

Avery, James, M. 2007. Race, Partisanship, and Political Trust Following *Bush v. Gore*. *Political Behavior* 29(3): 327–42.

Babbie, Earl. 2010. *The Practice of Social Research*, 12th edition. Belmont: Wadsworth, Cengage Learning.

Balkin, Jack. 2001. *Bush v. Gore* and the Boundary between Law and Politics. *Yale Law Journal* 110: 1407–58.

Baltimore Sun. "Reclaiming 'One Man, One Vote'" April 27, 2010. http://articles.baltimoresun.com/2010-04-27/news/bs-ed-baltimore-prisons-20100427_1_prison-inmates-residents-legislative.

Banducci, Susan A. and Jeffrey A. Karp. 2003. How Elections Change the Way Citizens View the Political System: Campaigns, Media Effects and Electoral Outcomes in Comparative Perspective. *British Journal of Political Science* 33(3): 433–67.

Banks, Christopher P., David B. Cohen, and John C. Green. 2005. *The Final Arbiter: The Consequences of Bush v. Gore for Law and Politics*. New York: State University of New York Press.

Barreto, Matt A., Bonnie Glaser, Karin MacDonald, Loren Collingwood, Francisco Pedraza, and Barry Pump. 2010. Online Voter Registration (OLVR) Systems in Arizona and Washington: Evaluating Usage, Public Confidence and Implementation Processes. Pew Center on the States.

Behrens, Angela, Christopher Uggen, and Jeff Manza. 2003. Ballot Manipulation and the "Menace of Negro Domination": Racial Threat and Felon Disenfranchisement in the United States, 1850–2002. *American Journal of Sociology* 109(3) (November): 559–605.

Beiser, Edward N. 1972. Lawyers Judge the Warren Court. *Law and Society Review* 7(1): 133–49.

Bensel, Richard Franklin. 2004. *The American Ballot Box in the Mid-Nineteenth Century*. New York: Cambridge University Press.

Berinsky, Adam J. 2005. The Perverse Consequences of Electoral Reform in the United States. *American Politics Research* 33(4): 471–91.

Berinsky, Adam J., Nancy Burns, and Michael W. Traugott. 2001. Who Votes By Mail? A Dynamic Model of the Individual-Level Consequences of Voting-by-Mail Systems. *Public Opinion Quarterly* 65(2): 18–198.

Brady, Henry E. 2000. Trust the People: Political Party Coalitions and the 2000 Election. In *The Unfinished Election of 2000*, ed. J. N. Rakove. New York: Basic Books.

Brickman, Danette and David A. M. Peterson. 2006. Public Opinion Reaction to Repeated Events: Citizen Response to Multiple Supreme Court Abortion Decisions. *Political Behavior* 28(1): 87–112.

Brown-Dean, Khalilah L. Forthcoming. *Once Convicted, Forever Doomed: Punishment, Citizenship, and Civil Death*. Yale University Press.

Bryant, Lisa A. 2010. *Voter Confidence and the Use of Absentee Ballots and Voter Assist Terminals: An Experimental Study.* University of New Mexico.

Bullock, Charles S., III and M. V. Hood III. 2002. One Person – No Vote; One Vote; Two Votes: Voting Methods, Ballot Types, and Undervote Frequency in the 2000 Presidential Election. *Social Science Quarterly* 83(4): 981–93.

Bullock, Charles III, M. V. Hood III, and Richard Clark. 2005. Punch Cards, Jim Crow, and Al Gore: Explaining Voter Trust in the Electoral System in Georgia, 2000. *State Politics and Policy Quarterly* 5(3): 283–94.

Burch, Traci. 2013. *Trading Democracy for Justice: Criminal Convictions and the Decline of Neighborhood Political Participation.* Chicago: University of Chicago Press.

Caldeira, Gregory A. 1986. Neither the Purse nor the Sword: Dynamics of Public Confidence in the Supreme Court. *American Journal of Political Science* 80(4): 1209–26.

Caldeira, Gregory A. and James L. Gibson. 1992. The Etiology of Public Support for the Supreme Court. *American Journal of Political Science* 36(3): 635–64.

Caltech/MIT Voting Technology Project. 2001a. *Residual Votes Attributable to Technology: An Assessment of the Reliability of Existing Voting Equipment.* Pasadena, CA and Cambridge, MA: California Institute of Technology and Massachusetts Institute of Technology.

2001b. *Voting: What Is, What Could Be.* Pasadena, CA and Cambridge, MA: California Institute of Technology and Massachusetts Institute of Technology.

Carter, James and Gerald Ford. 2002. *To Assure Pride and Confidence in the Electoral Process.* Washington, DC: Brookings Institution Press.

Casey, Gregory. 1974. The Supreme Court and Myth: An Empirical Investigation. *Law & Society Review* 8(3): 385–419.

Cemenska, Nathan, Jan E. Leighley, Jonathan Nagler, and Daniel P. Tokaji. 2009. Report on the 1972–2008 Early and Absentee Voting Dataset. The Pew Charitable Trusts.

Chemerinsky, Erwin. 2001. *Bush v. Gore* Was Not Justiciable. *Notre Dame Law Review* 76: 1093–112.

Citrin, Jack and Samantha Luks. 2001. Political Trust Revisited: Déjà Vu All Over Again? In *What Is It about Government that Americans Dislike?*, eds. J. R. Hibbing and E. Theiss-Morse. New York: Cambridge University Press.

Claassen, Ryan L., David B. Magelby, J. Quin Monson, and Kelly D. Patterson. 2008. At Your Service: Voter Evaluations of Poll Worker Performance. *American Politics Research* 36(4): 612–34.

Clarke, Harold D. and Alan C. Acock. 1989. National Elections and Political Attitudes: The Case of Political Efficacy. *British Journal of Political Science* 19(4): 551–62.

Clawson, Rosalee A., Elizabeth R. Kegler, and Eric N. Waltenburg. 2001. The Legitimacy – Conferring Authority of the United States Supreme Court: An Experimental Design. *American Politics Research* 29(6): 566–91.

2003. Supreme Court Legitimacy and Group – Centric Forces: Black Support for Capital Punishment and Affirmative Action. *Political Behavior* 25(4): 289–311.

Clayton, Cornell. 2002. The Supply and Demand Sides of Judicial Policymaking (Or, Why Be So Positive About the Judicialization of Politics?). *Law & Contemporary Problems* 65: 69–85.

Cobb, Rachael V., D. James Greiner, Kevin M. Quinn, Jerry Nickelsburg, Jeffrey F. Timmons, Matthew Groh, Casey Rothschild, and Michael L. Ross. 2012. "Can

Voter ID Laws Be Administered in a Race-Neutral Manner? Evidence from the City of Boston in 2008." *Quarterly Journal of Political Science* 7(1): 1–33.

Cohen, Michael D., James G. March, and Johan P. Olsen. 1972. A Garbage Can Model of Organizational Choice. *Administrative Science Quarterly* 17(1): 1–25.

Colvin, Nathan L. and Edward B. Foley. 2010. The Twelfth Amendment: A Constitutional Ticking Time Bomb. *University of Miami Law Review* 64: 475.

Commission on Federal Election Reform. 2005. Building Confidence in U.S. Elections. Center for Democracy and Election Management. American University. Available at: http://www1.american.edu/ia/cfer/.

Conrad, Frederick G., Benjamin B. Bederson, Brian Lewis, Emilia Peytcheva, Michael W. Traugott, Michael J. Hanmer, Paul S. Herrnson, and Richard G. Niemi. 2009. Electronic Voting Eliminates Hanging Chads But Introduces New Usability Challenges. *International Journal of Human-Computer Studies* 67: 111–24.

Cook, Timothy E. and Paul Gronke. 2005. The Skeptical American: Revisiting the Meanings of Trust in Government and Confidence in Institutions. *Journal of Politics* 67(3): 784–803.

Cooper, Michael. 2000. Contesting the Vote: Seminole County; Democrats Look to Another Trial. *New York Times*, December 6, 2000, A29.

Couper, Mick P. 2008. *Designing Effective Web Surveys*. Cambridge: Cambridge University Press.

Craig, Steven C., Richard C. Niemi, and G. E. Silver. 1990. Political Efficacy and Trust: A Report on the NES Pilot Study Items. *Political Behavior* 12(3): 289–314.

Dear, Jake and Edward W. Jessen. 2007. "Followed Rates" and Leading State Cases 1940–2005. *UC Davis Law Review* 41: 683–711.

Democratic National Committee. 2005. Democracy at Risk.

Dershowitz, Alan M. 2003. *Supreme Injustice: How the High Court Hijacked Election 2000*. Oxford: Oxford University Press.

Dillman, Don A. 2000. *Mail and Internet Surveys: The Tailored Design Method*. New York: John Wiley and Sons.

Dolbeare, Kenneth M. and Phillip E. Hammond. 1968. The Political Party Basis of Attitudes toward the Supreme Court. *Public Opinion Quarterly* 32(1): 16–30.

Dow, Jay K. and James W. Enderby. 2004. Multinomial Probit and Multinomial Logit: A Comparison of Choice Models in Voting Research. *Electoral Studies* 23(1): 106–22.

Driesen, David M. 2008. Firing U.S. Attorneys: An Essay. *Administrative Law Review* 60(3): 707–27.

Dugger, Ronnie. 1988. Annals of Democracy: Counting Votes. *New Yorker*, November 7, 1988, 31.

Easton, David. 1965. *A Systems Analysis of Political Life*. New York: John Wiley and Sons.

1975. A Re-Assessment of the Concept of Political Support. *British Journal of Political Science* 5(4): 435–37.

Ewald, Alec C. 2009. *The Way We Vote: The Local Dimensions of American Suffrage*. Nashville: Vanderbilt University Press.

Eversley, Melanie. 2012. Voter ID Laws are Growing; so are Challenges. *USA TODAY* (February 20).

Ferejohn, John. 2002. Judicializing Politics, Politicizing Law. 65 *Law & Contemp. Probs.* 41.

References   229

File, Thom. 2008. Voting and Registration in the Election of November 2006. U.S. Census Bureau. Current Population Reports. P20–557.

Flanders, Chad. 2006. Please Don't Cite This Case! The Precedential Value of *Bush v. Gore* 116 *Yale L.J.* Pocket Part 141, 144.

Foley, Edward N. 2007. The Future of *Bush v. Gore. Ohio State Law Journal* 68. Ohio State Public Law Working Paper No. 92.

Fortier, John C. 2006. *Absentee and Early Voting: Trends, Promises, and Perils.* Washington, DC: AEI Press.

Fountain, John W. 2000. The 2000 Elections: Missouri; Senator Refuses to Challenge Loss. *New York Times*, Nov. 9, 2000.

Franklin, Charles H. and Liane C. Kosaki. 1989. Republican Schoolmaster: The U.S. Supreme Court, Public Opinion and Abortion. *American Political Science Review* 83(3): 751–71.

Freeman, J. Leiper. 1955. *The Political Process: Executive Bureau-Legislative Committee Relations.* New York: Random House.

Frisina, Laurin, Michael C. Herron, James Honaker, Jeffrey B. Lewis. 2008. Ballot Formats, Touchscreens, and Undervotes: A Study of the 2006 Midterm Elections in Florida. *Election Law Journal* 7(1): 25–47.

Garner, Phillip and Enrico Spolaore. 2005. Why Chads? Determinants of Voting Equipment Use in the United States. *Public Choice* 123(3):363–92.

Garrett, Elizabeth. 2001. Leaving the Decision to Congress. In *The Vote: Bush, Gore, and the Supreme Court*, eds. C. Sunstein and R. Epstein, 38–54. Chicago: University of Chicago Press.

Gerken, Heather K. 2009. *The Democracy Index: Why Our Election System is Failing and How to Fix It.* Princeton, NJ: Princeton University Press.

Gibson, James L. 2007. The Legitimacy of the U.S. Supreme Court in a Polarized Polity. *Journal of Empirical Legal Studies* 4 (November): 507–38.

Gibson, James L. and Gregory A. Caldeira. 2009a. Confirmation Politics and the Legitimacy of the U.S. Supreme Court: Institutional Loyalty, Positivity Bias, and the Alito Nomination. *American Journal of Political Science* 53(1): 139–55.

2009b. Knowing the Supreme Court? A Reconsideration of Public Ignorance of the High Court. *Journal of Politics* 71(2): 429–41.

Gibson, James L., Gregory A. Caldeira, and Lester Kenyatta Spence. 2003a. Measuring Attitudes toward the United States Supreme Court. *American Political Science Review* 47(2): 354–67.

2003b. The Supreme Court and the Presidential Election of 2000: Wounds, Self-Inflicted or Otherwise? *British Journal of Political Science* 33(4): 535–56.

Gillman, Howard. 2001. *The Votes That Counted: How the Supreme Court Decided the 2000 Presidential Election.* Chicago: University of Chicago Press.

Ginsberg, Benjamin and Robert Weissberg. 1978. Elections and the Mobilization of Popular Support. *American Journal of Political Science* 22(1): 31–55.

Governor's Select Task Force on Election Procedures, Standards, and Technology. 2001. *Revitalizing Democracy in Florida.* Miami: Collins Center for Public Policy.

Greene, Jamal, Stephen Ansolabehere, and Nathaniel Persily. 2011. Profiling Originalism. *Columbia Law Review* 111(2): 356.

Griffin, Drew and Kathleen Johnston. 2008. Thousands of voter registration forms faked, officials say. CNN, October 9. Available at: http://articles.cnn.com/2008-10-09/politics/acorn.fraud.claims_1_acorn-officials-voter-fraud-voter-registration?_s=PM:POLITICS.

Gronke, Paul. 2005. Ballot Integrity and Voting By Mail: The Oregon Experience. Reed College. The Early Voting Information Center.

2008. Early Voting Reforms and American Elections. *William and Mary Law Review* 17(2): 423–51.

Gronke, Paul and Eva Galanes-Rosenbaum. 2008. The Growth of Early and Non-Precinct Place Balloting: When, Why, and Prospects for the Future. In *America Votes! A Guide to Election Law and Voting Rights*, ed. B. Griffith. American Bar Association.

Gronke, Paul and James Hicks. 2009a. N=1? The Anomalous 2008 Election and Lessons for Reform. Presented to the 2009 meeting of the American Political Science Association.

2009b. Reexamining Voter Confidence as a Metric for Election Performance. Presented at the Midwest Political Science Association's Annual Meeting, Chicago, Illinois, April 1–4.

Gronke, Paul and Charles Stewart III. 2008. Basic Principles of Data Collection. In *Data for Democracy: Improving Elections through Metrics and Measurements*. The Pew Center on the States.

Gronke, Paul and Daniel Toffey. 2008. The Psychological and Institutional Determinants of Early Voting. *Journal of Social Issues* 64(3): 503–24.

Grosskopf, Anke and Jeffrey L. Mondak. 1998. Do Attitudes toward Specific Supreme Court Decisions Matter? The Impact of *Webster* and *Texas v. Johnson* on Public Confidence in the Supreme Court. *Political Research Quarterly* 51(3): 633–54.

Hall, Thad E., J. Quin Monson, and Kelly D. Patterson. 2007. Poll Workers in American Democracy: An Early Assessment. *P.S.: Political Science and Politics* 40(4): 647–54.

2008. Poll Workers and American Democracy. In *Democracy in the States: Experiments in Election Reform*, eds. B. Cain, T. Donovan, and C. Tolbert, 35–54. Washington, DC: Brookings Institution Press.

2009. The Human Dimension of Elections: How Poll Workers Shape Public Confidence in Elections. *Political Research Quarterly* 62(2): 507–22.

Hall, Thad E. and Charles Stewart III. 2011. Voter Attitudes toward Poll Workers in the 2008 Election. University of Utah.

Harris, Joseph P. 1929. *Registration of Voters in the United States*. Washington, DC: Brookings Institution Press.

Hasen, Richard L. 2001. *Bush v. Gore* and the Future of Equal Protection Law in Elections. *Florida State University Law Review* 29: 377–406.

2004. A Critical Guide to *Bush v. Gore* Scholarship. *Annual Review of Political Science* 7: 297–313.

2005. Beyond the Margin of Litigation: Reforming U.S. Election Administration to Avoid Electoral Meltdown. *Washington and Lee Law Review* 6: 937–99.

2006. No Exit? The Roberts Court and the Future of Election Law. 57 *S.C. L. Rev*: 669, 685.

Hasen, Richard. 2007. The Untimely Death of *Bush v. Gore. Stanford Law Review* 60(1): 1–44.

Hasen, Rick. 2009. Felon Disenfranchisement Issue Heading to the Supreme Court? Election Law Blog. August 2. http://electionlawblog.org/archives/014188.html.

Heilke, Thomas, Mark R. Joslyn, and Alex Aguado. 2003. The Changing Readability of Introductory Political Science Textbooks: A Case Study of Burns and Peltason, Government by the People. *PS: Political Science and Politics* 36: 229–32.

Herrnson, Paul S., Michael J. Hanmer and Richard G. Niemi. 2012. The Impact of Ballot Type on Voter Errors. *American Journal of Political Science* 56(3): 716–730.

Herrnson, Paul S., Michael J. Hanmer and Richard G. Niemi. 2012. The Impact of Ballot Type on Voter Errors. *American Journal of Political Science* 56(3): 716–730.

Herrnson, Paul S., Richard G. Niemi, Michael J. Hanmer, Benjamin B. Bederson, Frederick G. Conrad, and Michael Traugott. 2008a. *Voting Technology: The Not-So-Simple Act of Casting a Ballot.* Washington, DC: Brookings Institution Press.

Herrnson, Paul S., Richard G. Niemi, Michael J. Hanmer, Peter L. Francia, Benjamin B. Bederson, Frederick G. Conrad, and Michael W. Traugott. 2008b. Voter Reactions to Electronic Voting Systems: Results from a Usability Field Test. *American Politics Research* 36: 580–611.

Hetherington, Marc J. 1998. The Political Relevance of Political Trust. *American Political Science Review* 92(4): 791–808.

Hiaasen, Scott, Gary Kane, and Elliot Jaspin. 2001. Felon Purge Sacrificed Innocent Voters. *Palm Beach Post.* May 27. http://www.palmbeachpost.com/news/content/news/election2000/election2000_felons2.html.

Hirschl, Ran. 2002. Resituating the Judicialization of Politics: *Bush v. Gore* as a Global Trend. *Canadian Journal of Law and Jurisprudence* 15: 191–218.

2004. *Towards Juristocracy: The Origins and Consequences of the New Constitutionalism.* Cambridge, MA: Harvard University Press.

Hofstadter, Richard. 1965. *The Paranoid Style of American Politics, and Other Essays.* New York: Knopf.

Hyde, Susan D. 2007. The Observer Effect in International Politics: Evidence from a Natural Experiment. *World Politics* 60(1): 37–63.

International Institute for Democracy and Electoral Assistance. 2002. *International Electoral Standards: Guidelines for Reviewing the Legal Framework of Elections.* Stockholm, Sweden.

Jenkins, Cleo R. and Don A. Dillman. 1997. Towards a Theory of Self-Administered Questionnaire Design. In *Survey Measurement and Process Quality*, eds. L. Lyberg, P. Biemer, M. Collins, E. deLeeuw, C. Dippo, N. Schwarz, and D. Trewin, 165–96. New York: Wiley Inter-Science.

Johnson, Timothy R. and Andrew D. Martin. 1998. The Public's Conditional Response to Supreme Court Decisions. *American Political Science Review* 92(2): 299–309.

Jones, Douglas W. 2000. Jones's Chad Page. Available at: http://www.cs.uiowa.edu/~jones/cards/chad.html.

Kam, Dara and Larry Keller. 2004. Early Vote Sites Report Intimidation. *Palm Beach Post*, October 25.

Kennedy, Robert F., Jr. 2006. Was the 2004 Election Stolen? *Rolling Stone 8*, June 15. Available at: http://www.rollingstone.com/news/story/10432334/was_the_2004_election_stolen.

Kessel, John H. 1966. Public Perceptions of the Supreme Court. *Midwest Journal of Political Science* 10(2): 167–91.

Key, V. O., Jr. 1949. *Southern Politics in State and Nation.* New York: Knopf.

Keyssar, Alexander. 2000. *The Right to Vote: The Contested History of Democracy in the United States.* New York: Basic Books.

Kimball, David C. and Edward B. Foley. 2009. Unsuccessful Provisional Voting in the 2008 General Election. Pew Charitable Trusts. The Center for the States. Provisional

Ballots: An Imperfect Solution. Available at: http://www.pewcenteronthestates.org/
initiatives_detail.aspx?initiativeID=54789.

Kimball, David C. and Martha Kropf. 2005. Ballot Design and Unrecorded Votes on
Paper-Based Ballots. *Public Opinion Quarterly* 69(4): 508–29.

2008. Voting Technology, Ballot Measures, and Residual Votes. *American Politics
Research* 36(4): 479–509.

2011. "Cumulative Voting: The Case of Port Chester, NY." Paper Presented at the
2011 Midwest Political Science Association Meeting, Chicago, IL.

Kimball, David C., Martha Kropf, and Lindsay Battles. 2006. Helping America Vote?
Election Administration, Partisanship, and Provisional Voting in the 2004 Election.
Election Law Journal 5(4): 447–61.

King, Ryan. 2006. A Decade of Reform: Felony Disenfranchisement Policy in the United
States. The Sentencing Project. Available at: http://www.sentencingproject.org/doc/
publications/fd_decade_reform.pdf.

Knack, Stephen. 1995. Does Motor Voter Work? Evidence from State-Level Data.
Journal of Politics 57(3): 796–811.

Knack, Stephen and Martha Kropf. 2003a. Roll-Off at the Top of the Ballot:
Intentional Undervoting in American Presidential Elections. *Politics & Policy*
31(4): 575–94.

2003b. Voided Ballots in the 1996 Presidential Election: A County-Level Analysis.
Journal of Politics 65(3): 881–97.

Kohno, Tadayoski, Adam Stubblefield, Aviel Rubin, and Dan Wallach. 2004. *Analysis
of an Electronic Voting System. IIE Symposium on Security and Privacy 2004.*
Piscataway, NJ: IEEE Society Press.

Koppelman, Alex. 2010. Election Fraud Charges Swirl Even Before Election Day.
ABC News, November 1. Available at: http://abcnews.go.com/Politics/vote-2010-
elections-voter-fraud-charges-election-day/story?id=11997231.

Kritzer, Howard M. 2001. The Impact of *Bush v. Gore* on Public Perceptions and
Knowledge of the Supreme Court. *Judicature* 85(1): 32–38.

Kropf, Martha. 2005. "Dogs and Dead People: Incremental Election Reform in
Missouri," in *Election Reform: Politics and Policy* (pp. 157–173), eds Daniel J.
Palazzollo and James W. Ceaser. Lanham: Lexington Books.

Kropf, Martha and David Kimball. 2012. *Helping America Vote: The Limits of Election
Reform.* Routledge.

Kruse, Douglas L., Kay Schriner, Lisa Schur, and Todd Shields. 1999. Empowerment
through Civic Participation: A Study of the Political Behavior of People with
Disabilities. Disability Research Consortium, Bureau of Economic Research,
Rutgers University and New Jersey Developmental Disabilities Council.

Lausen, Marcia. 2007. *Design for Democracy: Ballot and Election Design.* Chicago:
University of Chicago Press.

Leighley, Jan E. and Jonathan Nagler. 1992. Socioeconomic Class Bias in Turnout:
1964–1988: The Voters Remain the Same. *American Political Science Review*
86(3): 725–36.

2007. Unions, Voter Turnout, and Class Bias in the U.S. Electorate, 1964–2004.
Journal of Politics 69(2): 430–41.

2009. Electoral Laws and Turnout, 1972–2008. Presented at Fourth Annual
Conference on Empirical Legal Studies, November. SSRN eLibrary 1443556.

2014. *Who Votes Now: Demographics, Issues, Inequality, and Turnout in the United States*. Princeton, NJ: Princeton University Press.

Levinson, Sanford. 2002. *Bush v. Gore* and the French Revolution: A Tentative List of Some Early Lessons. *Law & Contemporary Problems* 65: 7–39.

Levitt, Justin, Wendy R. Weiser, and Ana Munoz. 2006. *Making the List: Database Matching and Verification Processes for Voter Registration*. New York: Brennan Center for Justice.

Liebschutz, Sarah and Daniel J. Palazzolo. 2005. HAVA and the State. *Publius* Fall: 497–514.

Litwin, Nathan P. 2003. Defending an Unjust System: How *Johnson v. Bush* Upheld Felon Disenfranchisement and Perpetuated Voter Inequality in Florida. *Connecticut Public Interest Law Journal*. Paper 8. http://lsr.nellco.org/uconn_cpilj/8.

Llewellyn, Morgan, R. Michael Alvarez, and Thad E. Hall. 2007. How Hard Can It Be: Do Citizens Think It Is Difficult to Register to Vote? *Stanford Law and Policy Review* 18(2): 282–409.

Long, William F., Ralph P. Garzia, Timothy Wingert, and Sylvia R. Garzia. 1996. The Ergonomics of Reading. In *Vision and Reading*, ed. R. P. Garzia, 71–110. St. Louis: Mosby.

Lowenstein, Daniel H. 2007. The Meaning of *Bush v. Gore*. *Ohio State Law Journal* 68. UCLA School of Law Research Paper No. 07–09.

Lowenstein, Daniel, Richard L. Hasen, and Daniel P. Tokaji. 2008. *Election Law: Cases and Materials*. Durham, NC: Carolina Academic Press.

Lowi, Theodore J. 1964. Review: American Business, Public Policy, Case-Studies, and Political Theory. *World Politics* 16(4): 677–715.

Magleby, David B., J. Quin Monson, and Kelly D. Patterson. 2008. Evaluating the Quality of the Voting Experience: A Cross Panel Pilot Study of the November 7 2006 Election in Franklin County OH, Summit County, OH, and the State of Utah. Center for the Study of Elections and Democracy. Brigham Young University.

Manza, Jeff and Christopher Uggen. 2004. Punishment and Democracy: Disenfranchisement of Nonincarcerated Felons in the United States. *Perspectives on Politics* 2(03): 491–505.

Mate, Manoj and Matthew Wright. 2008. The 2000 Presidential Election Controversy. In *Public Opinion and Constitutional Controversy*, eds. N. Persily, J. Citrin, and P. J. Egan, 333–52. New York: Oxford University Press.

McCormack, Conny. 2008. Florida's Transition from Touch Screens to OpScan Paper Ballots for Early Voting. Pew Center on the States. Available at: http://www.pew-centeronthestates.org/uploadedFiles/FLtripEVAug08.pdf.

McDonald, Michael P. 2008. Portable Voter Registration. *Political Behavior* 20(4): 491–501.

McDonald, Michael P. 2007. The True Electorate: A Cross-Validation of Voter File and Election Poll Demographics. *Public Opinion Quarterly* 71(4): 588–602.

Mebane, Walter R., Jr. 2004. The Wrong Man is President! Overvotes in the 2000 Presidential Election in Florida. *Perspectives on Politics* 2(3): 525–35.

2006. Election Forensics: The Second-Digit Benford's Law Test and Recent American Presidential Elections. Election Fraud Conference. Salt Lake City, Utah.

Miller, Arthur H. 1974. Political Issues and Trust in Government: 1964–1970. *American Political Science Review* 68: 989–1001.

Miller, Geralyn M. 2005. Methodology, Statistics, and Voting Error: An Exploration of 2000 Presidential Election data in Two States. *Policy Studies Journal* 33(1): 1–13.

Miles, Thomas. 2004. Felon Disenfranchisement and Voter Turnout. *Journal of Legal Studies* 33 University of Chicago (January).

Mockabee, Stephen T., J. Quin Monson, and Kelly D. Patterson. 2009. Evaluating On-line Training. Center for the Study of Democracy and Elections. Brigham Young University.

Mondak, Jeffrey J. and Shannon Ishiyama Smithey. 1997. The Dynamics of Public Support for the Supreme Court. *Journal of Politics* 59(4): 1114–12.

Monson, J. Quin, Kelly D. Patterson, and Tracy Warren. 2006. DRE Analysis for May 2006 Primary: Cuyahoga County, Ohio. Election Science Institute.

Montjoy, Robert. 2005. HAVA and the States. In *Election Reform: Politics and Policy*, eds. Daniel J. Palazzolo and James W. Ceaser, 16–34. Lanham, MD: Lexington Books.

Murphy, Chad, Martin Johnson, and Shaun Bowler. 2011. Partisan Bias in Evaluating U.S. Elections during the HAVA Decade: A Natural Experiment. University of California Riverside.

Murphy, Walter F. and Joseph Tanenhaus. 1968. Public Opinion and the Supreme Court: The Goldwater Campaign. *Public Opinion Quarterly* 32(1): 31–50.

Murphy, Walter F., Joseph Tanenhaus, and Daniel Kastner. 1973. *Public Evaluations of Constitutional Courts: Alternative Explanations*. Beverly Hills, CA: Sage Publications.

Nagler, Jonathan. 1991. The Effect of Registration Laws and Education on United States Voter Turnout. *American Political Science Review* 85(4): 1393–405.

National Commission on Federal Election Reform. 2001a. *Task Force Reports to Accompany the Report of the National Commission on Election Reform*. Charlottesville, VA and New York: Miller Center for Public Affairs and the Century Foundation.

2001b. *To Assure Price and Confidence in the Electoral Process*. Charlottesville, VA and New York: Miller Center of Public Affairs and The Century Foundation.

Navarro, Mireya. 1998. Fraud Ruling Invalidates Miami Mayoral Election. *New York Times*. March 5.

Neely, Francis and Corey Cook. 2008. Whose Votes Count? Undervotes, Overvotes, and Ranking in San Francisco's Instant-Runoff Elections. *American Politics Research* 36(4): 530–554.

New York Times Editorial. 2008. Expanding Democracy in Florida. June 30. http://www.nytimes.com/2008/06/30/opinion/30mon3.html.

New York Times Editorial. 2010a. Ex Offenders and the Vote. March 21. http://www.nytimes.com/2010/03/22/opinion/22mon3.html?ref=felonydisenfranchisement.

New York Times Editorial. 2010b. Their Debt Is Paid. October 19. http://www.nytimes.com/2010/10/20/opinion/20wed4.html.

Ngo, Nhu-Y. 2011. Delaware Inspires Maryland to Modernize its Voter Registration System. Brennan Center for Justice, March 28. Available at: http://www.brennancenter.org/blog/archives/delaware_inspires_maryland_vrm/.

Nicholson, Stephen P. and Robert M. Howard. 2003. Framing Support for the Supreme Court in the Aftermath of *Bush v. Gore. Journal of Politics* 65(3): 676–95.

Niemi, Richard G. and Paul S. Herrnson. 2003. Beyond the Butterfly: The Complexity of U.S. Ballots. *Perspectives on Politics* 1(2): 317–26.

Norden, Lawrence, David Kimball, Whitney Quesenbery, and Margaret Chen. 2008. *Better Ballots*. New York: Brennan Center for Justice.

Norris, Pippa. 1999. The Growth of Critical Citizens and Its Consequences. In *Critical Citizens: Global Support for Democratic Government*, ed. Pippa Norris, 257–72. Oxford: Oxford University Press.

Palast, Gregory. 2000. Florida's Flawed "Voter-Cleansing" Program. Salon.com, December 4. Available at: http://www.salon.com/news/politics/feature/2000/12/04/voter_file.

Palm Beach Post. 2004. Voting Early and Uniformly. January 27.

Pew Center on the States. 2007. HAVA at Five. Washington, DC. Available at: http://www.pewcenteronthestates.org/report_detail.aspx?id=34210.

Pildes, Richard H. 2004. The Constitutionalization of Democratic Politics. *Harvard Law Review* 118: 28–154.

Pitts, Michael J. and Matthew D. Neumann. Documenting Disfranchisement: Voter Identification at Indiana's 2008 General Election. Pew Charitable Trusts, The Center for the States, Provisional Ballots: An Imperfect Solution. Available at: http://www.pewcenteronthestates.org/initiatives_detail.aspx?initiativeID=54789.

Posner, Richard A. 2001. *Breaking the Deadlock: The 2000 Election, the Constitution and the Courts*. Princeton, NJ: Princeton University Press.

Price, Vincent and Anca Romantan. 2004. Confidence in Institutions before, during, and after Indecision 2000. *Journal of Politics* 66(3): 939–56.

Prison Policy Initiative "Census treatment of incarcerated felons unfairly dilutes voting strength of non – prison communities." June 22, 2005. http://www.prisonpolicy.org/news/pro6222005.html (Policy Initiative site also has the text of the three bills related to counting felons where they live).

Rattner, Benjamin. "Kentucky's Disturbing Disenfranchisement Numbers." Brennan Center at the NYU School of Law. http://www.brennancenter.org/blog/archives/kentuckys_disturbing_disenfranchisement_numbers.

Rhine, Staci L. 1995. Registration Reform and Turnout Change in the American States. *American Politics Quarterly* 23(4): 409–26.

Rosenberg, Jennifer, with Margaret Chen. 2009. *Expanding Democracy: Voter Registration around the World*. New York: Brennan Center for Justice.

Roth, Susan King. 1998. Disenfranchised by Design. *Information Design Journal* 9: 29–38.

Saltman, Roy G. 1975. *Effective Use of Computing Technology in Vote-Tallying*. Washington, DC: National Institute of Standards.

1988. *Accuracy, Integrity, and Security in Computerized Vote-Tallying*. Gaithersburg, MD: Institute for Computer Sciences and Technology. National Institute of Standards.

Sanders, Mark S. and Ernest J. McCormick. 1993. *Human Factors in Engineering and Design*, 7th Edition. New York: McGraw Hill.

Saphire, Richard B. and Paul Moke. 2006. Litigating *Bush v. Gore* in the States: Dual Voting Systems and the Fourteenth Amendment. *Villanova Law Review* 51: 229–98.

Schachter, Jason P. 2004. Geographic Mobility: 2002 to 2003, Population Characteristics. U.S. Census Bureau. P20–549.

Schattschneider, Elmer E. 1960. *The Semisovereign People: A Realist's View of Democracy in America*. New York: Holt, Rinehart and Winston.

The Sentencing Project Report. "Felon Disenfranchisement Laws in the United States." March 2011.

Shapiro, Martin and Alec Stone Sweet. 2002. *On Law, Politics, and Judicialization.* New York: Oxford University Press.

Shepsle, Kenneth A. 1992. Congress Is a "They," Not an "It": Legislative Intent as Oxymoron. *International Review of Law and Economics* 12(2): 239–56.

Sinclair, Betsy and R. Michael Alvarez. 2004. Who Overvotes, Who Undervotes, Using Punchcards? Evidence from Los Angeles County. *Political Research Quarterly* 57(1): 15–25.

Smith, Charles A. and Christopher Shortell. 2007. The Suits That Counted: The Judicialization of Presidential Elections after *Bush v. Gore Election Law Journal* *Aug* 6(3): 251–65.

Spriggs, II, James F. and Thomas G. Hansford. 2000. Measuring Legal Change: The Reliability and Validity of Shepard's Citations. *Political Research Quarterly* 53(2): 327–41.

Stein, Robert M. 1998. Introduction: Early Voting. *Public Opinion Quarterly* 62(1): 57–69.

Stein, Robert M. and P. A. García-Monet. 1997. Voting Early but Not Often. *Social Science Quarterly* 78(3): 657–71.

Stein, Robert M. and Greg Vonnahme. 2010. Early, Absentee, and Mail-In Voting. In *The Oxford Handbook of American Elections and Political Behavior*, ed. Jan Leighley. New York: Oxford University Press.

Stein, Robert M., Greg Vonnahme, Michael Byrne, and Daniel Wallach. 2008. Voting Technology, Election Administration, and Voter Performance. *Election Law Journal* 7(2): 123–235.

Stewart, Charles, III. 2004. The Reliability of Electronic Voting Machines in Georgia. Caltech/MIT Voting Technology Project.

2006. Residual vote in the 2004 election. *Election Law Journal* 5(2): 158–69.

2008a. Get a Grip on Elections. *Los Angeles Times*, October 27, 2008.

2008b. Improving the Measurement of Election System Performance in the United States. In *Mobilizing Democracy: A Comparative Perspective on Institutional Barriers and Political Obstacles*, eds. M. Levi, J. Johnson, J. Knight, and S. Stokes, 288–312. New York: Russell Sage.

2009. *Early- and Late-Adopters of Provisional Ballots.* Washington, DC: Pew Center on the States.

2010. Losing Votes by Mail. *Journal of Legislation and Public Policy* 13(3): 573–602.

2011a. Voting Technologies. *Annual Review of Political Science* 14: 355–80.

2011b. What Hath HAVA Wrought? Consequences, Intended and Not, of the Post–*Bush v. Gore* Reforms. In the Aftermath of *Bush v. Gore*: Ten Years Later. University of California, Irvine.

Stimson, James. 1985. Regression in Space and Time: A Statistical Essay. *American Journal of Political Science* 29(4): 914–47.

Stuart, Guy. 2004. Databases, Felons, and Voting: Bias and Partisanship of the Florida Felons List in the 2000 Elections. *Political Science Quarterly* 119(3): 453–75.

Suarez, Ray. 2004a. Florida Again. In Lehrer News Hour, PBS, October 26, 2004.

2004b. Voting Early. In Lehrer News Hour, PBS, October 18, 2004.

Sunstein, Cass R. and Richard A. Epstein, eds. 2001. *The Vote: Bush, Gore, and the Supreme Court.* Chicago: University of Chicago Press.

Tate, C. Neal and Torbjorn Vallinder, eds. 1995. *The Global Expansion of Judicial Power.* New York: New York University Press.

Tefki, Chafai. 1987. Readability Formulas: An Overview. *Journal of Documentation* 43: 261–73.

Tokaji, Daniel P. 2005. Early Returns on Election Reform: Discretion, Disenfranchisement, and the Help America Vote Act. *George Washington Law Review* 73: 1206–54.

Tomz, Michael and Robert P. Van Houweling. 2003. How Does Voting Equipment Affect the Racial Gap in Voided Ballots? *American Journal of Political Science* 47(1): 46–61.

Tomz, Michael, Jason Wittenberg, and Gary King. 2001. CLARIFY: Software for Interpreting and Presenting Statistical Results. Version 2.0. Cambridge, MA: Harvard University, June 1. Available at: http://gking.harvard.edu.

Tourangeau, Roger, Mick P. Couper, and Frederick Conrad. 2004. Spacing, Position, and Order: Interpretive Heuristics for Visual Features of Survey Questions. *Public Opinion Quarterly* 68(3): 368–93.

Traugott, Michael W. and Federick G. Conrad. 2012. "Confidence in the ELectoral System: Why We Do Auditing," in *Confirming Elections: Creating Confidence and Integrity through Election Auditing*, eds R. Michael Alvarez, Lonna Rae Atkeson and Thad E. Hall, New York: Palgrave and Macmillan.

Uggen, Christopher, Angela Behrens, and Jeff Manza. 2005. Criminal Disenfranchisement. *Annual Review of Law and Social Science.* 1: 307–22.

Uggen, Christopher and Jeff Manza, 2002. Democratic Contraction? Political Consequences of Felon Disenfranchisement in the United States. *American Sociological Review* 67(6) (Dec.): 777–803. Available at: http://as.nyu.edu/docs/IO/3858/Democratic_Contraction.pdf.

Urbina, Ian. 2007. Panel Said to Alter Finding on Voter Fraud. *New York Times*, April 11, 2007.

U.S. Census Bureau, Current Population Survey. 2002. Voting and Registration in the Election of November 2000. P20–542. Available at: http://www.census.gov/hhes/www/socdemo/voting/publications/p20/2000/index.html.

2010. Voting and Registration in the Election of November 2008. P20–562. Available at: http://www.census.gov/hhes/www/socdemo/voting/publications/p20/2008/index.html.

U.S. General Accounting Office. 2001. Voters with Disabilities: Access to Polling Places and Alternative Voting Methods. ed. U. S. GAO. Washington, DC: Government Printing Office.

Wand, Jonathan N., Kenneth W. Shotts, Jasjet S. Sekhon, Walter R. Mebane Jr., Michael C. Herron, and Henry E. Brady. 2001. The Butterfly Did It: The Aberrant Vote for Buchanan in Palm Beach County, Florida. *American Political Science Review* 95(4): 793–810.

Wang, Tova and Job Serebrov. 2007. Voting Fraud and Voter Intimidation, [Draft] Report to the U. S. Election Assistance Commission (EAC) on Preliminary Research and Recommendations (2006). *Election Law Journal* 6(3): 330–51.

Weiner, Jay. 2010. *This is Not Florida: How Al Franken Won the Minnesota Senate Recount.* Minneapolis: University of Minnesota Press.

Weiser, Wendy, Michael Waldman, and Renee Paradis. 2009. *Voter Registration Modernization: Policy Summary.* New York: Brennan Center for Justice.

Whitaker, L. Paige and Arthur Traldi. 2009. State Election Laws: Overview of Statutes Providing for Provisional Ballot Tabulation. Congressional Research Service. The Library of Congress.

Wolfinger, Raymond E. and Stephen J. Rosenstone. 1980. *Who Votes?* New Haven, CT: Yale University Press.

Word, Ron. 2004. *New Duval Elections Supervisor Quickly Adds Early Voting Sites.* Associated Press.

Yates, Jeffrey L. and Andrew B. Whitford. 2002. The Presidency and the Supreme Court after *Bush v. Gore*: Implications for Institutional Legitimacy and Effectiveness. *Stanford Law and Policy Review* 13(1): 101–18.

Zaller, John R. 1992. *The Nature and Origins of Mass Opinion.* New York: Cambridge University Press.

Index